WILLIAM BLAKE

ALSO EDITED BY HUGH J. LUKE

The Last Man by Mary Shelley (1965)

WILLIAM BLAKE

A Critical Essay

by

ALGERNON CHARLES SWINBURNE

Edited with an introduction by Hugh J. Luke

UNIVERSITY OF NEBRASKA PRESS · LINCOLN

CONTENTS

INTRODUCTION

William Blake: A Critical Essay, the longest, the most ambitious, and undoubtedly the finest of Algernon Charles Swinburne's prose works—and the first full-length critical study of Blake to be published—was begun as a review article on Alexander Gilchrist's *Life of William Blake: "Pictor Ignotus";* and its roots lie deep within the tangled history of that biography. Gilchrist had begun work on the *Life* about 1855. By 1860 the course of his research had led him inevitably to Dante Gabriel Rossetti, who had as early as 1847 purchased (with ten shillings borrowed from his brother William Michael) the manuscript notebook of Blake's poems which came to be known as the Rossetti Manuscript, and who had made Blake known to other members of the Pre-Raphaelite Brotherhood. Gilchrist and Rossetti rapidly became close friends; and when Gilchrist suddenly died of scarlet fever in November, 1861, with about one-third of the *Life* yet to be completed, Dante Gabriel and his brother, together with other members of the Pre-Raphaelite Brotherhood, went to the aid of Gilchrist's widow Anne to complete the work.[1]

---

[1] For an account of the writing of the Gilchrist *Life,* see G. E. Bentley, Jr. and Martin K. Nurmi, *A Blake Bibliography* (Minneapolis: University of Minnesota Press, 1964), p. 12.

Swinburne was asked by the Rossettis to revise the portions of the *Life* dealing with Blake's Prophetic Books.[2] The choice was natural enough. Swinburne must have seen the Blake manuscripts soon after he had met Rossetti, in the late 1850's. Certainly he was a Blake enthusiast by December, 1859, when—at the age of twenty-two—we find him writing to William Bell Scott that he has just "written a new ballad so indecent that it beats all the rest and is nearly up to Blake's Klopstock. N. B.," he adds, "I have got Blake's Dante—seven plates—stunners. Also his Job. I shall bring them north next year." [3] By 1862, Rossetti can describe Swinburne to Mrs. Gilchrist as the man who "has made, next to your husband, the most diligent research of any one into the more recondite side of Blake." [4] In a subsequent letter to Mrs. Gilchrist, a few weeks later, Rossetti is discussing a "further instalment of the Blake proofs," and writes: "Mr. Swinburne, of whose interest in the subject I was speaking to you (and indeed you know how great it is) , read them with me and was equally delighted with them. In Chap. XII however (relating to the Prophetic Books, of which Swinburne has made a very special study) he found a good deal which he thought might be improved by rearrangement, addition, and even omission. I am not sure from what you said to me, whether this is all by your husband, or some of it your own additional work, as I remember that this section of

---

[2] *The Swinburne Letters*, ed. Cecil Y. Lang (New Haven: Yale University Press, 1959–1962; cited hereafter as *Letters*), I, 59, note.

[3] *Letters*, I, 28–29.

[4] *Letters of Dante Gabriel Rossetti*, ed. Oswald Doughty and John Robert Wahl (Oxford: Oxford University Press, 1965–1967), II, 452; letter of August 25, 1862.

the work was the one left imperfect. Would there be any opportunity of reconsidering this chapter, as well as the part relating to the *Marriage of Heaven and Hell*—especially as regards the extracts? If so, I know that Swinburne would be glad to take any pains in connexion with them, and also I doubt not with the *Jerusalem* if necessary. He is far more competent for this than I am." [5]

But finally Swinburne decided against any attempt to revise that portion of the *Life*. After further discussion with Dante Gabriel, he wrote William Michael on October 6, 1862, "the result we both at once came to was that, as the weather stands by this time, it would be at least useless to attempt patching or padding the book, even if one's patchwork were to come under no further supervision from a chaste publisher. [6] . . . To give a decent revision of the leading prophetic books, it would first of all be necessary to entirely melt down and recast the chapters printed. To leave these as they are and then stick on a supplement at the end would be absurd. . . .

"What I now want to do," Swinburne adds, in his first reference to what ultimately grew to be his full-length study of William Blake, "and mean to set about this year if I can, is the making of a distinct small commentary of a running kind, but as full and satisfactory as it could well be made, on Blake's work. . . . I have spoken to Gabriel about the way and means, and we want you in the

---

[5] Ibid., p. 455; letter of September 13, 1862.

[6] The reference, of course, is to Alexander Macmillan. See Swinburne's angry letter of July, 1864, where, writing to Seymour Kirkup, he says that "the *publisher* of the biography (a very contemptible cur) took fright and would not forsooth *allow* them to be dully analysed" (*Letters*, 1, 202).

council. May I come to you or could you come here at any time to talk it over?" [7]

Swinburne's original intention, clearly enough, was to write and publish the "small running commentary" in the form of a magazine review of the *Life*. But he set to work with a Blakean energy and enthusiasm, and soon found (setting, perhaps, the first precedent for a now well-established tradition of Blake scholarship—for a note to become an article, an article a book, and a book a life's work) that "the complete work has swollen beyond all periodical limits." [8]

By January of 1864, the work had taken what was to be, for the most part, its final shape. "Being now within sight of land," he wrote William Michael, "I can see that it falls naturally into three main divisions 1) a revisal of the life and published designs, as distinct from any publication with a text of Blake's own; but touching upon his early poems and later controversial notes on art etc. as stages or landmarks in the narrative. 2) A review of his Poems and the illustrative work belonging to them; i.e., of the 'Songs' and the great MS. 3) The Prophetic books." [9] The first and second parts, he wrote, were virtually complete; the third "of course imperfect, as I had to leave it unfinished in the summer; but a week would suffice to break the back of it." [10]

But he continued to work on the third part for some two years longer: partly, no doubt, because he was also readying *Poems and Ballads* for the press during this

---

[7] *Letters*, I, 59–60.
[8] *Letters*, I, 94; letter of January 31, 1864, to William Michael Rossetti.
[9] Ibid.
[10] Ibid.

period; partly because he continued to acquire new fragments of information about Blake, mostly from Blake's
surviving acquaintance Seymour Kirkup; partly because of
the immense difficulty of those Prophetic Books through
which he was traveling a course at that time quite completely unexplored. But at least as important as any of
those reasons must have been Swinburne's determination
to write a critical volume which would be answerable to
his own conviction of Blake's greatness in poetry, in
painting, and in moral vision. "I have given my best
powers to the subject . . . ," he wrote William Michael
in the letter just quoted. "You will see that I have not
slighted or slurred over the subject. Coming after you
and Gabriel, I wanted to do something durable also for
Blake, if of less direct value than your work and his;
I have for once taken the same pains in arranging and
designing the parts of this essay as if I had been dealing
with a poem. . . . I have worked into it with real care,
and sometimes not without much labour, all the elucida-
tions and expressions of thought or feeling on the matter
that I could put into reasonable form or coherent shape."

In January or February of 1866, Swinburne sent the
manuscript of his *Essay* to his publisher,[11] complete save
for a few missing pages containing his transcript of passages
from *The Marriage of Heaven and Hell,* and by April
19 he was correcting proof both of the *Essay* and of his
Poems and Ballads.[12] The *Essay* would undoubtedly have
been published in 1866 but for the journalistic outburst

---

[11] See *Letters,* I, 149, and I, 156. In a letter of January 5, 1866, Swinburne speaks of his plans to send the manuscript in; in a letter of
February 17 he speaks of having done so.
[12] *Letters,* I, 164 and note.

which greeted the appearance in July of *Poems and Ballads:* John Morley's attack in the *Saturday Review* labelled Swinburne "the libidinous laureate of a pack of Satyrs," and other reviewers sounded much the same note.[13] J. Bertrand Payne, acting for the firm of Moxon, promptly and without ceremony withdrew the volume from sale, and Swinburne found himself in search of a new publisher. The best he was able to do was to accept the offer of John Camden Hotten, that entrepreneur whose one saving virtue was that he was available. Finally, in December of 1867, almost two years after the body of the volume was complete, and under the imprint of John Camden Hotten, Piccadilly, *William Blake: A Critical Essay* found its way to the public.[14]

In the Preface to their edition of *The Works of William Blake,* William Butler Yeats and Edwin John Ellis described Swinburne in his role of Blake critic as "the one-eyed man of the proverb among the blind";[15] more recently, G. E. Bentley, Jr. and Martin K. Nurmi have suggested much the same thing, perhaps, when they label Swinburne's *Essay* as "a work of its author and time." [16] It is true enough, certainly, that Swinburne was at least half-blind to a number of things which have come

---

[13] Quoted in Samuel C. Chew, *Swinburne* (London: John Murray, 1931) , p. 71. See Georges Lafourcade, *Swinburne: A Literary Biography* (London: G. Bell & Sons, 1932) , pp. 134–36, for an account of the concerted attack in the public press on *Poems and Ballads,* an attack which Lafourcade calls the most "dishonourable episode in the history of literary journalism."

[14] *Letters,* I, 279 and note. Although actually published in December, 1867, the volume is dated 1868.

[15] London, 1893, I, viii.

[16] *A Blake Bibliography,* p. 15.

to the light of day during our own century of Blake studies. His vision was limited by personal predilection and by cultural myopia, by the remnants of a theory of "art for art's sake," by the dark and cloudy ways of an untrodden land into which he alone had yet dared to venture. (All of which, perhaps, is merely to state the obvious: that Swinburne's was a pioneering work.) But what is more to the point (if the figure will bear pressing one step more) is that with his one good eye he saw many things for the first time, that he saw them (sometimes) clearly, and that he expressed what he saw in the vibrant and compelling prose of a practising poet.

Swinburne was the first, for example, to stress the importance of at least making the attempt to read *all* of Blake, including the Prophetic Books: "Whatever a good poet or a good painter has thought worth representing by verse or design must probably be worth considering before one deliver judgment on it," he writes. "What is true of all poets and artists worth judging is especially true of him; that critics who attempt to judge him piecemeal do not in effect judge him at all, but some one quite different from him, and some one (to any serious student) probably more inexplicable than the real man. For what are we to make of a man whose work deserves crowning one day and hooting the next? If the 'Songs' be so good, are not those who praise them bound to examine and try what merit may be latent in the 'Prophecies'? bound at least to explain as best they may how the one comes to be worth so much and the other worth nothing?" [17]

Swinburne was the first to make use of insights gained

---

[17] See p. 105.

from a reading of the Prophetic Books to enlarge our understanding of the shorter poems. See, for example, in his discussion of "The Human Abstract," his understanding that "the vision of the wise man or poet is wider than both" innocence and experience.[18]

Swinburne was the first to understand that the Prophetic Books must be read as myth, not allegory. See, for example, in his discussion of *Milton:* "To this plea of 'an Eternal' before the assembly succeeds the myth of Leutha 'offering herself a ransom for Satan': a myth, not an allegory; for of allegory pure and simple there is scarcely a trace in Blake." [19]

Not least important, Swinburne remains one of the few critics of Blake to observe his capacity for laughter: [20] the Blake who "hated scarce smiles" and "loved laughing" would no doubt have forgiven Swinburne much for that understanding.

In his *Notes on Poems and Reviews,* published in 1866, Swinburne wrote, "I have never been able to see what should attract men to the profession of criticism but the noble pleasure of praising." [21] And the editors of *A Blake Bibliography* are undoubtedly right in their comment that the chief importance of the *Essay* is as an appreciation of *Blake.*[22] Again and again throughout his "running commentary" on Blake's work, Swinburne singles out passages, poems, and entire works for en-

---

[18] See p. 147, note.

[19] See pp. 264–65.

[20] See, for example, p. 198.

[21] *The Complete Works of Algernon Charles Swinburne,* ed. Sir Edmund Gosse and Thomas J. Wise (London: William Heineman, 1925–27), XVI, 372.

[22] P. 14–15.

thusiastic, detailed, and infectious praise. Quoting the first three stanzas of the lines beginning "Silent, Silent Night," he comments: "Verse more nearly faultless and of a more difficult perfection was never accomplished." [23] Or, quoting the opening stanzas of the "Garden of Love," he observes: "The sharp and subtle change of metre here and at the end of the poem has an audacity of beauty and a justice of impulse proper only to the leaders of lyrical verse; unfit alike for definition and for imitation, if any copyist were to try his hand at it." [24] Or, on the lines beginning "I asked a thief to steal me a peach": this song "is lighter in tone than usual, and admirable for humorous imagination; a light of laughter shines and sounds through the words." [25] Or, he writes, *The Marriage of Heaven and Hell* is "the greatest of all his books; a work indeed which we rank as about the greatest produced by the eighteenth century in the line of high poetry and spiritual speculation. . . . None of his lyrical writings show the same sustained strength and radiance of mind; . . . small things he could often do perfectly, and great things often imperfectly; here for once he has written a book as perfect as his most faultless song, as great as his most imperfect rhapsody." [26] Whatever the faults of the *Essay*, it does most certainly fulfill what must be one of the ideal functions of literary criticism: it stimulates the desire on the part of the reader to turn back to the work under discussion.

For the literary scholar (whether he is interested primarily in Blake or in Swinburne), the *Essay* holds still

---

[23] See pp. 132–33.
[24] See p. 141.
[25] See p. 141.
[26] See pp. 204–05.

another fascination, a kind of fascination which Swinburne could hardly have intended, and of which he himself may well have been quite completely unaware. We can see, that is to say, at various levels just below the surface of the text, an evolution and growth of Swinburne's critical and poetic sensibility, as well as of his stance toward William Blake within the context of that sensibility. To put the matter as briefly as may be, Swinburne begins the critical sections of the Essay with an extended defense of "art for art's sake," contrasting that position with "the heresy of instruction," or what he calls "the great moral heresy," and arguing that the former is "the real point of view taken during life by Blake." [27] In the final pages of the volume, he has left the opposition of "morality" and "art" far behind. "In Blake," he writes, "above all other men, the moral and the imaginative senses were so fused together as to compose the final artistic form." [28] In a parallel kind of movement, Swinburne begins his Essay by examining Blake in the context of the Elizabethan lyric, with his principal emphasis on a kind of perfection of form; he ends the volume by stressing Blake's close similarities to Walt Whitman, and therefore his importance as a contemporary force bearing on contemporary problems and contemporary modes of thought and action.

Almost fifteen years after the publication of the Essay, Swinburne looked back to describe the reception of

---

[27] See pp. 91–93.

[28] See p. 298. Thomas E. Connolly has also observed (Swinburne's Theory of Poetry [Albany: State University of New York Press, 1964], p. 15) that the Essay "reflects the struggle that was going on within him during this period."

what he called "the most unlucky and despised of all my brain-children." Writing to Richard Henry Horne, on July 15, 1882, he says, "I need not say how much more than gratified I am by what you say of my book on Blake. . . . The only point on which I feel confidence is that it does deserve the credit of unsparing industry. I spent days in the print-room of the British Museum scribbling in pencil the analysis of Blake's 'prophetic books,' and hours at Lord Houghton's in the same labour with pen and ink— to produce a book which was received with general contumely, ridicule, and neglect, and has never yet, I believe, paid half its expenses, or struggled into a second edition." [29]

It is possible to discern at least three reasons for the poor reception of the *Essay*. Most obvious is the immediate context of its publication: the concerted attack in the journals on *Poems and Ballads*, the abrupt withdrawal of that volume by the reputable firm of Moxon, and Swinburne's subsequent association with the disreputable firm of John Camden Hotten, left his reputation at its nadir.

A second reason must lie in the fact that much of what Swinburne included in the *Essay* of Blake's works ran counter to the deep grain of Victorian values. One can—just barely—imagine the Queen's reaction to this

---

[29] *Letters*, IV, 284. A so-called "Second Edition" was issued in 1869 (dated 1868), according to T. J. Wise, but it consisted merely of new title pages bound up with the original sheets. Copies of the volume with its original title page, Wise claimed, "were still on sale more than twenty years later," and "this manipulation was merely a trick on the part of John Camden Hotten to excite or stimulate interest in the book." (*A Bibliography of the Writings in Prose and Verse of Algernon Charles Swinburne, Works*, XX, 94–95.)

excerpt, for example, from Swinburne's discussion of *The Visions of the Daughters of Albion:* "Oothoon is no harlot, but 'a virgin filled with virgin fancies, open to joy and to delight wherever it appears; if in the morning sun I find it, there my eyes are fixed in happy copulation:' and so forth—further than we need follow." [30] And still a third reason, no doubt, is that the *Essay,* with its largest section devoted to Swinburne's discussion of Blake's Prophetic Books, would have been a difficult volume for most readers.

The poor reception of his *Essay* must have saddened Swinburne, but it neither dampened his large admiration for the poet nor discouraged him in his continuing efforts to further Blake's cause. Even a casual inspection of Swinburne's letters throughout the remainder of his long life is enough to show that William Blake had entered into the very fibers of his language and thought. In June of 1871, for example, Swinburne has just been vaccinated. Writing to William Michael Rossetti, he comments, "I will merely say that pox in all its branches of cow, chicken, and man is an Emanation worthy of the 'mistaken demon of heaven,' at whose vegetating and spectrous birth the Eternal Female groaned," a sentence which the editor of Swinburne's *Letters* correctly identifies as containing a "potpourri of lines from Blake's Prophetic Books." [31] In a letter to his mother, he points to Blake as "*the* one man of all others who were alive in any part of this century (except, perhaps, Shelley) that I should most have liked to see and speak to in person." [32] And in the long

---

[30] See p. 233.

[31] *Letters,* II, 148 and note.

[32] *Letters,* II, 350; letter of November 2, 1874.

autobiographical letter to E. C. Stedman, written February 20, 1875, he says, "I might call myself if I wished a kind of Christian (of the Church of Blake and Shelley).[33]

His letters are also filled with his involvement in other Blake projects—urging his publishers (generally without success) to issue facsimile editions of Blake, in whole or part; describing days spent in feverish work on William Michael Rossetti's Aldine edition of Blake; writing a long essay in French for Stéphane Mallarmé to publish in *La République des Lettres*.[34]

By 1906, the time was finally right for a new edition of Swinburne's *Essay*, thirty-eight years after the first. Swinburne's final comment on Blake in his published letters—a comment which may stand as a fitting conclusion to the Introduction to this edition of the *Essay*—concerns that edition of 1906. "Your kindness to my old Blake book," he writes William Michael Rossetti, to whom the *Essay* was dedicated and with whom he had shared an enthusiasm for Blake for almost half a century, "—so very old, and so very young—is most delightful to me, as expressed alike in your last book and in your last note. I suppose you have seen the last edition of Blake's works in two volumes. Have you tackled 'Vala' yet? I might have tackled it in my twenties. I don't think I shall at the close of my sixties, though I have not at all outgrown the fascination of Blake." [35]

---

[33] *Letters*, III, 14.

[34] See *Letters*, III, 134, 137, 193; and V, 61. Swinburne apparently abandoned the project. Lafourcade (*Swinburne*, pp. 238–243) argues that two articles which did appear in *La République des Lettres*, signed "Herbert Harvey," were actually written by Swinburne; but almost certainly they were not.

[35] *Letters*, VI, 203; letter of October 29, 1906.

A NOTE ON THE TEXT

This edition of *William Blake: A Critical Essay* reproduces the text of the first edition, first issue, as described in *A Bibliography of the Writings in Prose and Verse of Algernon Charles Swinburne,* by Thomas James Wise (vol. 20 of *The Complete Works of Algernon Charles Swinburne,* ed. Sir Edmund Gosse and Thomas J. Wise, London, 1925–1927, known as the Bonchurch Edition). The "List of Authorities" and "Note Added by the Author in 1906" are reproduced from the text of *William Blake: A Critical Essay* included in vol. 16 of the Bonchurch Edition. The Editor's Notes, beginning on page 309, locate Swinburne's citations from Blake in the standard editions edited by Sir Geoffrey Keynes and by David V. Erdman. The notes are keyed to the text by page and line.

I should like to express my thanks to Professor Stanley Vandersall of the Classics Department of the University of Nebraska for his translation of the Greek and Latin phrases appearing in the text.

WILLIAM BLAKE

DEDICATION.

To WILLIAM MICHAEL ROSSETTI.

THERE are many reasons which should make me glad to inscribe your name upon the forefront of this book. To you, among other debts, I owe this one—that it is not even more inadequate to the matter undertaken; and to you I need not say that it is not designed to supplant or to compete with the excellent biography of Blake already existing. Rather it was intended to serve as complement or supplement to this. How it grew, idly and gradually, out of a mere review into its present shape and volume, you know. To me at least the subject before long seemed too expansive for an article ; and in the leisure of months, and in the intervals of my natural work, the first slight study became little by little an elaborate essay. I found so much unsaid, so much unseen, that a question soon rose before me of simple alternatives : to do nothing, or to do much. I chose the latter ; and you, who have done more than I to serve and to exalt the memory of Blake, must know better how much remains undone.

Friendship needs no cement of reciprocal praise ; and this

book, dedicated to you from the first, and owing to your guidance as much as to my goodwill whatever it may have of worth, wants no extraneous allusion to explain why it should rather be inscribed with your name than with another. Nevertheless, I will say that now of all times it gives me pleasure to offer you such a token of friendship as I have at hand to give. I can but bring you brass for the gold you send me; but between equals and friends there can be no question of barter. Like Diomed, I take what I am given and offer what I have. Such as it is, I know you will accept it with more allowance than it deserves; but one thing you will not overrate—the affectionate admiration, the grateful remembrance, which needs no public expression on the part of your friend

A. C. SWINBURNE.

November, 1866.

WILLIAM BLAKE.

Tous les grands poëtes deviennent naturellement, fatalement, critiques. Je plains les poëtes que guide le seul instinct ; je les crois incomplets. Dans la vie spirituelle des premiers, une crise se fait infailliblement, où ils veulent raisonner leur art, découvrir les lois obscures en vertu desquelles ils ont produit, et tirer de cette étude une série de préceptes dont le but divin est l'infaillibilité dans la production poétique. Il serait prodigieux qu'un critique devînt poëte, et il est impossible qu'un poëte ne contienne pas un critique.—CHARLES BAUDELAIRE.

I.—LIFE AND DESIGNS.

In the year 1827, there died, after a long dim life of labour, a man as worthy of remark and regret as any then famous. In his time he had little enough of recognition or regard from the world ; and now that here and there one man and another begin to observe that after all this one was perhaps better worth notice and honour than most, the justice comes as usual somewhat late.

Between 1757 and 1827 the world, one might have thought, had time to grow aware whether or not a man were worth something. For so long there lived and laboured in more ways than one the single Englishman of supreme and simple poetic genius born before the closing years of the eighteenth century ; the one man of that date fit on all accounts to rank with the old great names. A man perfect in his way, and beautifully unfit for walking in the way of any other man. We have

now the means of seeing what he was like as to face in
the late years of his life : for his biography has at the
head of it a clearly faithful and valuable likeness. The
face is singular, one that strikes at a first sight and grows
upon the observer ; a brilliant eager old face, keen and
gentle, with a preponderance of brow and head ; clear
bird-like eyes, eloquent excitable mouth, with a look of
nervous and fluent power ; the whole lighted through as
it were from behind with a strange and pure kind of
smile, touched too with something of an impatient pro-
spective rapture. The words clear and sweet seem the
best made for it ; it has something of fire in its composition, and something of music. If there is a want of
balance, there is abundance of melody in the features ;
melody rather than harmony ; for the mould of some is
weaker and the look of them vaguer than that of others.
Thought and time have played with it, and have nowhere pressed hard ; it has the old devotion and desire
with which men set to their work at starting. It is not
the face of a man who could ever be cured of illusions ;
here all the medicines of reason and experience must
have been spent in pure waste. We know also what
sort of man he was at this time by the evidence of living
friends. No one, artist or poet, of whatever school, who
had any insight or any love of things noble and lovable,
ever passed by this man without taking away some pleasant
and exalted memory of him. Those with whom he had
nothing in common but a clear kind nature and sense of
what was sympathetic in men and acceptable in things
—those men whose work lay quite apart from his—
speak of him still with as ready affection and as full

remembrance of his sweet or great qualities as those nearest and likest him. There was a noble attraction in him which came home to all people with any fervour or candour of nature in themselves. One can see, by the roughest draught or slightest glimpse of his face, the look and manner it must have put on towards children. He was about the hardest worker of his time ; must have done in his day some horseloads of work. One might almost pity the poor age and the poor men he came among for having such a fiery energy cast unawares into the midst of their small customs and competitions. Unluckily for them, their new prophet had not one point they could lay hold of, not one organ or channel of expression by which to make himself comprehensible to such as they were. Shelley in his time gave enough of perplexity and offence ; but even he, mysterious and rebellious as he seemed to most men, was less made up of mist and fire than Blake.

He was born and baptized into the church of rebels ; we can hardly imagine a time or scheme of things in which he could have lived and worked without some interval of revolt. All that was accepted for art, all that was taken for poetry, he rejected as barren symbols, and would fain have broken up as mendacious idols. What was best to other men, and in effect excellent of its kind, was to him worst. Reynolds and Rubens were daubers and devils. The complement or corollary of this habit of mind was that he would accept and admire even small and imperfect men whose line of life and action seemed to run on the same tramway as his own. Barry, Fuseli, even such as Mortimer—these were men he would allow and approve of. The devils had not entered into them ; they worked, each to himself, on the same ground as Michael Angelo. To such effect he would at times prophesy, standing revealed for a brief glimpse on the cloudy and tottering height of his theories, before the incurious eyes of a public which had no mind to inhale such oracular vapour. It is hard to conjecture how his opinions, as given forth in his *Catalogue* or other notes on art, would have been received—if indeed they had ever got hearing at all. This they naturally never did ; by no means to Blake's discouragement. He spoke with authority ; not in the least like the Scribes of his day.

So far one may at least see what he meant ; although at sight of it many would cover their eyes and turn away. But the main part of him was, and is yet, simply inexplicable ; much like some among his own designs, a maze of cloudy colour and perverse form, without a clue for the hand or a feature for the eye to lay hold of. What he meant, what he wanted, why he did this thing or not that other, no man then alive could make out. Nevertheless it was worth the trying. In a time of critical reason and definite division, he was possessed by a fervour and fury of belief ; among sane men who had disproved most things and proved the rest, here was an evident madman who believed a thing, one may say, only insomuch as it was incapable of proof. He lived and worked out of all rule, and yet by law. He had a devil, and its name was Faith. No materialist has such belief in bread and meat as Blake had in the substance underlying appearance which he christened god or spectre, devil or angel, as the fit took him ; or rather as he saw it from one or the other side. His faith was absolute and hard, like a pure fanatic's; there was no speculation in him. What could be made of such a man in a country fed and clothed with the teapot pieties of Cowper and the tape-yard infidelities of Paine? Neither set would have to do with him; was he not a believer? and was he not a blasphemer? His licence of thought and talk was always of the maddest, or seemed so in the ears of his generation. People remember at this day with horror and pity the impression of his daring ways of speech, but excuse him still on the old plea of madness. Now on his own ground no man was ever more sane or more reverent. His outcries on various matters of art or morals were in effect the mere expression, not of reasonable dissent, but of violent belief. No artist of equal power had ever a keener and deeper regard for the meaning and teaching—what one may call the moral—of art. He sang and painted as men write or preach. Indifference was impossible to him. Thus every shred of his work has some life, some blood, infused or woven into it. In such a vast tumbling chaos of relics as he left behind to get in time disentangled and cast into shape, there are naturally inequalities enough; rough sides and loose sides, weak points and helpless knots, before which all mere human patience or comprehension recoils and reels back. But in all, at all times, there is the one invaluable quality of actual life.

Without study of a serious kind, it is hopeless for any man to get at the kernel of Blake's life and work. Nothing can make the way clear and smooth to those who are not at once drawn into it by a sincere instinct of sympathy. This cannot be done ; but what can be done has been thoroughly and effectually well done in this present biography.* A trained skill, an exquisite admiration, an almost incomparable capacity of research and care in putting to use the results of such long and refined labour, no reader can fail to appreciate as the chief gifts of the author : one who evidently had at once the power of work and the sense of selection in perfect order. The loss of so admirable a critic, so wise and altogether competent a workman, is a loss to be regretted till it can be replaced—a date we are not likely to see in our days. At least his work is in no danger of following him. This good that he did is likely to live after him ; no part of it likely to be interred in his grave. For the book, unfinished, was yet not incomplete, when the writer's work was broken short off. All or nearly all the biographical part had been ably carried through to a good end. It remained for other hands to do the editing ; to piece together the loose notes left, and to supply all that was requisite or graceful in the way of remark or explanation. With what excellent care and taste this has been done, no one can miss of seeing. Of the critical and editorial part there will be time to speak further in its own place. All, in effect, which could be done for a book thus left suddenly and sadly to itself, has been done as well as possible ; no tenderness of labour grudged, no power and skill spared to supply or sustain it. So that we now have it in a fair and sufficient form, and can look with reasonable hope for this first critical Life of Blake and selected edition of

* Gilchrist's "Life of Blake."

his Works to make its way and hold its place among the precious records and possessions of Englishmen.

What has been once well done need not be tried at again and done worse. No second writer need now recapitulate the less significant details of Blake's life : space and skill wanting, we can but refer readers to the complete biography. That the great poet and artist was a hosier's son,* born near Golden Square, put to school in the Strand to learn drawing at ten of one Pars, apprenticed at fourteen to learn engraving of one Basire ; that he lived " smoothly enough" for two years, and was then set to work on abbey monuments, " to be out of harm's way," other apprentices being " disorderly," " mutinous," and given to " wrangling ; " these facts and more, all of value and weight in their way, Mr. Gilchrist has given at full in his second and third chapters, adding just enough critical comment to set the facts off and give them their proper relief and significance. His labours among Gothic monuments, and the especial style of his training as an engraver, left their marks on the man afterwards. Two things here put on record are worthy of recollection : that he began seeing visions at " eight or ten ;" and that he took objections to Ryland (a better known engraver than Basire), when taken to be apprenticed to him, on a singular

---

° It may be as well set down here as at any further stage of our business, that the date of Blake's birth appears, from good MS. authority, to have been the 20th of November (1757), not the 28th ; that he was the second of five children, not four ; James, the hosier in Broad Street, being his junior, not, as the biography states, his senior by a year and a half. The eldest son was John, a favourite child who came to small good, enlisted, and died it seems in comparative youth ; of him Mr. Gilchrist evidently had not heard. In some verses of the Felpham period (written in 1801, printed in vol. ii. p. 189 of the "Life and Selections ") Blake makes mention, hitherto unexplained, of " my brother John the evil one," which may now be comprehensible enough.

ground : "the man's face looks as if he will live to be hanged :" which the man was, ten years later. But the first real point in Blake's life worth marking as of especial interest is the publication of his *Poetical Sketches;* which come in date before any of his paintings or illustrative work, and are quite as much matters of art as these. Though never printed till 1783, the latest written appears to belong to 1777, or thereabouts.

Here, at a time when the very notion of poetry, as we now understand it, and as it was understood in older times, had totally died and decayed out of the minds of men ; when we not only had no poetry, a thing which was bearable, but had verse in plenty, a thing which was not in the least bearable ; a man, hardly twenty years old yet, turns up suddenly with work in that line already done, not simply better than any man could do then ; better than all except the greatest have done since: better too than some still ranked among the greatest ever managed to do. With such a poet to bring forward it was needless to fall back upon Wordsworth for excuse or Southey for patronage. The one man of genius alive during any part of Blake's own life who has ever spoken of this poet with anything like a rational admiration is Charles Lamb, the most supremely competent judge and exquisite critic of lyrical and dramatic art that we have ever had. All other extant notices down to our own day, even when well-meaning and not offensive, are to the best of our knowledge and belief utterly futile, incapable and valueless : burdened more or less with chatter about "madness" and such-like, obscured in some degree by mere dullness and pitiable assumption.

There is something too rough and hard, too faint and formless, in any critical language yet devised, to pay tribute with the proper grace and sufficiency to the best works of the lyrical art. One can say, indeed, that some of these earliest songs of Blake's have the scent and sound of Elizabethan times upon them; that the song of forsaken love—"My silks and fine array"—is sweet enough to recall the lyrics of Beaumont and Fletcher, and strong enough to hold its own even beside such as that one of Aspatia—"Lay a garland on my hearse"—which was cut (so to speak) out of the same yew; that Webster might have signed the "Mad Song," which falls short only (as indeed do all other things of the sort) of the two great Dirges in that poet's two chief plays; that certain verses among those headed "To Spring," and "To the Evening Star," are worthy even of Tennyson for tender supremacy of style and noble purity of perfection; but when we have to drop comparison and cease looking back or forward for verses to match with these, we shall hardly find words to suit our sense of their beauty. We speak of the best among them only; for, small as the pamphlet is (seventy pages long, with title-page and prefatory leaf), it contains a good deal of chaff and bran besides the pure grain and sifted honeymeal. But these best things are as wonderful as any work of Blake's. They have a fragrance of sound, a melody of colour, in a time when the best verses produced had merely the arid perfume of powder, the twang of dry wood and adjusted strings; when here the painting was laid on in patches, and there the music meted out by precedent; colour and sound never mixed together into the perfect scheme of poetry. The texture of these songs

has the softness of flowers ; the touch of them has nothing
metallic or mechanical, such as one feels in much excellent and elaborate verse of this day as well as of that.
The sound of many verses of Blake's cleaves to the sense
long after conscious thought of the meaning has passed
from one : a sound like running of water or ringing of
bells in a long lull of the wind. Like all very good
lyrical verse, they grow in pleasurable effect upon the
memory the longer it holds them—increase in relish the
longer they dwell upon the taste. These, for example,
sound singularly plain, however sweet, on a first hearing;
but in time, to a reader fit to appreciate the peculiar properties and merits of a lyric, they come to seem as perfect
as well can be :

> " Thou the golden fruit dost bear,
>   I am clad in flowers fair;
>   Thy sweet boughs perfume the air,
>   And the turtle buildeth there.
>   There she sits and feeds her young:
>   Sweet I hear her mournful song;
>   And thy lovely leaves among,
>   There is love, I hear his tongue."

The two songs " To Memory," and " To the Muses " are
perhaps nearer being faultless than any others in the book.
This last especially should never be omitted in any professedly complete selection of the best English lyrics. So
beautiful indeed is its structure and choice of language
that its author's earlier and later vagaries and erratic
indulgences in the most lax or bombastic habits of speech
become hopelessly inexplicable. These unlucky tendencies
do however break out in the same book which contains
such excellent samples of poetical sense and taste ; giving

terrible promise of faults that were afterwards to grow
rank and run riot over much of the poet's work. But
even from his worst things here, not reprinted in the
present edition, one may gather such lines as these :

> " My lord was like a flower upon the brows
> Of lusty May: ah life as frail as flower!
> My lord was like a star in highest heaven,
> Drawn down to earth by spells and wickedness;
> My lord was like the opening eye of day;
> But he is darkened; like the summer moon
> Clouded; fall'n like the stately tree, cut down:
> The breath of heaven dwelt among his leaves."

Verses not to be despised, when one remembers that the
boy who wrote them (evidently in his earlier teens) was
living in full eighteenth century. But for the most part
the blank verse in this small book is in a state of incredible
chaos, ominous in tone of the future " Prophetic Books,"
if without promise of their singular and profound power
or menace of their impenetrable mistiness, the obscurity of
confused wind and cloud. One is thankful to see here
some pains taken in righting these deformed limbs and
planing off those monstrous knots, by one not less qualified
to decide on such minor points of execution than on the
gravest matters of art ; especially as some amongst these
blank verse poems contain things of quite original and
incomparable grandeur. Nothing at once more noble and
more sweet in style was ever written, than part of this
" To the Evening Star" :

> " Smile on our loves; and while thou drawest round
> The sky's blue curtains, scatter silver dew
> On every flower that closes its sweet eyes
> In timely sleep. Let thy west wind sleep on
> The lake : *speak silence with thy glimmering eyes,*
> *And wash the dusk with silver.*"

The two lines, or half lines, which make the glory of this extract resemble perfectly, for vigorous grace and that subtle strength of interpretation which transfigures the external nature it explains, the living leader of English poets. Even he has hardly ever given a study of landscape more large and delicate, an effect of verse more exquisite and sonorous. Of the "Spring" we have already said something; but for that poem nothing short of transcription would be adequate. The "Autumn," too, should hardly have been rejected: it contains lines of perfect power and great beauty, though not quite up to the mark of "Spring" or "Summer." From another poem, certainly not worthier of the place it has been refused, we have extracted two lines worth remembering for their terseness and weight of scorn, recalling certain grave touches of satire in Blake's later work:

> " For ignorance is folly's leasing nurse,
> And love of folly needs none other's curse."

All that is worth recollection in the little play of " Edward the Third " has been here reproduced with a judicious care in adjusting and rejecting. Blake had probably never seen the praiseworthy but somewhat verbose historical drama on the same subject, generously bestowed upon Shakespeare by critics of that German acuteness which can accept as poetry the most meritorious powers of rhetoric. His own disjointed and stumbling fragment, deficient as it is in shape or plan or local colour, has far more of the sound and savour of Shakespeare's style in detached lines: more indeed than has ever been caught up by any poet except one to whom his editor has seized

the chance of paying tribute in passing—the author of
"Joseph and his Brethren ;" a poem which, for strength
of manner and freshness of treatment, may certainly recall
Blake or any other obscurely original reformer in art ;
although we may not admit the resemblance claimed for
it on spiritual grounds to the works of Blake, in whose
eyes the views taken by the later poet of the mysteries
inherent in matters of faith or morality, and generally of
the spiritual side of things, would, to our thinking, probably have appeared shallow and untrue by the side of his
own mystic personal creed. In dramatic passion, in
dramatic character, and in dramatic language, Mr. Wells'
great play is no doubt far ahead, not of Blake's work only,
but of most other men's : in actual conception of things
that lie beyond these, it keeps within the range of common
thought and accepted theory ; falling therefore far short,
in its somewhat over frequent passages of didactic and
religious reflection, of much less original thinkers than
Blake.

One other thing we may observe of these "Sketches ;"
that they contain, though only in the pieces rejected from
our present collection, sad indications of the inexplicable
influence which an early reading of the detestable pseudo-
Ossian seems to have exercised on Blake. How or why
such lank and lamentable counterfeits of the poetical style
did ever gain this luckless influence—one, too, which in
after years was to do far worse harm than it has done
here—it is not easy to guess. Contemporary vice of taste,
imperfect or on some points totally deficient education,
may explain much and more than might be supposed, even
with regard to the strongest untrained intellect ; but on

the other hand, the songs in this same volume give evidence of so rare a gift of poetical judgment, such exquisite natural sense and art, in a time which could not so much as blunder except by precedent and machinery, that such depravity of error as is implied by admiration and imitation of such an one as Macpherson remains inconceivable. Similar puzzles will, however, recur to the student of Blake's art; but will not, if he be in any way worthy of the study, be permitted for a minute to impair his sense of its incomparable merits. Incomparable, we say advisedly: for there is no case on record of a man's being quite so far in advance of his time, in everything that belongs to the imaginative side of art, as Blake was from the first in advance of his.

In 1782 Blake married, it seems after a year or two of engaged life. His wife Catherine Boucher deserves remembrance as about the most perfect wife on record. In all things but affection, her husband must have been as hard to live with as the most erratic artist or poet who ever mistook his way into marriage. Over the stormy or slippery passages in their earlier life Mr. Gilchrist has passed perhaps too lightly. No doubt Blake's aberrations were mainly matters of speech or writing; it is however said, truly or falsely, that once in a patriarchal mood he did propose to add a second wife to their small and shifting household, and was much perplexed at meeting on one hand with tears and on all hands with remonstrances. For any clandestine excursions or furtive eccentricities he had probably too much of childish candour and impulse; and this one hopeful and plausible design he seems to have sacrificed with a good grace, on finding it really objectionable to the run of erring men. As to the rest, Mrs. Blake's belief in him was full and profound enough to endure some amount of trial. Practically he was always, as far as we know, regular, laborious, immaculate to an exception; and in their old age she worked after him and for him, revered and helped and obeyed him, with an exquisite goodness.

For the next eighteen years we have no continuous or available record under Blake's own hand of his manner of life; and of course must not expect as yet any help from those who can still, or could lately, remember the man himself in later days. He laboured with passionate steadiness of energy, at work sometimes valueless and sometimes invaluable; made, retained, and lost friends of a varying quality. Even to the lamentable taskwork of bad comic engravings for dead and putrescent "Wit's Magazines" his biographer has tracked him and taken note of his doings. The one thing he did get published —his poem, or apology for a poem, called "The French Revolution" (the first of seven projected books)—is, as far as I know, the only original work of its author worth little or even nothing; consisting mainly of mere wind and splutter. The six other books, if extant, ought nevertheless to be looked up, as they can hardly be without some personal interest or empirical value, even if no better in workmanship than this first book. During these years however he produced much of his greatest work; among other things, the "Songs of Innocence and Experience," and the prophetic books from "Thel" to "Ahania;" of all which we shall have to speak in due time and order. The notes on Reynolds and Lavater, from which we have here many extracts given, we must hope to see some day printed in full. Their vivid and vigorous style is often a model in its kind ; and the matter, however violent and eccentric at times, always clear, noble, and thoughtful ; remarkable especially for the eagerness of approbation lavished on the meanest of impulsive or fanciful men, and the fervour of scorn excited by the best works and the best intentions of others. The watery wisdom and the bland absurdity of Lavater's axioms meet with singular tolerance from the future author of the " Proverbs of Hell ; " the considerate regulations and suggestions of Reynolds' " Discourses " meet with no tolerance at all from the future illustrator of Job and Dante. In all these rough notes, even we may say in those on Bacon's Essays, there is always a bushel of good grain to an ounce of chaff. What is erroneous or what seems perverse lies for the most part only on the surface ; what is falsely applied is often truly said ; what is unjustly worded is often justly conceived. A man insensible to the perfect manner and noble matter of Bacon, while tolerant of the lisping and slavering imbecilities of Lavater, seems at first sight past hope or help ; but subtract the names or alter the symbols given, and much of Blake's commentary will seem, as it is, partially true and memorable even in its actual form, wholly true and memorable in its implied meaning. Again, partly through ingrained humour, partly through the rough shifts of his imperfect and tentative education, Blake was much given to a certain perverse and defiant habit of expression, meant rather to scare and offend than to allure and attract the common run of readers or critics. In his old age we hear that he would at times try the ironic method upon objectionable reasoners; not, we should imagine, with much dexterity or subtlety.

The small accidents and obscure fluctuations of luck during these eighteen years of laborious town life, the changes of residence and acquaintance, the method and result of the day's work done, have been traced with much care and exhibited in a direct distinct manner by the biographer. Nothing can be more clear and sufficient than the brief notices of Blake's favourite brother and pupil, in character seemingly a weaker and somewhat violent *replica* of his elder, not without noble and amiable qualities; of his relations with Fuseli and Flaxman, with Johnson the bookseller, and others, whose names are now fished up from the quiet comfort of obscurity, and made more or less memorable for good or evil through their connection with one who was then himself among the obscurest of men. His alliance with Paine and the ultra-democrats then working or talking in London is the most curious episode of these years. His republican passion was like Shelley's, a matter of fierce dogmatic faith and rapid assumption. Looking at any sketch of his head and face one may see the truth of his assertion that he was born a democrat of the imaginative type. The faith which accepts and the passion which pursues an idea of justice not wholly attainable looks out of the tender and restless eyes, moulds the eager mobile-seeming lips. Infinite impatience, as of a great preacher or apostle—intense tremulous vitality, as of a great orator—seem to me to give his face the look

of one who can do all things but hesitate. We need
no evidence to bid us believe with what fervour of spirit
and singleness of emotion he loved the name and followed the likeness of freedom, whatever new name or
changed likeness men might put upon her. Liberty and
religion, taken in a large and subtle sense of the words,
were alike credible and adorable to him ; and in nothing
else could he find matter for belief or worship. His
forehead, largest (as he said) just over the eyes, shows an
eager steadiness of passionate expression. Shut off any
single feature, and it will seem singular how little the
face changes or loses by the exclusion. With all this, it
is curious to read how the author of " Urizen" and
" Ahania" saved from probable hanging the author of
the " Rights of Man " and " Age of Reason." Blake had
as perfect a gift of ready and steady courage as any
man : was not quicker to catch fire than he was safe to
stand his ground. The swift quiet resolution and fearless instant sense of the right thing to do which he
showed at all times of need are worth notice in a man of
such fine and nervous habit of mind and body.

In the year after Paine's escape from England, his
deliverer published a book which would probably have
been something of a chokepear for the *conventionnel.*
This set of seventeen drawings was Blake's first series of
original designs, not meant to serve as merely illustrative
work. Two of the prophetic books, and the " Songs of
Innocence," had already been engraved ; but there the
designs were supplementary to the text ; here such text
as there was served only to set out the designs ; and
even these " Keys" to the " Gates of Paradise," some-

what of the rustiest as they are, were not supplied in every copy. The book is itself not unavailable as a key to much of Blake's fitful and tempestuous philosophy; and it would have been better to re-engrave the series in full than to give random selections twisted out of their places and made less intelligible than they were at first by the headlong process of inversion and convulsion to which they have here been subjected.

The frontispiece gives a symbol of man's birth into the fleshly and mutable house of life, powerless and painless as yet, but encircled by the likeness and oppressed by the mystery of material existence. The pre-existent spirit here well-nigh disappears under stifling folds of vegetable leaf and animal incrustation of overgrowing husk. It lies dumb and dull, almost as a thing itself begotten of the perishable body, conceived in bondage and brought forth with grief. The curled and clinging caterpillar, emblem of motherhood, adheres and impends over it, as the lapping leaves of flesh unclose and release the human fruit of corporeal generation. With mysterious travail and anguish of mysterious division, the child is born as a thing out of sleep; the original perfect manhood being cast in effect into a heavy slumber, and the female or reflective element called into creation. This tenet recurs constantly in the turbulent and fluctuating evangel of Blake; that the feminine element exists by itself for a time only, and as the shadow of the male; thus Space is the wife of Time, and was created of him in the beginning that the things of lower life might have air to breathe and a place to hide their heads; her moral aspect is Pity. She suffers through the lapse of obscure and painful centuries with the sufferings of her children; she is oppressed with all their oppressions; she is plagued with all the plagues of transient life and inevitable death. At sight of her so brought forth, a wonder in heaven, all the most ancient gods or dæmons of pre-material life were terrified and amazed, touched with awe and softened with passion; yet endured not to look upon her, a thing alien from the things of their eternal life; for as space is impredicable of the divine world, so is pity impredicable of the dæmonic nature. (See the "First Book of Urizen.") For of all the minor immortal and uncreated spirits Time only is the friend of man; and for man's sake has given him Space to dwell in, as under the shadow and within the arms of a great compassionate mother, who has mercy upon all her children, tenderness for all good and evil things. Only through his help and through her pity can flesh or spirit endure life for a little, under the iron law of the maker and the oppressor of man. Alone among the other co-equal and co-eternal dæmons of his race, the Creator is brought into contact and collision with Space and Time; against him alone they struggle in Promethean agony of conflict to deliver the children of men; and against them is the Creator compelled to fight, that he may reach and oppress those whose weakness is defended by all the warring hands of Time, sheltered by all the gracious wings of Space.

In the first plate of the " Gates of Paradise," the woman finds the child under a tree, sprung of the earth like a mandrake, which he who plucks up and hears groan must go mad or die; grown under the tree of physical life, which is rooted in death, and the leaf of it is poisonous, and it bears as fruit the wisdom of the serpent, moral reason or rational truth, which invents the names of virtue and vice, and divides moral life into good and evil. Out of earth is rent violently forth the child of dust and clay, naked, wide-eyed, shrieking ; the woman bends down to gather him as a flower, half blind with fierce surprise and eagerness, half smiling with foolish love and pitiful pleasure ; with one hand she holds other children, small and new-blown also as flowers, huddled in the lap of her garment; with the other she plucks him up by the hair, regardless of his deadly shriek and convulsed arms, heedless that this uprooting of the mandrake is the seal of her own death also. Then follow symbols of the four created elements from which the corporeal man is made ; the water, blind and mutable as doting age, emblem of ignorant doubt and moral jealousy ; the heavy melancholy earth, grievous to life, oppressive of the spirit, type of all sorrows and tyrannies that are brought forth upon it, saddest of all the elements, tightest as a curb and painfullest as a load upon the soul : then the air wherein man is naked, the fire wherein man is blind ; ashamed and afraid of his own nature and its nakedness, surrounded with similitudes of severance and strife : overhung by rocks, rained upon by all the storms of heaven, lighted by unfriendly stars, with clouds spread under him and over; " a dark hermaphrodite," enlightened by the light within him, which is darkness—the light of reason and morality ; evil and good, who was neither good nor evil in the eternal life before this generated existence ; male and female, who from of old was neither female nor male, but perfect man without division of flesh, until the setting of sex against sex by the malignity of animal creation. Round the new-created man revolves the flaming sword of Law, burning and dividing in the hand of the angel, servant of the cruelty of God, who drives into exile and debars from paradise the fallen spiritual man upon earth. Round the woman (a double type perhaps at once of the female nature and the "rational truth" or law of good and evil) roar and freeze the winds and snows of prohibition, blinding, congealing, confusing; and in that tempest of things spiritual the shell of material things hardens and thickens, excluding all divine vision and obscuring all final truth with solid-seeming walls of separation. But death in the end shall enlighten all the deluded, shall deliver all the imprisoned; there, though the worm weaves, the Saviour also watches; the new garments of male and female to be there assumed by the spirit are so woven that they shall no longer be as shrouds or swaddling-clothes to hamper the newly born or consume the newly dead, but free raiment and fair symbol of the spirit. For the power of the creative dæmon, which began with birth, must end with death; upon the perfect and eternal man he had not power till he had created the earthly life to bring man into subjection; and shall not have power upon him again any more when he is once resumed by death. Where the Creator's power ends, there begins the Saviour's power; where oppression loses strength to divide, mercy gains strength to reunite. For the Creator is at most God of this world only, and belongs to the life which he creates; the God of this world is a thing of this world, but the Saviour or perfect man is of eternity, belonging to the spiritual life which was before birth and shall be after death.

In these first six plates is the kernel of the book ; round these the subsequent symbols revolve, and toward these converge. The seventh we may assume to be an emblem of desire as it is upon earth, blind and wild, glad and sad, destroying the pleasures it catches hold of, losing those it lets go. One Love, a moth-like spirit, lies crushed at the feet of the boy who pursues another, flinging his cap towards it as though to trap a butterfly ; startled with the laugh of triumphant capture even at his lips, as the wingless flying thing eludes him and soars beyond the enclosure of summer leaves and stems toward upper air and cloud. To the original sketch was appended this quotation from Spenser, Book 2, Canto 2, v. 2 :

> " Ah luckless babe, born under cruel star,
> And in dead parents' baleful ashes bred ;
> Full little weenest thou what sorrows are
> Left thee for portion of thy livelyhed."

Again, Youth, with the bow of battle lifted in his right hand, turns his back upon Age, and leaves him lamenting in vain remonstrance and piteous reclamation : the fruit of vain-glory and vain teaching, ending in rebellion and division of spirit, when the beliefs and doctrines of a man turn against him and he becomes at variance with himself and with his own issue of body or of soul. In the ninth plate, men strive to set a ladder against the moon and climb by it through the deepest darkness of night ; a white segment of narrow light just shows the sharp tongue of precipitous land upon which they are gathered together in vain counsel and effort. This was originally a satirical sketch of " amateurs and connoisseurs," emblematic merely of their way of studying art, analyzing all great things done with ready rule and line, and scaling with ladders of logic the heaven of invention; here it reappears enlarged and exalted into a general type of blind belief and presumptuous reason, indicative also of the helpless hunger after spiritual things ingrained in those made subject to things material; the effusion and eluctation of spirits sitting in prison towards the truth which should make them free. In the tenth plate, the half-submerged face and outstretched arm of a man drowning in a trough of tumbling sea show just above the foam, against the glaring and windy clouds whose blown drift excludes the sky. Perhaps the noble study of sea registered in the Catalogue as No. 128 of the second list was a sketch for this design of man sinking under the waves of time. Of the two this sketch is the finer; a greater effect of tempest was never given by the work of any hand than in this weltering and savage space of sea, with the aimless clash of its breakers and blind turbulence of water veined and wrinkled with storm, enridged and cloven into drifting array of battle, with no lesser life visible upon it of man or vessel, fish or gull : no land beyond it conceivable, no heaven above it credible. This drawing, which has been reproduced by photography, might have found a place here or later in the book. In the eleventh plate, emblematic of religious restraint and the severities of artificial holiness, an old man, spectacled and strait-mouthed, clips with his shears the plumes of a winged boy, who writhes

vainly in a passionate attempt at self-release, his arm
hiding his face, his lithe slight limbs twisting with pain
and fear, his curled head bent upon the curve of his
elbow, his hand straining the air with empty violence of
barren agony; a sun half risen lights up the expansion
of his half-shorn wings and the helpless labour of his
slender body. The twelfth plate continues this allegory
under the type of father and sons, the vital energy and
its desires or passions, thrust down into prison-houses
of ice and snow. Next, man as he is upon earth attains
for once to the vision of that which he was and shall be ;
his eyes open upon the sight of life beyond the mundane
and mortal elements, and the chains of reason and
religion relax. In the evening he travels towards the
grave ; a figure stepping out swiftly and steadily, staff
in hand, over rough country ground and beside low
thick bushes and underwood, dressed as a man of Blake's
day ; a touch of realism curious in the midst of such
mystical work. Next in extreme age he passes through
the door of death to find the worm at her work ; and in
the last plate of the series, she is seen sitting, a worm-
like woman, with hooded head and knees drawn up, the
adder-like husk or shell of death at her feet, and behind
her head the huge rotting roots and serpentine nether
fibres of the tree of life and death : shapes of strange
corruption and conversion lie around her, and between
the hollow tree-roots the darkness grows deep and
hard. " I have said to corruption, thou art my father ;
to the worm, thou art my mother and my sister."
This is she who is nearest of kin to man from his birth
to his death :

> " Weaving to dreams the sexual strife,
> And weeping over the web of life."

I have given thus early a rough and tentative analysis of this set of designs, rather than leave it to find a place among the poems or prophecies, because it does in effect belong rather to art than poetry, the verses being throughout subordinate to the engravings, and indeed scarcely to be accounted of as more than inscriptions or appendages. It may however be taken as being in a certain sense one of the prophetic or evangelic series which was afterwards to stretch to such strange lengths. In this engraved symbolic poem of life and death, most of Blake's chief articles of faith are advanced or implied ; noticeably, for example, that tenet regarding the creative deity and his relations to time and to the sons of men. Thus far he can see and no farther ; for so long and no longer he has power upon the actions and passions of created and transient life. Him let no Christians worship, nor the law of his covenant ; the written law which its writer wept at and hid beneath his mercy-seat ; but instead let them write above the altars of their faith a law of infinite forgiveness, annihilating in the measureless embrace of its mercy the separate existences of good and evil. So speaks Blake in his prologue ; and in his epilogue thus :

To the Accuser, who is the God of this World.

> Truly, my Satan, thou art but a dunce,
> And dost not know the garment from the man ;
> Every harlot was a virgin once,
> Nor canst thou ever change Kate into Nan.

Though thou are worshipped by the names divine
Of Jesus and Jehovah, thou art still
The Son of Morn in weary night's decline ;
The lost traveller's dream under the hill.

Upon the life which is but as a vesture, and as a vesture shall be changed, he who created it has power till the end ; appearances and relations he can alter, and turn a virgin to a harlot ; but not change one individual life to another, reverse or rescind the laws of personality. Virtue and vice, chastity and unchastity, are changeable and perishable ; "they all shall wax old as doth a garment :" but the underlying individual life is imperishable and intangible. All qualities proper to human nature are inventions of the Accuser ; not so the immortal prenatal nature, which is the essence of every man severally from eternity. That lies beyond the dominion of the God of this world ; he is but the Son of Morning, that having once risen, will set again ; shining only in the darkness of spiritual night ; his light is but a light seen in dreams before the dawn by men belated and misled, which shall pass away and be known no more at the advent of the perfect day.

All these mystical heresies may seem turbid and chaotic ; but the legend or subject-matter of the present book is transparent as water, lucid as flame, compared to much of Blake's subsequent work. The designs, even if taken apart from their significance, are among his most inventive and interesting. They were done "for children," because, in Blake's mind, the wise innocence of children was likeliest to appreciate and accept the message involved in them ; "for the sexes," that they might be at once enlightened to see beyond themselves, and enfranchised from the bondage of pietism or materialism. Interpreted according to Blake's intention, the book was a small leaf or chapter of the inspired gospel of deliverance which he was charged to preach through the organs of his art; a gospel not easily to be made acceptable or comprehensible.

Of the prophetic books produced about this time we shall not as yet speak; nor have we much to say of the next set of designs, those illustrative of "Young's Night Thoughts," which were done, as will be surmised, on commission. Power, invention, and a certain share of beauty, these designs of course have; but less, as it seems to me, of Blake's great qualities and more of his faults or errors than usual. That the text which serves as a peg to hang them on, or a finger-post to point them out, is itself a thing dead and rotten, does not suffice to explain this; for Blake could do admirable work by way of illustration to the verse of Hayley.

This name brings us to a new and singular division of our present task. During the four important years of Blake's residence at Felpham we can trace his doings and feelings with some fulness and with some confidence. They were probably no busier than other years of his life; but by a happy accident we hear more concerning the sort of labour done. In August 1800 Blake moved out of London for the first time; he returned "early in 1804."

Hayley's patronage of Blake is a piece of high comedy perfect in its way. The first act or two were played out with sufficient liking on either side. "Mr. Hayley acts

like a prince" towards "his good Blake," not it seems in
the direct way of pecuniary gifts or loans, but in such
smaller attentions as he could easily show to the husband
and wife on their first arrival close at hand.   It must be
remarked and remembered that throughout this curious
and incongruous intercourse there is no question whatever of obligation on Blake's part for any kindness shown
beyond the equal offices of friend to friend.   It is for
"Mr. Hayley's usual brotherly affection" that he expresses
such ready gratitude.   That the poor man's goodwill
was genuine we need not hesitate to allow ; but the
fates never indulged in a freak of stranger humour than
when it seemed good to their supreme caprice to couple in
the same traces for even the shortest stage a man like
Hayley with a man like Blake, and bracket the " Triumphs
of Temper" with the "Marriage of Heaven and
Hell."

England, with a deplorable ingratitude, has apparently
forgotten by this time what her Hayley was once like.
It requires a certain strength of imagination to realise the
assured fact that he was once a "greatest living poet ; "
retrospection collapses in the effort, and credulity loses
heart to believe.   Such, however, was in effect his profession ; he had the witness of his age under hand and
seal to the fact, that on the death of his friend Cowper
the supreme laurels of the age or day had fallen by inheritance to that poet's accomplished and ingenious biographer.
There is something pathetic and almost piteous in his
perfect complacency and his perfect futility.   A moral
country should not have forgotten that to Mr. Hayley,
when at work on his chief poem, "it seemed to be a kind

of duty incumbent on those who devote themselves to poetry to render a powerful and too often a perverted art as beneficial to life and manners as the limits of composition and the character of modern times will allow." Although the ages, he regretted to reflect, were past, in which poetry was idolized for *miraculous effects*, yet a poem intended to promote the cultivation of good humour, and designed to unite the special graces of Ariosto, of Dante, and of Pope, might still be of service to society ; or, he added with a chaste and noble modesty, "if this may be thought too chimerical and romantic by sober reason, it is at least one of those pleasing and innocent illusions in which a poetical enthusiast may be safely indulged ; " who will deny it ?

This was the patron to whom Flaxman introduced Blake as an available engraver, and, on occasion, a commendable designer. Hayley was ready enough to cage and exhibit among the flock of tame geese which composed his troop of swans this bird of foreign feather ; and until the eagle's beak and claws came into play under sharp provocation, the Felpham coop and farmyard were duly dignified by his presence and behaviour as a "tame villatic fowl." The master bantam-cock of the hen-roost in person fluttered and cackled round him with assiduous if perplexed patronage. But of such alliances nothing could come in the end but that which did come. "Mr. H.," writes Blake in July 1803 to Mr. Butts, his one purchaser (on the scale of a guinea per picture), "approves of my designs as little as he does of my poems. I have been forced to insist on his leaving me, in both, to my own self-will ; for I am determined to be no longer

pestered with his genteel ignorance and polite disapproba-
tion. His imbecile attempts to depress me only deserve
laughter." Let a compassionate amateur of human
poultry imagine what confusion must by this time have
been reigning in the poor hen-roost and dove-cote of
Eartham! Things, however, took some time in reaching
the tragic pitch of these shrill discords. For months or
years they appear to have run through various scales of very
tolerable harmony. Blake, in the intervals of incessant
engraving and occasional designing, was led by his good
Hayley into the greenest pastures of literature and beside
the stillest waters of verse; he was solicited to help in
softening and arranging for public inspection the horrible
and pitiful narrative of Cowper's life; he was prevailed
upon to listen while Hayley "read Klopstock into English
to Blake," with what result one may trust he never knew.
For it was probably under the sting of this infliction that
Blake scratched down in pencil a brief lyrical satire on
the German Milton, which modern humanity would refuse
to read in public if transcribed; although or because it
might be, for grotesque ease and ringing breadth of
melodious extravagance, a scrap saved from some tattered
chorus of Aristophanes, or caught up by Rabelais as the
fragment of a litany at the shrine of the *Dive Bouteille*.
Let any man judge, from the ragged shred we can afford
to show by way of sample, how a sight or handling of the
stuff would have affected Hayley;

> " The moon at that sight blushed scarlet red,
> The stars threw down their cups and fled,
> And all the devils that were in hell
> Answered with a ninefold yell.

Klopstock felt the intripled turn,
And all his bowels began to churn ;
And his bowels turned round three times three,
And locked in his soul with a ninefold key ;
*   *   *

Then again old Nobodaddy swore
He never had seen such a thing before
Since Noah was shut in the ark,
Since Eve first chose her hell-fire spark,
Since 'twas the fashion to go naked,
Since the old Anything was created ;
And   *   *   "

Only in choice Attic or in archaic French could the rest
be endured by modern eyes ; but Panurge could hardly
have improved on the manner of retribution devised
for flaccid fluency and devout sentiment always running
at the mouth.

For the rest, when out of the shadow of Klopstock or
Cowper, Blake had enough serious work on hand.   His
designs for various ballads of Hayley's, strays of sick
verse long since decomposed, were admirable enough to
warrant a hope of general admiration.   This they failed
of ; but Blake's head and hands were full of other work.
" Miniature," he writes to Mr. Butts, " is become a goddess
in my eyes."   He did not serve her long ; but while his
faith in her godhead lasted he seems to have officiated
with some ardour in the courts of her temple.   He speaks
of orders multiplying upon him, of especial praise received
for proficiency in this style of work ; not, we may suppose, from any who had much authority to praise or dispraise.   It is impossible to imagine that Hayley knew a
really great work of Blake's when he saw it ; a clever com-
minution of great power must have seemed to him the
worthiest use of it ; whereas the design and the glory of

Blake was to concentrate and elevate his talent: all he did and all he touched with profit has an air and a savour of greatness. In miniature and such things he must probably have worked with half his heart and less than half his native skill or strength of eye and hand.

There is a certain pathos in the changes of tone which come one by one over Blake's correspondence at this time. All at first is sunlit and rose-coloured. "The villagers are not mere rustics; they are polite and modest. Meat is cheaper than in London; but the sweet air and the voices of winds, trees, and birds, and the odours of the happy ground, make it a dwelling for immortals." This intense and eager pleasure in the freshness of things, this sharp relish of beauty in all the senses, which must needs run over and lapse into sudden musical expression, will recall the passages in Shelley's letters where some delight of sound or sight suddenly felt or remembered forces its way into speech, and makes music of the subservient words. "Work will go on here with God-speed. A roller and two harrows lie before my window." This passion for hints and types, common to all men of highly toned nerves and rapid reflectiveness of spirit, was not with Blake a matter of fugitive impulse or casual occasion. In his quietest moods of mind, in his soberest tempers of fancy, he was always at some such work. At this time, too, he was living at a higher strain of the senses than usual. So sudden a change of air and change of world as had come upon him filled his nerves and brain at every entrance with keen influences of childlike and sensitive satisfaction. Witness his first sweet and singular verses to Flaxman and to Butts—"such as Felpham produces

by me, though not such as she produces by her eldest
son," he remarks, with some reason ; that eldest son and
heir of every Muse being her good Hayley.   Witness too
the simple and complete pleasure with which he writes
invitations and descriptions, transcribes visions and expe-
riences.   Probably too in some measure, could we trace
the perfect relation of flesh with spirit and blood with
brain, we should find that this first daily communion with
the sea wrought upon him at once within and without ;
that the sharp sweetness of the salted air was not without
swift and pungent effect ; that the hourly physical delight
lavished upon every sense by all tunes and odours and
changes and colours of the sea—the delight of every
breath or sound or shadow or whisper passing upon it—
may have served at first to satiate as well as to stimulate,
before the pressure of enjoyment grew too intense and the
sting of enjoyment too keen.   Upon Blake, of all men,
one may conjecture that these influences of spirit and
sense would act with exquisite force.   It is observable
that now, and not before, we hear of visions making manifest to him the spiritual likeness of dead men : that the
scene of every such apocalypse was a sea-beach ; the shore
of a new Patmos, prolific as was the first of splendid and
enormous fancies, of dreams begotten and brought forth
in a like atmosphere and habit of mind.*   Now too the
illimitable book of divine or dæmonic revelation called

* Our greatest poet of the later days may be cited as a third witness. Through
the marvellous last book of the *Contemplations* the breath and sound of the sea is
blown upon every verse ;. when he heard as it were the thunder and saw as it
were the splendour of revelation, it was amid the murmur and above the motion
of the Channel ;

près du dolmen qui domine Rozel,
À l'endroit où le cap se prolonge en presqu'île.

"Jerusalem" was dictated by inspiration of its authors, who "are in eternity :" Blake "dares not pretend to be any other than the secretary." Human readers, if such indeed exist beyond the singular or the dual number, will wish that the authors had put themselves through a previous course of surgical or any other training which might have cured a certain superhuman impediment of speech, very perplexing to the mundane ear ; a habit of huge breathless stuttering, as it were a Titanic stammer, intolerable to organs of flesh. "Allegory," the too obedient secretary writes to his friend, "addressed to the intellectual powers, while it is altogether hidden from the corporeal understanding, is my definition of the most sublime poetry." A better perhaps could not be given ; as far that is as relates to the "spirit of sense" which is to be clothed in the beautiful body of verse ; but when once we have granted the power of conception, the claims of form are to be first thought of. It is of small moment how the work thus done may strike the heavy ear of vulgarity or affect the torpid palate of prurience ; against mere indolence or mere misconstruction it is waste of time to contrive precautions or rear defences ; but the laws and the dues of art it is never permissible to forget. It is in fact only by innate and irrational perception that we can apprehend and enjoy the supreme works of verse and colour ; these, as Blake indicates with a noble accuracy, are not things of the understanding ; otherwise, we may add, the whole human world would appreciate them alike or nearly alike, and the high and subtle luxuries of exceptional temperaments would be made the daily bread of the poor and hungry ; the *vinum dæmonum* which now the few only can digest safely and relish ardently would be found medicinal instead of poisonous, palatable instead of loathsome, by the run of eaters and drinkers ; all specialties of spiritual office would be abolished, and the whole congregation would communicate in both kinds. All the more, meantime, because this " bread of sweet thought and wine of delight" is not broken or shed for all, but for a few only—because the sacramental elements of art and poetry are in no wise given for the sustenance or the salvation of men in general, but reserved mainly for the sublime profit and intense pleasure of an elect body or church—all the more on that account should the ministering official be careful that the paten and chalice be found wanting in no one possible grace of work or perfection of material.

That too much of Blake's written work while at Felpham is wanting in executive quality, and even in decent coherence of verbal dress, is undeniable. The Pythoness who delivers these stormy and sonorous oracles is at once exposed and hampered as it were by her loose and heavy raiment ; the prophetic robe here slips or gapes, there muffles and impedes ; is now a tatter that hardly hides the contorted limbs, and now an encumbrance that catches or trips up the reeling feet. Everything now written in the fitful impatient intervals of the day's work bears the stamp of an overheated brain and of nerves too intensely strung. Everything may well appear to confirm the suggestion that, as high latitudes and climates of rarefied air affect the physical structure of inhabitants or travellers, so in this case did the sudden country life, the taste and savour of the sea, touch sharply and irritate deliciously the more susceptible and intricate organs of mind and nature. How far such passive capacity of excitement differs from insanity; how in effect a temperament so sensuous, so receptive, and so passionate, is further off from any risk of turning unsound than hardier natures carrying heavier weight and tougher in the nerves; need scarcely be indicated. For the rest, our concern at present shall still be mainly with the letters of this date; and by their light we may be enabled to see light shed upon many things hitherto hopelessly dark. As no other samples of Blake's correspondence worth mention have been allowed us by the jealousy of fate and divine parsimony, we must be duly grateful and careful in dealing with all we have; gathering the fragments into commodious baskets, and piecing the shreds into available patchwork.

These letters bear upon them the common stamp of all Blake's doings and writings; the fiery and lyrical tone of mind and speech, the passionate singleness of aim, the heat and flame of faith in himself, the violence of mere words, the lust of paradox, the loud and angry habits of expression which abound in his critical or didactic work, are not here missing; neither are clear indications wanting of his noblest qualities; the great love of great things, the great scorn of small men, the strong tenderness of heart, the tender strength of spirit, which won for him honour from all that were honourable. Ready even in a too fervent manner to accept, to praise, to believe in worth and return thanks for it, he will have no man or thing impede or divert him, either for love's sake or hate's. Small friends with feeble counsels to suggest must learn to suppress their small feelings and graceful regrets, or be cleared out of his way with all their powers to help or hinder ; lucky if they get off without some label of epigram on the forehead or sting of epigram in the flesh. Upon Hayley, as we may see by collation of Blake's note-book with his letters, the lash fell at last, after long toler-ation of things intolerable, after "great objections to my doing anything but the mere drudgery of business," (as for instance engraving illustrations to Hayley's poems designed by Flaxman's sister—not by his wife, as stated at p. 171 of the "Life" by some momentary slip of a most careful pen), "and intimations that if I do not confine myself to this I shall not live. This," adds Blake, "has always pursued me. You will understand by this the source of all my uneasiness. This from Johnson and Fuseli brought me down here, and this from Mr. H. will bring me back again." In a sharper mood than this, he appended to the decent skirts of Mr. Hayley one of the best burlesque epigrams in the language :—

> " Of Hayley's birth this was the happy lot :
> His mother on his father him begot."

With this couplet tied to his tail, the ghost of Hayley may perhaps run further than his own strength of wind or speed of foot would naturally have carried him : with this hook in his nose, he may be led by "his good Blake" some way towards the temple of memory.

What is most to be regretted in these letters is the wonderful tone of assertion respecting the writer's own pictures and those of the great Italian schools. This it would be difficult enough to explain, dishonest to over-look, easy to ridicule, and unprofitable to rebuke. All

that need be said of this singular habit of Blake's has
been said with admirable clearness and fairness in the
prefatory note to the prose selections in Vol. II. Higher
authority than the writer's of that note no man can have
or can require. And as Blake's artistic heresies are in
fact mere accidents—the illegitimate growth of chance
and circumstance—we may be content to leave them
wholly to the practical judgment and the wise charity of
such artists as are qualified to pass sentence upon the
achievements and the shortcomings of this great artist.
Their praise can alone be thoroughly worth having ; their
blame can alone be of any significance : and in no other
hands than theirs may we safely leave the memory and
the glory of a fellow-labourer so illustrious as Blake.

Other points and shades of character not less singular
it is essential here to take notice of. These are not matters of accident, like the errors of opinion or perversities
of expression which may distort or disfigure the notes and
studies on purely artistic matters ; they compose the vital
element and working condition of Blake's talent. From
the fifth to the tenth letter especially, it becomes evident
that the writer was passing through strange struggles of
spirit and passionate stages of faith. As early as the
fourth letter, dated almost exactly a year later than the
first written on his arrival at Felpham, Blake refers in a
tone of regret and perplexity to the "abstract folly"
which makes him incapable of direct practical work,
though not of earnest and continuous labour. This action
of the nerves or of the mind he was plainly unable to
regulate or modify. It hurries him while yet at work
into "lands of abstraction ;" he "takes the world with

him in his flight." Distress he knows would make the
world heavier to him, which seems now "lighter than a
ball of wool rolled by the wind;" and this distress material
philosophies or methodical regulations would "prescribe
as a medicinal potion" for a mind impaired or diseased
merely by the animal superflux of spirits and childlike
excess of spiritual health. But this medicine the strange
and strong faculty of faith innate in the man precludes
him from taking. Physical distress "is his mock and
scorn; mental no man can give; and if Heaven inflicts
it, all such distress is a mercy." It is not easy, but it is
requisite, to realise the perpetual freshness and fulness of
belief, the inalterable vigour and fervour of spirit with
which Blake, heretic and mystic as he may have been,
worshipped and worked; by which he was throughout
life possessed and pursued. Above all gods or dæmons of
creation and division, he beheld by faith in a perfect man a
supreme God. "Though I have been very unhappy, I am
so no longer. I am again emerged into the light of day;
I still (and shall to eternity) embrace Christianity, and
adore Him who is the express image of God." In the
light of his especial faith all visible things were fused into
the intense heat and sharpened into the keen outline of
vision. He walked and laboured under other heavens, on
another earth, than the earth and the heaven of material
life :

> " With a blue sky spread over with wings,
> And a mild sun that mounts and sings;
> With trees and fields full of fairy elves
> And little devils who fight for themselves;
> With angels planted in hawthorn bowers,
> And God Himself in the passing hours."

All this was not a mere matter of creed or opinion, much less of decoration or ornament to his work. It was, as we said, his element of life, inhaled at every breath with the common air, mixed into his veins with their natural blood. It was an element almost painfully tangible and actual ; an absolute medium or state of existence, inevitable, inexplicable, insuperable. To him the veil of outer things seemed always to tremble with some breath behind it : seemed at times to be rent in sunder with clamour and sudden lightning. All the void of earth and air seemed to quiver with the passage of sentient wings and palpitate under the pressure of conscious feet. Flowers and weeds, stars and stones, spoke with articulate lips and gazed with living eyes. Hands were stretched towards him from beyond the darkness of material nature, to tempt or to support, to guide or to restrain. His hardest facts were the vaguest allegories of other men. To him all symbolic things were literal, all literal things symbolic. About his path and about his bed, around his ears and under his eyes, an infinite play of spiritual life seethed and swarmed or shone and sang. Spirits imprisoned in the husk and shell of earth consoled or menaced him. Every leaf bore a growth of angels ; the pulse of every minute sounded as the falling foot of God ; under the rank raiment of weeds, in the drifting down of thistles, strange faces frowned and white hair fluttered ; tempters and allies, wraiths of the living and phantoms of the dead, crowded and made populous the winds that blew about him, the fields and hills over which he gazed. Even upon earth his vision was " twofold always ;" singleness of vision he scorned and feared as the sign of

mechanical intellect, of talent that walks while the soul
sleeps, with the mere activity of a blind somnambulism.
It was fourfold in the intervals of keenest inspiration and
subtlest rapture ; threefold in the paradise of dreams
lying between earth and heaven, lulled by lighter airs
and lit by fainter stars ; a land of night and moonlight,
spectral and serene. These strange divisions of spirit
and world according to some dim and mythologic
hierarchy were with Blake matters at once serious and
commonplace. The worlds of Beulah and Jerusalem,
the existence of Los god of Time and Enitharmon goddess
of Space, the fallen manhood of Theotormon, the imprisoned womanhood of Oothoon, were more to him even
than significant names ; to the reader they must needs
seem less. This monstrous nomenclature, this jargon of
miscreated things in chaos, rose as by nature to his lips,
flowed from them as by instinct. Time, an incarnate
spirit clothed with fire, stands before him in the sun's
likeness ; he is threatened with poverty, tempted to
make himself friends of this world ; and makes answer
as though to a human tempter :

> " My hands are laboured day and night
> And rest comes never in my sight ;
> My wife has no indulgence given
> Except what comes to her from heaven ;
> We eat little, we drink less ;
> This earth breeds not our happiness."

He beheld, he says, Time and Space as they were eternally, not as they are seen upon earth ; he saw nothing
as man sees : his hopes and fears were alien from all
men's ; and upon him and his the light of prosperous
days and the terrors of troubled time had no power.

" When I had my defiance given
    The sun stood trembling in heaven;
    The moon, that glowed remote below,
    Became leprous and white as snow ;
    And every soul of man on the earth
    Felt affliction and sorrow and sickness and dearth."

In all this we may see on one side the reflection and
refraction of outer things, on the other side the pro-
jection of his own mind, the effusion of his individual
nature, throughout the hardest and remotest alien matter.
Strangely severed from other men, he was, or he conceived himself, more strangely interwoven with them.
The light of his spiritual weapons, the sound of his
spiritual warfare, was seen, he believed, and was heard
in faint resonance and far reverberation among men who
knew not what such sights and sounds might mean. If,
worsted in this " mental fight," he should let " his sword
sleep in his hand," or " refuse to do spiritual acts
because of natural fears and natural desires," the world
would be the poorer for his defection, and himself
" called the base Judas who betrays his friend." Fear of
this rebuke shook and wasted him day and night; he
was rent in sunder with pangs of terror and travail.
Heaven was full of the dead, coming to witness against
him with blood-shedding and with shedding of tears :

" The sun was hot
    With the bows of my mind and with arrows of thought."

In this spirit he wrought at his day's work, seeing
everywhere the image of his own mood, the presence of
foes and friends. Nothing to him was neutral ; nothing
without significance. The labour and strife of soul in

which he lived was a thing as earnest as any bodily
warfare. Such struggles of spirit in poets or artists
have been too often made the subject of public study;
nay, too often the theme of chaotic versifiers. A theme
more utterly improper it is of course impossible to
devise. It is just that a workman should see all sides of
his work, and labour with all his might of mind and
dexterity of hand to make it great and perfect; but to
use up the details of the process as crude material for
cruder verse—to invite spectators as to the opening of a
temple, and show them the unbaked bricks and untem-
pered mortar—to expose with immodest violence and
impotent satisfaction the long revolting labours of mental
abortion—this no artist will ever attempt, no craftsman
ever so perform as to escape ridicule. It is useless for
those who can carve no statue worth the chiselling to
exhibit instead six feet or nine feet of shapeless plaster
or fragmentary stucco, and bid us see what sculptors
work with; no man will accept that in lieu of the
statue. Not less futile and not less indecent is it for
those who can give expression to no great poem to dis-
gorge masses of raw incoherent verse on the subject of
verse-making : to offer, in place of a poem ready wrought
out, some chaotic and convulsive story about the way in
which a poet works, or does not work.

To Blake the whole thing was too grave for any such
exposure of spiritual nudity. In these letters he records
the result of his " sore travail;" in these verses he com-
memorates the manner of his work " under the direction
of messengers from heaven daily and nightly, not without
trouble or care;" but he writes in private and by pure

instinct; he speaks only by the impulse of confidence,
in the ardour of faith. What he has to say is said
with the simple and abstract rapture of apostles or prophets; not with the laborious impertinence and vain
obtrusion of tortuous analysis. For such heavy play
with gossamer and straws his nature was too earnest
and his genius too exalted. This is the mood in which
he looks over what work he has done or has to do :
and in his lips the strange scriptural language used has
the sincerity of pure fire. "I see the face of my
Heavenly Father; He lays His hand upon my head, and
gives a blessing to all my work. Why should I be
troubled? why should my heart and flesh cry out? I
will go on in the strength of the Lord; through hell
will I sing forth His praises; that the dragons of the
deep may praise Him, and that those who dwell in darkness and in the sea-coasts may be gathered into His
kingdom." So did he esteem of art, which indeed is not
a light thing; nor is it wholly unimportant to men that
they should have one capable artist more or less among
them. How it may fare with artisans (be they never so
pretentious) is a matter of sufficiently small moment.
One blessing there assuredly was upon all Blake's work ;
the infinite blessing of life ; the fervour of vital blood.

In spite however of all inspiration and of all support,
sickness and uncongenial company impeded his hours of
labour and corroded his hours of repose. A trial on the
infamous charges of sedition and assault, brought by a
private soldier whose name of Scholfield was thus made
shamefully memorable, succeeded finally in making the
country unendurable to him. It must be said here of

the hapless Hayley that he behaved well in this time of vexation and danger : coming forward to bail " our friend Blake," and working hard for the defence in a tumultuous and spluttering way : he " would appear in public at the trial, living or dying," and did, with or without leave of doctors, appear and speak up for the accused. Blake's honourable acquittal does not make it less disgraceful that the charge should at all have been entertained. His own courage, readiness of wit, and sincerity of spirit are fully shown in the letter relating this short and sharp episode in his quiet life. Some months later he returned to London once for all, and once for all broke off relations with Felpham : commending, it may be hoped, Hayley to the Muses and Scholfield to the halberts.

Having read these letters, we are not lightly to judge of Blake as of another man. Thoughts and creeds peculiar to his mind found expression in ways and words peculiar to his lips. It was no vain or empty claim that he put forward to especial insight and individual means of labour. If he spoke strangely, he had great things to speak. If he acted strangely, he had great things to do. "Mount Sinai was altogether on a smoke, because the Lord descended on it in fire." Let the tree be judged by its fruit. If the man who wrote thus had nothing to do or to say worth the saying or the doing, it may fairly be said that he was mad or foolish. The involving smoke, here again, implied the latent fire. Where the particles of dust are mere hardened mud, where the cloud is mere condensing fog hatched from the stagnation of a swamp, one may justly complain of the obstruction and the obscurity. There is here indeed too much of mist, but it is at least clear ; the air that breeds it is high, the moisture that feeds it is pure. This man had never lived in the low places of thought. In the words of a living poet,* whose noble verses are worthy to stand thus near Blake's own—

> " He had seen the moon's eclipse
> By the fire from Etna's lips,
> With Orion had he spoken,
> His fast with honey-dew had broken."

His dialect was too much the dialect of a far country ; but it was from a far country that he came, from a lofty station that he spoke. To a poet who has given us so much, to an artist who has done great things to such great purpose, we may give at least some allowance and some toleration. The distance is great which divides a fireside taper from the eclipsed moon on Etna. Rules which are useful or necessary for household versifiers may well be permitted to relax or even to dissolve when applied to one who has attained to see with unblinded eyes and to speak with adequate words of matters so far above them.

The next point noticeable by us in the story of Blake's life is his single-handed duel with Cromek and Stothard ; and of this we need not wish to speak at much length. The engraver, swift and sharp in all his dealings—never scrupulous, insolent sometimes, and always cunning—had

---

* W. B. Scott. The few and great words cited above occur, it will be observed, in a poem affording throughout no inapt allegory of Blake's life and works. More accurate and more admirable expression was never given to a theme so pregnant and so great. The whole "fable" may be well applied by students of the matter in hand to the history of Blake's relations with minor men of more turn for success ; which, as Victor Hugo has noted in his royal manner, is so often "a rather hideous thing."

an easy game to play, and played it without shame ; not even taking the trouble to hide his marked cards or to load his dice in private.　In spite or in consequence of this rapacity and mendacity,* Cromek was evidently of

* It appears that some effort, laudable if wholly sincere, and not condemnable if partly coloured by personal feeling, has been made to rebut the charges brought against Stothard and Cromek by the biographer of Blake.　What has been written in the text is of course based upon the assumption that Mr. Gilchrist has given an account of the matter as full and as fair as it was assuredly his desire to make it.　As junior counsel (so to speak) on behalf of Blake, I have followed the lead of his biographer ; for me in fact nothing remained but to revise and restate, with such clearness and brevity as I could, the case as laid down by him.　This, finding on the face of it nothing incoherent or incredible, I have done ; whether any man can disprove it remains to be seen. Meantime we are not left to our own choice in the matter of epithets.　There is but one kind of phrase that will express such things and the doers of such things. Against Stothard no grave charge has been brought ; none therefore can be re-futed.　Any reference to subsequent doings or sufferings of his must be unspeakably irrelevant to the matter in hand.　Against Cromek a sufficiently heavy indict-ment has been laid ; one which cannot be in the least degree lightened by counter-charges of rash violence on Blake's part or blind hastiness on Mr. Gilchrist's. One thing alone can avail him in the way of whitewash.　He is charged with theft ; prove that he did not steal.　He is charged with breach of contract ; prove that his contract was never broken.　He is charged with denying a commission given by him ; prove that he did not deny it.　For no man, it is to be feared, will now believe that Blake, sleeping or waking, forged the story of the com-mission or trumped up the story of the contract.　That point of the defence the counsel for Cromek had best give up with all convenient speed ; had better indeed not dream at all of entering upon it.　Again : he is charged, as above, with adding to his apparent perfidy a superfetation of insolence, an accretion or excrescence of insult.　Prove that he did not write the letter published by Mr. Cunningham in 1852.　It is undoubtedly deplorable that any one now living should in any way have to suffer for the misdoings of a man, whom, were it just or even possible, one would be willing to overlook and to forget.　But time is logical and equable; and this is but one among many inevitable penalties which time is certain to bring upon such wrong-doers in the end ; penalties, or rather simple results of the thing done.　Had this man either dealt honestly or while dealing dishonestly been but at the pains to keep clear of Walter Scott and William Blake, no writer would have had to disturb his memory.　But now, however strong or sincere may be our just sense of pity for all to whom it may give pain, truth must be spoken ; and the truth is that, unless the authorities cited can be utterly upset and broken down by some palpable proof in his favour, Cromek was what has been stated. Mr. Gilchrist also, in the course of his fair and lucid narrative, speaks once of "pity."　Pity may be good, but proof is better.　Until such proof come, the

some use to Blake. And even for the exercise of these special talents he is perhaps not to be blamed ; the man did but work with such qualities as he had ; did but put out to use his natural gifts and capacities. But that he should have done this at Blake's expense is and must remain unpardonable : and therefore he must be left to hang with the head downwards from the memorial gallows to which biography has nailed him ; a warning to all such others to choose their game more warily. A

best that can be done for Cromek is to let well alone. Less could not have been said of him than equitable biography has here been compelled to say ; no more need be said now and for ever, if counsel will have the wisdom to let sleeping dogs lie. This advice, if they cannot refute what is set down without more words, we must give them ; μὴ κίνει Καμάριναν. The waters are muddy enough without that. Vague and vain clamour of deprecation or appeal may be plaintive but is not conclusive. As to any talk of cruelty or indelicacy shown in digging up the dead misdeeds of dead men, it is simply pitiable. Were not reason wasted on such reasoners it might be profitable (which too evidently it is not) to reply that such an argument cuts right and left at once. Suppress a truth, and you suggest a lie ; and a lie so suggested is the most "indelicate" of cruelties possible to inflict on the dead If, for pity's sake or contempt's or for any other reason, the biographer had explained away the charges against Cromek which lay ready to his hand, he must have left upon the memory of Scott and upon the memory of Blake the stain of a charge as grave as this : if Cromek was honest, they were calumniators. To one or two the good name of a private man may be valuable ; to all men the good name of a great man must be precious. This difference of value must not be allowed to weigh with us while considering the evidence ; but the fact seems to be that no evidence in disproof of the main charges has been put forward which can be seriously thought worth sifting for a moment. This then being the sad case, to inveigh against Blake's biographer is utterly idle and hardly honest. If the stories are not true, any man's commentary which assumes their truth must be infinitely unimportant. If the stories are true, no remark annexed to the narrative can now blacken the accused further. Those alone who are responsible for the accusation brought can be convicted of unfairness in bringing it ; Mr. Gilchrist, it must be repeated, found every one of the charges which we now find in his book, given under the hand and seal of honourable men. These he found it, as I do now, necessary to transcribe in a concise form ; adding, as I have done, any brief remarks he saw fit to make in the interest of justice and for the sake of explanation. Let there be no more heard of appeal against this exercise of a patent right, of invective against this discharge of an evident duty. Disproof is the one thing that will now avail; and to anything short of that no one should again for an instant listen.

tradesman who, by their own account, swindled Blake
and robbed Scott can hardly expect to be allowed safe
harbourage under the compassionate shelter of complete
oblivion or behind the weather-tight screen of simple
contempt. It may be worth while to condense the
evidence as to his dealings with Blake and Stothard.
One alone of these three comes out clear from the
involved network of suspicious double-dealing. In the
matter of the engravings to Blair, Cromek had en-
trapped and cheated Blake from the first. In the matter
of the drawing from Chaucer, he had gone a step
further down the steep slope of peculation. After the
proposal to employ Schiavonetti, Blake might at once
have thrown him over as a self-detected knave. He did
not; and was accordingly plundered again in a less
dexterous and a more direct manner. It is fortunate
that the shameful little history has at last been tracked
through all its scandalous windings by so keen an eye
and so sure a hand as Mr. Gilchrist's. Two questions
arise at first sight; did Cromek give Blake a commission
for his design of the "Pilgrims"? did Stothard, when
Cromek proposed that he should take up the same subject, know that the proposal was equivalent to the
suggestion of a theft? Both these questions Blake would
have answered in the affirmative; and in his dialect the
affirmative mood was distinct and strong. Further evidence on the first head can be wanted by no one of
decent insight or of decent candour. That Cromek,
with more than professional impudence, denied the
charge, is an incident in the affair neither strange nor
important. The manner of his denial may be matched

for effrontery with the tone of his insolent letter to Blake on the subject of the designs to Blair. With the vulgarities and audacities, the shifts and the doubles of this shuffling man of prey, no one need again be troubled. That a visitor caught with the spoons in his pocket should bluster, stammer, and grin as he pleads innocence or affects amazement, is natural and desirable; for every word and gesture, humble or shameless, incoherent or intrepid, serves to convict him twice over. Undoubtedly he saw Blake's sketch, tried to conjure it into his pocket, and failed; undoubtedly, finding that the artist would not again give up his work to be engraved by other hands, he made such approach to an honest offer as was compatible with his character; undoubtedly also he then made money in his uncleanly way out of the failure by tossing the subject to another painter as a bait. No man has a right to express wonder that Blake refused to hold Stothard blameless. It is nothing whatever to the purpose that, while Cromek's somewhat villainous share in the speculation was as yet under cover, Blake may have bestowed on Stothard's unfinished design his friendly counsel and his frank applause. After the dealer's perfidy had been again bared and exposed by his own act, it was, and it is yet, a stretch of charity to suppose that his associate was not likewise his accomplice. And the manner of Stothard's retort upon Blake, when taxed by him with unfair dealing, was not of a sort qualified to disperse or to allay suspicion. He charged, and he permitted Cromek to charge, the plundered man with the act of plunder. Even though we, who can now read the whole account without admixture of personal feeling, may acquit Stothard of active or actual treachery, as all must gladly do who remember how large a debt is due from all to an artist of such exquisite and pleasurable talent, it is hopeless to make out for him a thoroughly sufficient case. The fellowship of such an one as Cromek leaves upon all who take his part at least the suspicion of a stain. All should hope that Stothard on coming out of the matter could have shown clean hands ; none can doubt that Blake did. That on Stothard's part irritation should have succeeded to surprise, and rancour to irritation, is not wonderful. If he was indeed injured by the fault of Cromek and the misfortune of Blake, it would doubtless have been admirably generous to have controlled the irritation and overcome the rancour ; but in that case the worst that should be said of him is that he did not adopt the noblest course of action possible to him. Admitting this, he is not blameable for choosing to throw in his lot with Cromek ; but we must then suppose not merely that Cromek had abstained from any avowal of his original treachery, but that Stothard was unhappily able to accept in good faith the bare assertion of Cromek in preference to the bare assertion of Blake. If we believe this, we are bound to admit no harsher feeling than regret that Cromek should so have duped and blinded his betters ; but in common fairness we are also bound to restrict the question within these limits. For Stothard a door of honourable escape stands open ; and all must desire rather to widen than to narrow the opening. No one can wish to straiten his chance of acquittal, or to inquire too curiously whether there be not a pretext for closing the door that now stands ajar. But for the rest,

it is simply necessary to choose between Blake's authority
and Cromek's ; and to consider this alternative seriously
for a moment would be at once an act of condescension
towards Cromek and of impertinence towards Blake,
equally unjustifiable on either side. It is possible that
Blake was not wronged by Stothard ; it is undeniable
that he was wronged through him. It is probable that
Stothard believed himself to be not in the wrong ; it is
certain that Blake was in the right.*

* It is to be regretted that the share taken in this matter by Flaxman, who
defended Stothard from the charge of collusion with Cromek, appears to have
alienated Blake from one of his first friends. Throughout the MS. so often cited
by his biographer, he couples their names together for attack. In one of his
rough epigrams, formless and pointless for the most part, but not without value
for the sudden broken gleams of light they cast upon Blake's character and
history, he reproaches both sculptor and painter with benefits conferred by himself and disowned by them : and the blundering stumbling verses thus jotted
down to relieve a minute's fit of private anger are valuable as evidence for his
sincere sense of injury.

To F. AND S.

> " I found them blind : I taught them how to see ;
> And now they know neither themselves nor me.
> 'Tis excellent to turn a thorn to a pin,
> A fool to a bolt, a knave to a glass of gin."

Whether or not he had in fact thus utilized his rivals by making the most out
of their several qualities, may be questionable. If so, we must say he managed
to scratch his own fingers with the pin, to miss his shot with the bolt, and to
spill the liquor extracted from the essence of knavery. The following dialogue
has equal virulence and somewhat more sureness of aim.

MR. STOTHARD TO MR. CROMEK.

> " For fortune's favour you your riches bring ;
> But fortune says she gave you no such thing.
> Why should you prove ungrateful to your friends,
> Sneaking, and backbiting, and odds-and-ends ? "

MR. CROMEK TO MR. STOTHARD.

> " Fortune favours the brave, old proverbs say ;
> But not with money ; that is not the way :
> Turn back, turn back ; you travel all in vain ;
> Turn through the iron gate down Sneaking Lane."

About the close of this quarrel, and before the publication of Blake's designs to Blair as engraved for Cromek
by Schiavonetti, a book came out which would have
deserved more notice and repaid more interest than has
yet been shown it.   The graceful design by Blake on its
frontispiece is not the only or even the chief attraction
of Dr. Malkin's "Memoirs of his Child."   The writer
indeed treads ponderously and speaks thickly ; but there
is extant no picture at once so perfect and so quaint of
a purely childlike talent.   Even supreme genius, which
usually has a mind now and then to try, has never given
us the complete and vivid likeness which a child has for
once given of himself.   Even Shakespeare, even Hugo,
even Blake, has not done this.   The husky dialect of his
father suffices to express something ; and the portrait is
significant and pleasant, reproducing as it does the solid
grace and glad gravity proper to children ; a round and
bright figure, with no look of over-training or disease.
But the child's own scraps and scrawls contain the kernel
and jewel of the book.   His small drawings are certainly
firmer, clearer, more inventive than could have been
looked for in a six-year-old artist.   Any slight imitative
work in a child implies the energy which impels invention in a man.   His little histories and geographies are
delightful for illogical sequence of events and absurd
coherence of fancy.   Only a child could have invented
and combined such unimaginable eccentricities of innocence.   The language and system of proper names strongly

For the "iron gate" of money-making the brazen-browed speaker was no
unfit porter.   The crudity of these rough notes for some unfinished satire is not,
let it be remembered, a fair sample of Blake's capacity for epigram ; and it
would indeed be unfair to cite them but for their value as to the matter in hand.

recall Blake's own habits of speech. The province of Malleb and the city of Tumblebob are no unfit abodes for Hand and Hyle, Kwantok and Kotope. The moral polity of Allestone is not unlike that which prevails among the Emanations "who in the aggregate are called Jerusalem." The pamphlet, condensed and compressed into a form more thoroughly readable, would be worth republishing.

It seems probable that the verses following were written by Blake about this time, as Mr. Gilchrist refers the design of the "Last Judgment," executed on commission for Lady Egremont, to the year 1807. They are evidently meant to match the beautiful dedication of the designs to Blair, which were not brought out till the next year. Less excellent in workmanship, they are not less important by way of illustration. The existence of some mythical or symbolic island of Atalantis, where the arts were to be preserved as in paradise, now walled round or washed over by the blind and bitter waters of time, was a favourite vision with Blake. At a first reading some of these verses seemed to refer to the subsequent series of designs from Dante; but there is no evidence of any such later commission as we must in that case take for granted.

> " The caverns of the grave I've seen,
> And these I showed to England's queen;
> But now the caves of Hell I view,
> Who shall I dare to show them to?
> What mighty soul in beauty's form
> Shall dauntless view the infernal storm?
> Egremont's Countess can control
> The flames of hell that round me roll.

> If she refuse, I still go on,
> Till the heavens and earth are gone;
> Still admired by noble minds,
> Followed by Envy on the winds.
> Re-engraved time after time,
> Ever in their youthful prime,
> My designs unchanged remain ;
> Time may rage, but rage in vain ;
> For above Time's troubled fountains,
> On the great Atlantic mountains,
> In my golden house on high,
> There they shine eternally."

Blake was always looking westward for his islands of the blest. All transatlantic things appear to have a singular hold upon his fancy. America was a land of misty and stormy morning, struck by the fierce and fugitive fires of intermittent war and nascent freedom. In a dim confused manner, he seems to mix up the actual events of history with the formless and labouring legends of his own mythology ; or rather to cast circumstances into the crucible of vision, and extract a strange amalgam of metals unfit for mortal currency and difficult to bring to any test.

In 1808 the illustrations to "Blair's Grave" appeared, and found some acceptance ; a success on which the shameful soul of Cromek fed exultingly and fattened scandalously. The ravenous gamester had packed his cards from the first with all due care, and was able now to bluster without fear as he had before swindled without shame. Twenty pounds of the profits fell to the share of the designer for some of the most admirable works extant in that line. The sweetness and vivid grace of these designs are as noticeable as the energy and rapidity of imagination implied by them. Even in Blake's lifetime their tender and lofty beauty drew down some recognition; and incautious criticism, as it praised them, forgot that the artist was not dead yet. The generous oversight was afterwards amply and consistently redeemed. For the moment it was perhaps not wonderful that even so much excellence should obtain something of mistrustful admiration. The noble passion and exaltation of spirit here made visible burnt its way into notice for a time; and Cromek was allowed to claim applause for his invention of Blake. We will choose two designs only for reference. None who have seen can well forget the glorious violence of reunion between soul and body, meeting with fierce embraces, with glad agony and rage of delight; with breasts yearning and eyes wide, with sweet madness of laughter at their lips; the startled and half-arisen body not less divine already than the descending soul, though the earth clings yet about his knees and feet, and though she comes down as with a clamour of rushing wind and prone impulse of falling water, fresh from the stars and the highest air of heaven. But for perfect beauty nothing of Blake's can be matched against the design of the soul departing; in this drawing the body lies filled as it were and clothed with the supreme sleep of flesh, no man watching by it; with limbs laid out and covered, with eyelids close; and the soul, with tender poise of pausing feet, with painless face and sad pure eyes, looks back as with a serene salutation full of pity, before passing away into the clear air and light left at the end of sunset on heaven and the hills; where outside the opened lattice a soft cold land of rising fields and ridged moorland bears upon it the barren

beauty of shadow and sleep, the breath and not the
breeze of evening. The sweet and grave grace of this
background, with a bright pallor in the sky and an effect
upon field and moor of open air without wind, brings
with it a sense as of music.

A year later Blake advertised and opened his exhibition; which he was about as qualified to manage as
little Malkin might have been. Between anger, innocence, want of funds and sense of merit, he would
assuredly have ruined a better chance than he ever had.
With the exception of his *Canterbury Pilgrims*, the
choice of pictures and designs for exhibition seems to
have been somewhat unhappy.* The admirable power
and high dramatic quality of that singular but noble
picture, the latent or superincumbent beauty which
corrects and redeems its partial ugliness, the strong
imagination and the fanciful justice of the entire work,
were invisible to all but such spectators as Charles Lamb;
if indeed there were ever another capable of seeing
them to such purpose. Whatever portion of the like
merit there may have been in the other works exhibited
was still more utterly lost upon the few who saw them
at all; for of these we have scarcely any record beyond
Blake's own. One journal alone appears to have noticed
the exhibition. An angry allusion of Blake's to some

---

* Since writing the lines above I have been told by Mr. Seymour Kirkup that
one picture at least among those exhibited at this time was the very noblest of all
Blake's works; the "Ancient Britons." It appears to have dropped out of sight,
but must be still hidden somewhere. Against the judgment of Mr. Kirkup there
can be no appeal. The saviour of Giotto, the redeemer of Dante, has power to
pronounce on the work of Blake. I allow what I said to stand as I said it at
first, only that I may not miss the chance of calling attention to the loss and
paying tribute to the critic.

assault of the *Examiner* newspaper upon his works and character has been hitherto left unexplained, presumably through a not irrational contempt. That Blake may be cleared from any charge of perversity, a brief account of the quarrel is here appended. Contemptible as are both the journeyman writer and his poor day's work, they have been found worth tracking down on account of the game flown at.

In the thirtieth number of the *Examiner* (August 7th, 1808) there is a review (signed R. H.) of the *Blair's Grave*, sufficiently impudent in manner and incapable in matter to have provoked a milder spirit than Blake's. Fuseli's prefatory note is cited with a tone of dissentient patronage not lightly to be endured; " none but such a visionary as Mr. Blake or such a frantic (*sic*) as Mr. Fuseli could possibly fancy," and so forth; then follows some chatter about the failures of great poets, "utter impossibility of representing *Spirit* to the eye" (except by means of italic type), "insipid," "absurd," "all the wise men of the East would not possibly divine," " *small* assistance of the title" (italics again), "how are we to find out?" (might not one reply with Thersites, " Make that demand of thy Maker ?"), "how absurd," "more serious censure," "most heterogeneous and serio-fantastic," " most indecent," " appearance of libidinousness," "much to admire, but more to censure," and all the common-places of that pestilent old style which, propped on italics and points of exclamation, halts at every sentence between a titter, a shrug, and a snarl. Schiavonetti also "has done more than justice" to Blake, and Blair and his engraver are finally bidden to divide the real palm. Who this reviewer was, no man need either know or care; but all may now understand the point of Blake's allusion. Next year however the real batteries were opened. It is but loathsome labour to shovel out this decomposed rubbish from the catacombs of liberal journalism; but if thus only we can explain an apparently aimless or misplaced reference on the great artist's part, it may be worth while to throw up a few spadefuls.

This second article bears date September 17th, 1809, No. 90 of the *Examiner*, and is labelled "Mr. Blake's Exhibition." The contributor has already lapsed from simple fatuity into fatuity compound with scurrility. Blake here figures as "an unfortunate lunatic, whose personal inoffensiveness secures him from confinement, and consequently of whom no public notice would have been taken, if he was not" (the man's grammar here goes mad on its own account, but what then?) "forced on the notice and animadversion of the *Examiner* in having been held up" (the case by this time is fairly desperate) "to public admiration;" such is the eccentricity of human error. The *Blair* of last year "was a futile endeavour *by* bad drawings to represent immateriality *by* bodily personifications," and so forth; once again, "the tasteful hand of Schiavonetti," one regrets to remember, was employed to bestow "an exterior charm on deformity and nonsense. Thus encouraged, the poor man" (to wit, Blake) "fancies himself a great master, and has painted a few wretched pictures, some of which are"—any one may finish that for the critic. The catalogue is "a farrago of nonsense, unintelligibleness (*sic*), and egregious vanity." Stothard and the irrepressible Schiavonetti are of course held up in contrast to the "distempered brain" which produced Blake's *Pilgrims*. The picture of *The Ancient Britons* "is a complete caricature; the colour of the flesh is exactly like hung beef." Here we will pull the man up short and have done with him. He shirks a signature this time; and whether or no he were the same as last year's critic, those may find out who care.

"Arcadiæ pecuaria rudere dicas;" would not one say that this mingling bray and howl had issued through the throat and nostril of some one among the roving or browsing cattle of our own daily or weekly literature, startled at smelling some incongruous rose in his half-eaten thistle-heap? Such feeders were always one in voice and one in palate: it were waste of wood and iron to cudgel or to prod them. Even when their clamour becomes too intolerably dissonant we may get out of hearing and solace our vexed ears and spirits with reflection on that axiom of Blake's, which, though savouring in such a case of excessive optimism, we will strive to hope is true :

> " The bleat, the bark, bellow, and roar,
> Are waves that beat on Heaven's shore."

This was not Blake's only connexion or collision with the journals of his day. An adverse notice of Fuseli had excited him to more direct reprisals than the attack upon himself now did. The *Monthly Magazine* for July 1st, 1806 (vol. xxi. pp. 520, 521), contains the following letter, which is now first unearthed and seems worth saving. It is not without perversities; neither is it wanting in vigour and fervour of thought.

" To the Editor of the ' Monthly Magazine.'

" Sir,—My indignation was exceedingly moved at reading a criticism in *Bell's Weekly Messenger* (25th May) on the picture of Count Ugolino, by Mr. Fuseli, in the Royal Academy Exhibition; and your magazine being as extensive in its circulation as that paper, and as it also must from its nature be more permanent, I take the advantageous opportunity to counteract the widely-diffused malice which has for many years, under the pretence of admiration of the arts, been assiduously sown and planted among the English public against true art, such as it existed in the days of Michael Angelo and Raphael. Under pretence of fair criticism and candour, the most wretched taste ever produced has been upheld for many, very many years; but now, I say, now its end has come. Such an artist as Fuseli is invulnerable, he needs not my defence; but I should be ashamed not to set my hand and shoulder, and whole strength, against those wretches who, under pretence of criticism, use the dagger and the poison.

" My criticism on this picture is as follows : ' Mr. Fuseli's Count Ugolino is the father of sons of feeling and dignity, who would not sit looking in their parent's face in the moments of his agony, but would rather retire and die in secret while they suffer him to indulge his passionate and innocent grief, his innocent and venerable madness, and insanity, and fury, and whatever paltry cold-hearted critics cannot, because they dare not, look upon. Fuseli's Count Ugolino is a man of wonder and admiration, of resentment against man and devil, and of humiliation before God : prayer and parental affection fills the figure from head to foot. The child in his arms, whether boy or girl signifies not (but the critic must be a fool who has not read Dante, and who does not know a boy from a girl); I say, the child is as beautifully drawn as it is coloured—in both, inimitable; and the effect of the whole is truly sublime, on account of that very colouring which our critic calls black and heavy. The German-flute colour, which was used by the Flemings (they call it burnt bone), has [? so] possessed the eye of certain connoisseurs, that they cannot see appropriate colouring, and are blind to the gloom of a real terror.

" The taste of English amateurs has been too much formed upon pictures imported from Flanders and Holland, consequently our countrymen are easily brow-beat on the subject of painting; and hence it is so common to hear a man say, ' I am no judge of pictures;' but, O Englishmen ! know that every man ought to be a judge of pictures, and every man is so who has not been connoisseured out of his senses.

"A gentleman who visited me the other day said, 'I am very much surprised at the dislike which some connoisseurs show on viewing the pictures of Mr. Fuseli; but the truth is, he is a hundred years beyond the present generation.' Though I am startled at such an assertion, I hope the contemporary taste will shorten the hundred years into as many hours; for I am sure that any person consulting his own eyes must prefer what is so supereminent; and I am as sure that any person consulting his own reputation, or the reputation of his country, will refrain from disgracing either by such ill-judged criticisms in future.

"Yours, WM. BLAKE."

This ready championship, erratic and excessive as it may be, is not less characteristic of the man than is that outspoken violence which helped to make his audience often deaf and unfriendly. The letter, as we said, did not happen to turn up in time for insertion in any niche of the *Life* or *Appendix*: it will not seem a valueless windfall if read by the light of the Catalogue, the Address, and other notes on art embalmed in the second volume.

No part of Blake's life was nobler in action or is yet worthier of study than the period of neglected labour and unbroken poverty which followed. Much of the work done is now, it appears, irretrievably lost. New friends gathered about him as the old ones died out; for indeed all men capable of seeing the beauty of greatness and goodness were drawn at once to such a man as he was. Violent and petulant as he may have seemed on some rare occasions of public protest, he endured all the secret slights and wants of his latter life with a most high patience, and with serene if not joyous acceptance of his fate. Without brute resignation, nay with keen sense of neglect shown and wrong done, he yet laboured gladly and without ceasing. Sick or well, he was at work; his utmost rest was mere change of labour. To relax the intense nerve or deaden the travailing brain would have been painful and grievous to him. Fervent incessant action was to him as the breath of every moment, the bread of every day. His talk was eager and eloquent; his habits of life were simple and noble, alike above compassion and beyond regret. To all the poor about him—and among the poor he had to live out all his latter days of life—he showed all the supreme charities of courtesy. From one or two things narrated of him, we may all see and be assured that a more perfect and gentle excellence of manner, a more royal civility of spirit, was never found in any man. Fearless, blameless, and laborious, he had also all tender and exquisite qualities of breeding, all courteous and gracious instincts of kindness. As there was nothing base in him, so was there nothing harsh or weak. This old man, whose hand academicians would not take because he had to fetch his own porter, had the habit and spirit of the highest training. He was born a knight and king among men, and had the great and quiet way of such. To say that he was not ashamed or afraid of his poverty seems an expression actually libellous by dint of inadequacy. Fear and shame of any base kind are inconceivable of him. The great and sleepless soul which impelled him to work and to speak could take no taint and no rest in this world. Conscious as he was of the glory of his gift and capacity, he was apparently unconscious how noble a thing was his own life. The work which he was able and compelled to perform he knew to be great; that his manner of living should be what it was, he seems to have thought but simple. "Few," his biographer has well said, " are so persistently brave." But his was the supreme valour which ignorantly assumes and accepts itself. It was natural to him not to cease from doing well or complain of faring ill, as it is natural to a soldier not to turn tail. That he should do great things for small wages was a condition of his life. Neither, with all his just and distinct self-assertion, did he assume any special credit for this. He did not ask for more of meat and drink, more of leisure or praise ; he demanded only such recognition as might have enabled him to do more work and greater while strength and sight were left in him. That neglect, and the necessities of mere handiwork involved by neglect, should thus shorten his time and impair his capacity for higher labours, he did at times complain, not without an audible undertone of scornful and passionate rebuke. " Let not that nation," he says once, " where less than nobility is the ' reward,' pretend that Art is encouraged by that nation." There was no angry prurience for fame or gold underlying such complaints.

His famous drawings, burlesque or serious, of visionary heads are interesting chiefly for the evidence they give of Blake's power upon his own mind and nerves, and of the strong and subtle mixture of passion with humour in his temperament. Faith, invention, and irony are here mingled in a rare and curious manner. The narrow leer of stolid servile vigour, the keen smirk of satisfied and brutish achievement, branded upon the grotesque face of the "Man who built the Pyramids," implies a good satire on workmen of base talent and mean success.

Several others, such as "The Accusers" and the celebrated "Ghost of a Flea," are grotesque almost to
grandeur, and full of strength and significance. More
important than hundreds of these are the beautiful
designs to Virgil—or to Phillips. Reproduced at page 271
of Vol. I. with the utmost care and skill, they have of
course lost something by the way ; enough remains, and
would remain had less favour been shown them, to give
great and keen pleasure. In the first, the remote sweet
curve of hill against a sky filled with evening, seen far
above the rows of folded sheep, may recall a splendid
former design in the "Blair." In the second, which
perhaps has lost more than any in course of transference,
the distance of winding road and deepening gorge, woods
and downs and lighted windy sky, is among the noblest
inventions of imaginative landscape. Highest of all in
poetical quality I should class the third design. Upon the
first two, symbolic as they are of vision and of pilgrim-
age, the shadow of peace is cast like a garment ; rest
lies upon them as a covering. In the third, a splendour
of sweet and turbulent moonlight falls across blown
bowed hedgerows, over the gnarled and labouring
branches of a tough tortuous oak, upon soft ears of laid
corn like long low waves without ripple or roll ; every
bruised blade distinct and patient, every leaf quivering
and straightened out in the hard wind. The stormy
beauty of this design, the noble motion and passion in
all parts of it, are as noticeable as its tender sense of
detail and grace in effect of light. Not a star shows
about the moon ; and the dark hollow half of her glimmering shell, emptied and eclipsed, is faint upon the

deep air. The fire in her crescent burns high across
the drift of wind. Blake's touch in this appears to me
curiously just and perfect ; the moon does not seem to
quail or flicker as a star would ; but one may feel and
see, as it were, the wind passing beneath her ; amid the
fierce fluctuation of heaven in the full breath of tempest,
blown upon with all the strength of the night, she stands
firm in the race of winds, where no lesser star can stand ;
she hangs high in clear space, pure of cloud ; but no
likeness of the low-hung labouring moon, no blurred and
blinking planet with edges blotted and soiled in fitful
vapour, would have given so splendid a sense of storm
as this white triumphal light seen above the wind.
Small and rough as these half-engraved designs may be,
it is difficult to express in words all that is latent, even
all that is evident, in the best of them. Poets and
painters of Blake's kind can put enough into the slightest
and swiftest work they do to baffle critics and irritate
pretenders.

Friends, as we have said, were not wanting to Blake in
his old age ; to one of them we owe, among other more
direct obligations, an inestimable debt for the "Illustrations to Job," executed on his commission. Another
worthy of notice here was, until our own day called forth
a better, the best English critic on art ; himself, as far
as we know, admirable alike as a painter, a writer, and a
murderer. In each pursuit, perhaps, there was a certain
want of solid worth and fervour, which at times impeded
or impaired the working of an excellent faculty ; but
in each it is evident there was a noble sense of things
fair and fit ; a seemliness and shapeliness of execution,

a sensitive relish of excellence, an exquisite aspiration after goodness of work, which cannot be overpraised. With pen, with palette, or with poison, his hand was never a mere craftsman's. The visible vulgarities and deficiencies of his style went hardly deeper than the surface. Excess of colour and levity of handling have not unjustly been charged against him ; he does not seem to have always used the material on hand, whether strychnine or mere ink, to the best purpose ; his work has a certain crudity and violence of tone ; his articles and his crimes are both too often wanting in the most delightful qualities of which finished art is capable ; qualities which a more earnest man of lesser genius might have given them. The main object in both seems wrong, or at best insufficient ; in the one case he looked less to achievement than to effect ; in the other he aimed rather at money-getting than at enjoyment ; which is the more deplorable, as a man so greatly gifted must have been in every way fitted to apprehend, to relish, and to realize all noble and subtle pleasure in its more vigorous forms and in its more delicate sense. What he has done however is excellent ; and we need not inquire with a captious ingratitude whether another could have done better : that meaner men have since done worse, we know and lament. Too often the murderer is not an artist ; and the converse defect is no doubt yet more unhappily frequent. On all accounts we may suppose that in days perhaps not remote a philosophic posterity, mindful that the harvest of art has few reapers worthy of their hire, and well aware that what is exalted must also be exceptional, will inscribe with due honour upon

the list of men who have deserved well of mankind the
name of Wainwright. Those who would depreciate his
performance as a simple author must recollect that in
accordance with the modern receipt he "lived his poems;"
that the age prefers deeds to songs; that to do great
things is better than to write; that action is of eternity,
fiction of time; and that these poems were doubtless
the greater for being "inarticulate." Remembering which
things, the sternest critic will not deny that no kaiser or
king ever "polished his stanza" to better purpose with
more strenuous will.

What concerns us at present is, that there grew up
between Blake and Wainwright an intimacy not unpleasing
to commemorate. An artist in words, in oils, and in
drugs, Wainwright had an exquisite power of recognition, and a really noble relish of all excellence. No
good work came in his way but he praised it with all
his might. The mixture of keen insight with frank
pleasure, innate justice of eye with fresh effusion of
enjoyment, gives to his papers on art a special colour or
savour which redeems the offences of a tricked and
tinselled style. Clearly too he did what he could for
Blake in the way of journalism; but a super-editorial
thickness of hide and head repelled the light sharp
shafts loosed from a bow too relaxed by too unsteady
a hand. It is lamentable that the backstroke of a recal-
citrant hoof should have broken this bowman's arm
when it might have done good service. Help shown
to Blake about this time, especially help of the swift
efficient nature that Wainwright would have given, might
have been infinitely important; it was no light thing

to come so near and yet fall short of. Exposition of the beloved "Song of Jerusalem," adequate at least on the side of pure art, would assuredly have given the great old man pleasure beyond words and beyond gold. This too he was not to have. There are men set about the ways of life who seem made only to fulfil the office of thorns; it is difficult for retrospection to observe that they have·done anything but hurt and hinder the feet of higher men. Doubtless they have had their use and taken their pleasure. These have left no trace; we can still see the scars they made on the hand and the fragments they rent from the cloak of a great man as he passed by them. A little of the honour which he has lately received would have been to Blake in his life a great and pleasant thing to attain; praise of his work now leaves an after-taste of bitterness on the lips which utter it. His work, not done for wages, hardly repaid with thanks, we can touch and handle and remark upon as ability is given us; "nothing can touch him further." Those who might have done what we would give much to do left it undone. And even to men who enjoy such power to do and such wisdom to choose greatly as were the inheritance of Blake it is not a thing worth no regret to have been allowed upon earth no comprehension and no applause. He had a better part in life than the pleasure that comes of such things; but these also he might have had. He would not come down to chaffer for them or stoop to gather them up from unclean or unsafe ground; but they might have been laid at his feet freely and with thanks; which they never were.

Foiled as he had been in his good purpose, the critic

at least won full gratitude from the gentle and great nature of his friend, who repaid him in a kingly manner with praise worth gold. One may hope that a picture painted by Wainwright and commended by Blake will yet be traced somewhere, in spite of the singular fate which hung upon so much of their lives, and which still obscures 'so much of their work. At least its subject and quality should be sought out and remembered. But for the strange collision with social laws which broke up his life and scattered his designs, it might also be hoped that some other relics of Wainwright would be found adrift in manuscript or otherwise, and a collection of his stray works be completed and published, with an adequate notice of his life, well weeded of superfluous lamentations, duly qualified to put an end to perversion and foolish fancies, clear of deprecation or distortion, just, sufficient, and close to the purpose, Few things would be better worth doing by a competent editor.

Even of the " Inventions to the Book of Job," as far as I know, no especial notice was taken. Upon these, the greatest of all Blake's designs, such noble exposition has now at length been bestowed that further remark may henceforward well be spared. This commentary has something of the stately beauty and vigorous gravity of style which distinguish the work spoken of. Blake himself, had he undertaken to write notes on his designs, must have done them less justice than this. The perfect apprehension and the perfect representation of the great qualities which all men, according to their capacity, must here in some degree perceive, give to these notes

a value beyond that of mere eloquence or of mere
sympathy. The words chosen do not merely render the
subject with fluency and fitness ; they attain a choiceness
and exaltation of expression, which give to the writing
much of the character of the designs. Whether or not
from any exceptional aptitude in the material, these
designs are more lucid and dramatic in effect than perhaps any of Blake's works. His specialties of belief or
sentiment hardly show in this series at all ; except perhaps in the passionate and penitent character which
seems here to supplant the traditional divine look of
patience and power. The whole work has in it a vibra-
tion as of fire ; even the full stars and serene lines of hill
are set in frameworks of fervent sky or throbbing flame.
But for the most part those intense qualities of sleepless
invention which in many of Blake's other works impel
him into fierce aberration and blind ecstasy, through ways
which few can tread and mists which few can pierce, are
now happily diverted and kept at work upon the exquisite borders and appendages. In these there is enough
of fiery fancy and tender structure of symbol to employ
the whole wide and vivid imagination of the artist.
And throughout the series there is a largeness and a
loftiness of manner which sustain the composition at
the height of the poem. In the highest flights of spiritual
passion and speculation, in the subtle contention with
fate and imperious agony of appeal against heaven, Blake
has matched himself against his text, and translated its
sharp and profound harmonies into a music of design not
less adorable.

Those who have read with any care or comprehension

the excellent chapters on Blake's personal life will regret, not it may be without a keen suppressed sense of vain vexation, that the author did not live to get sight of the letters which have since been found and published. They will at least observe with how much reason the editor of the *Life* has desired us to notice the close and complete confirmation given by that correspondence to the accuracy of these chapters. No tribute more valuable could be devised to the high sincerity, the clear sagacity, the vigorous sense of truth and lucid power of proof, which have left us for the first time an acceptable and endurable portrait of Blake. All earlier attempts were mere masses of blot and scratch, evidently impossible and false on the face of them, and even pitifully conscious that they could not be true, not being human. The bewildered patronage, fear, contempt, goodwill and despair which Blake had excited among those hapless biographers have left in their forlorn failures a certain element of despicable pathos. We have now, thanks to no happier chance, but solely to the strenuous ability and fidelity of a man qualified to study and to speak upon the matter, a trustworthy, perspicuous, and coherent summary of the actual facts of Blake's life, of the manner in which he worked, and of the causes which made his work what it was.

Among these late labours of Blake the "Dante" may take a place of some prominence. The seven published plates, though quite surprisingly various in merit, are worth more notice than has yet been spared them. Three at least, for poetical power and nobility of imaginative detail, are up to the artist's highest mark.

Others have painted the episode of Francesca with more or less of vigour and beauty ; once above all an artist to whom any reference here must be taken as especially apposite has given with the tenderest perfection of power, first the beauty of beginning love in the light and air of life on earth, then the passion of imperishable desire under the dropping tongues of flame in hell. To the right the lovers are drawn close, yearning one toward another with touch of tightened hands and insatiable appeal of lips ; behind them the bower lattice opens on deep sunshine and luminous leaves ; to the left, they drift before the wind of hell, floated along the misty and straining air, fastened one upon another among the fires, pale with perpetual division of pain ; and between them the witnesses stand sadly, as men that look before and after. Blake has given nothing like this : of personal beauty and special tenderness his design has none ; it starts from other ground. Often as the lovers had been painted, here first has any artist desired to paint the second circle itself. To most illustrators, as to most readers, and (one might say) to Dante himself, the rest are swallowed up in those two supreme martyrs. Here we see, not one or two, but the very circle of the souls that sinned by lust, as Dante saw it ; and as Keats afterwards saw it in the dream embalmed by his sonnet ; the revolution of infinite sorrowing spirits through the bitter air and grievous hurricane of hell. Through strange immense implications of snake-shaped fold beyond fold, the involved chain of figures that circle and return flickers in wan white outline upon the dense dark. Under their feet is no stay as on earth ; over their heads is no light as in heaven. They have no rest, and no resting-place : they revolve like circles of curling foam or fire. The two witnesses, who alone among all the mobile mass have ground whereon to set foot, stand apart upon a broken floor-work of roots and rocks, made rank with the slime and sprawl of rotten weed and foul flag-leaves of Lethe. Detail of drawing or other technical work is not the strong point of the design ; but it does incomparably well manage to render the sense of the matter in hand, the endless measured motion, the painful and fruitless haste as of leaves or smoke upon the wind, the grey discomforted air and dividing mist. Blake has thoroughly understood and given back the physical symbols of this first punishment in Dante ; the whirling motion of his figures has however more of blind violence and brute speed than the text seems to indicate : they are dashed and dragged one upon another like weed or shingle torn up in the drift of a breaking sea : overthrown or beaten down, haled or crushed together, as if by inanimate strength of iron or steam : not moved as we expect to see them, in sad rapidity of stately measure and even time of speed. The flame-like impulse of idea natural to Blake cannot absolutely match itself against Dante's divine justice and intense innate forbearance in detail ; nor so comprehend, as by dint of reproduction to compete with, that supreme sense of inward and outward right which rules and attunes every word of the *Commedia*.

Two other drawings in this series are worth remark and praise ; the sixth and seventh in order. In the sixth, Dante and Virgil, standing in a niche of rifted rock faced

by another cliff up and down which a reptile crowd of
spirits swarms and sinks, look down on the grovelling and
swine-like flocks of Malebolge ; lying tumbled about the
loathsome land in hateful heaps of leprous flesh and dishevelled deformity, with limbs contorted, clawing nails,
and staring horror of hair and eyes : one figure thrown
down in a corner of the crowded cliff-side, her form and
face drowned in an overflow of ruined raining tresses.
The pure grave folds of the two poets' robes, long and
cleanly carved as the straight drapery of a statue, gain
chastity of contrast from the swarming surge and monstrous mass of all foulest forms beneath, against the reek
of which both witnesses stop their noses with their gowns.
Behind and between, huge outlines of dark hill and sharp
curves of crag show like stiffened ridges of solid sea,
amid heaving and glaring motion of vapour and fire.
Slight as the workmanship is of this design also, alien as
is perhaps its structure of precipice and mountain from
the Dantesque conception of descending circles and narrowing sides, it has a fiery beauty of its own ; the background especially, with its climbing or crawling flames,
the dark hard strength and sweep of its sterile ridges,
seen by fierce fits of reflected light, washed about with surf
and froth of tideless fire, and heavily laden with the lurid
languor of hell. In the seventh design we reach the
circle of traitors ; the foot of the passenger strikes against
one frost-bound face ; others lie straight, with crowned
congealing hair and beard taken in the tightening rivets
of ice. To the right a swarm of huge and huddled figures
seems gathering with moan or menace behind a veil of
frozen air, a mask of hardening vapour ; and from each

side the bitter light of ice or steel falls grey in cruel
refraction. Into the other four designs we will not enter;
some indeed are too savagely reckless in their ugly and
barren violation of form or law, to be redeemed by even
an intenser apprehension of symbol and sense; and one at
least, though with noble suggestions dropped about it, is
but half sketched in. In that of the valley of serpents
there is however a splendid excess of horror and prodigal
agony; the ravenous delight of the closing and laughing
mouths, the folded tension of every scale and ring, the
horrible head caught and crushed with the last shriek
between its teeth and the last strain upon its eyelids, in
the serrated jaws of the erect serpent—all have the brand
of Blake upon them.

These works were the last he was to achieve; out of
the whole Dantesque series, seven designs alone have ever
won their way into such notice as engraving could earn
for them. The latest chapters of Blake's life are perhaps
also the noblest. His poverty, if that word implies anything of a destitute or sordid way of living, seems to have
grown and swollen somewhat beyond its actual size in the
dim form of report. Stories have come to hand of late,
which, being seemingly accurate in the main, though not
as yet duly fixed in detail or date, remove any such ground
of fear. They do better; they bring proof once again of
the noble charity, the tender exaltation of mind, the swift
bounty of hand, which would have made memorable a man
meaner in talent. Once, it is said, he lent £40 to some
friend in distress, which friend's wife, having laid out most
of her windfall in dress, thought Mrs. Blake might like to
see *that* by way of change for her husband's money.

Once too they received into their lodging (into which does not yet seem certain) a young student of art, sick and poor, who died some time after upon their hands. These things, and such as these, we know dimly.   One or two such deeds, seen through such dull vague obstruction, in the midst of so many things forgotten, should be taken to imply much.   How few we know of, it is easy to say ; how many there must have been, it is not easy.   This also may be remembered, that the man so liberal when he had little might once have had much to give, and would not take it at the price.   It is recorded on the authority of a personal friend, that some proposal had once been made to " engage Blake as teacher of drawing to the royal family"; a proposal declined on his part from no folly or vulgarity of prepossession, but from a simple and noble sense of things reasonable and right.   For once, it is also said, some samples of his work were laid before the king, not then, unluckily, in his strait-waistcoat ; "Take them away !" spluttered the lunatic—not quite as yet "blind, mad, despised, and dying," as when Byron and Shelley embalmed him in corrosive rhymes ; not all of these as yet. But as a great man then alive and yet living * has well asked—"What mortal ever heard Any good of George the Third ?"   Blake's MSS. contain an occasional allusion expressive of no ardent reverence for the person or family of that insane Dagon, so long left standing as the leaden rather than brazen idol of hypocrites and dunces. As to the arts, it was well for Blake to keep clear of the patron of West.   All he ever got from government was the risk of hanging, or such minor penalty as that

---

* Written in 1863.   Mr. Landor died Sept. 17th, 1864.

equitable time might have inflicted on seditious laxity of speech and thought.

In smaller personal matters, Blake was as fearless and impulsive as in his conduct of these graver affairs. Seeing once, somewhere about St. Giles's, a wife knocked about by some husband or other violent person, in the open street, a bystander saw this also—that a small swift figure coming up in full swing of passion fell with such counter violence of reckless and raging rebuke upon the poor ruffian, that he recoiled and collapsed, with ineffectual cudgel; persuaded, as the bystander was told on calling afterwards, that the very devil himself had flown upon him in defence of the woman ; such Tartarean overflow of execration and objurgation had issued from the mouth of her champion. It was the fluent tongue of Blake which had proved too strong for this fellow's arm : the artist, doubtless, not caring to remember the consequences, proverbial even before Molière's time, of such interference with conjugal casualties.

These things, whenever it was that they happened, were now of the past ; as were many labours of many days, to be followed by not many more. Among a few good friends, and not without varieties of changed scene and company, Blake drew daily nearer to death. Of all the records of these his latter years, the most valuable perhaps are those furnished by Mr. Crabb Robinson, whose cautious and vivid transcription of Blake's actual speech is worth more than much vague remark, or than any commentary now possible to give. A certain visible dislike and vexation excited by the mystic violence of Blake's phrases, by the fierce simplicity of his mental bearing, have not been allowed to impair the excellent justice of tone and evident accuracy of report which give to these notes their singular value. In his correspondence, in his conversation, and in his prophecies, Blake was always at unity with himself; not, it seems to us, actually inconsistent or even illogical in his fitful varieties of speech and expression. His faith was large and his creed intricate; in the house of his belief there were many mansions. In these notes, for instance, the terms "atheism" and "education" are wrested to peculiar uses; education must mean not exactly training, but moral tradition and the retailed sophistries of artificial right and wrong; atheism, as applicable to Dante, must mean adherence to the received "God of this world"—that confusion of the Creator with the Saviour which was to Blake the main rock of offence in all religious systems less mystic than his own; being indeed, together with "Deism," the perpetual butt of his prophetic slings and arrows. All this, however, we must leave now for time to enlighten in due course as it best may; meanwhile some last word has to be said concerning Blake's life and death.

To a life so gentle and great, so brave and stainless, there could be but one manner of end, come when and how it might; a serene and divine death, full of placid ardour and hope unspotted by fear. Having lived long without a taint of shame upon his life, having long laboured without a stain of falsehood upon his work, it was no hard task for him to set the seal of a noble death upon that noble life and labour. He, it might be said, whom the gods love well need not always die young; for this man died old in years at least, having done work enough for three men's lives of strenuous talent and spirit. After certain stages of pain and recovery and relapse, the end came on the second Sunday in August 1827. A few days before he had made a last drawing of his wife— faithful to him and loving almost beyond all recorded faith and love. Forty-five years she had cloven to him and served him all the days of her life with all the might of her heart ; for a space of four years and two months they were to be divided now. He did not draw her like, it appears : that which "she had ever been to him," no man could have drawn. Of her, out of just reverence and gratitude that such goodness should have been, we will not say more. All words are coarse and flat that men can use to praise one who has so lived.* It has been told

* Since the lines above were written, I have been informed by a surviving friend of Blake, celebrated throughout Italy as over England, in a time nearer our own, as (among other things) the discoverer of Giotto's fresco in the Chapel of the Podestà, that after Blake's death a gift of £100 was sent to his widow by the Princess Sophia, who must not lose the exceptional honour due to her for a display of sense and liberality so foreign to her blood. At whose suggestion it was made is not known, and worth knowing. Mrs. Blake sent back the money with all due thanks, not liking to take or keep what (as it seemed to her) she could dispense with, while many to whom no chance or choice was given might have been kept alive by the gift ; and, as readers of the " Life" know, fell to work in her old age by preference. One complaint only she was ever known to make during her husband's life, and that gently. "Mr. Blake" was so little with her, though in the body they were never separated ; for he was incessantly away "in Paradise"; which would not seem to have been far off. Mr. Kirkup also speaks of the courtesy with which, on occasion, Blake would waive the question of his spiritual life, if the subject seemed at all incomprehensible or offensive to the friend with him : he would no more obtrude than suppress his faith, and would practically accept and act upon the dissent or distaste of his companions without visible vexation or the rudeness of a thwarted fanatic. It was in the time of this intimacy (see note at p. 58) that Mr. Kirkup also saw, what seems long since to have dropped out of human sight, the picture of *The Ancient Britons ;* which, himself also an artist, he thought and thinks the finest work of the painter : remembering well the fury and splendour of energy there contrasted with the serene ardour of simply beautiful courage ; the violent life of the design, and the fierce distance of fluctuating battle.

more than once in print—it can never be told without a sense of some strange and sweet meaning—how, as Blake lay with all the tides of his life setting towards the deep final sleep, he made and sang new fragments of verse, the last oblations he was to bring who had brought so many since his first conscience of the singular power and passion within himself that impels a man to such work. Of these songs not a line has been spared us ; for us, it seems, they were not made. In effect, they were not his, he said. At last, after many songs and hours, still in the true and pure presence of his wife, his death came upon him in the evening like a sleep.*

* The direct cause of Blake's death, it appears from a MS. source, "was the mixing of the gall with the blood." It may be worth remark, that one brief notice at least of Blake's death made its way into print ; the "Literary Gazette" (No. 552 ; the "Gentleman's Magazine" published it in briefer form but nearly identical words as far as it went) of August 18, 1827, saw fit to "record the death of a singular and very able man," in an article contributed mainly by "the kindness of a correspondent," who speaks as an acquaintance of Blake, and gives this account of his last days, prefaced by a sufficiently humble reference to the authorities of Fuseli, Flaxman, and Lawrence. "Pent, with his affectionate wife, in a close back-room in one of the Strand courts, his bed in one corner, his meagre dinner in another, a ricketty table holding his copper-plates in progress, his colours, books (among which his Bible, a Sessi Velutello's Dante, and Mr. Carey's translation, were at the top), his large drawings, sketches, and MSS. ; his ankles frightfully swelled, his chest disordered, old age striding on, his wants increased, but not his miserable means and appliances ; even yet was his eye undimmed, the fire of his imagination unquenched, and the preternatural never-resting activity of his mind unflagging. He had not merely a calmly resigned, but a cheerful and mirthful countenance. He took no thought for his life, what he should eat or what he should drink ; nor yet for his body, what he should put on ; but had a fearless confidence in that Providence which had given him the vast range of the world for his recreation and delight. Blake died last Monday ; died as he had lived, piously, cheerfully, talking calmly, and finally resigning himself to his eternal rest like an infant to its sleep. He has left nothing except some pictures, copper-plates, and his principal work, a series of a hundred large designs from Dante. . . . . He was active" (the good correspondent adds, further on) "in mind and body, passing from one occupation to another without an intervening minute of repose. Of an ardent, affectionate, and grateful temper, he was simple in manner and address, and displayed an inbred courteous-

Only such men die so ; though the worst have been
known to die calmly and the meanest bravely, this pure
lyric rapture of spirit and perfect music of sundering
soul and body can only be given to these few. Knowing
nothing of whence and whither, the how and the when of
a man's death we can at least know, and put the knowy-
ledge to what uses we may. In this case, if we will, it
may help us to much in the way of insight and judgment ;
it may show us many things that need not be wrought
up into many words. For what more is there now to say
of the man ? Of the work he did we must speak gradually,
if we are to speak adequately. Into his life and method
of work we have looked, not without care and veneration;
and find little to conclude with by way of comment. If
to any reader it should not by this time appear that he
was great and good among the chief of good and great
men, it will not appear for any oration of ours. Most
funeral speeches also are cheap and inconclusive. Especially they must be so, or seem so, when delivered over
the body of a great man to whom his own generation
could not even grant a secure grave. In 1831 his wife
was buried beside him : where they are laid now no man
can say : it seems certain only that their graves were
violated by hideous official custom, and their bones cast

ness of the most agreeable character." Finally, the writer has no doubt that
Mrs. Blake's " cause will be taken up by the distributors of those funds which are
raised for the relief of distressed artists, and also by the benevolence of private
individuals " : for she " is left (we fear, from the accounts which have reached us)
in a very forlorn condition, Mr. Blake himself having been much indebted for
succour and consolation to his friend Mr. Linnell the painter." The discreet
editor, " when further time has been allowed him for inquiry, will probably
resume the matter :" but, we may now more safely prophesy, assuredly will
not.

out into some consecrated pit among other nameless relics of poor men. It might not have hurt them even to foresee this ; but nevertheless the doers of such a thing had better not have done it. Having missed of a durable grave, Blake need not perhaps look for the " weak witness" of any late memorial. Such things in life were indifferent to him ; and should be more so now. To be buried among his nearest kin, and to have the English burial service read over him, he did, we are told, express some wish ; and this was done. The world of men was less by one great man, and was none the wiser ; while he lived he was called mad and kept poor ; after his death much of his work was destroyed; and in course of time not so much as his grave was left him. All which to him must matter little, but is yet worth a recollection more fruitful than regret. The dead only, and not the living, ought, while any trace of his doings remains, to forget what was the work and what were the wages of William Blake.

II.—LYRICAL POEMS.

—◆—

WE must here be allowed space to interpolate a word of the briefest possible comment on the practical side of Blake's character. No man ever lived and laboured in hotter earnest; and the native energy in him had the property of making all his atmosphere of work intense and keen as fire—too sharp and rare in quality of heat to be a good working element for any more temperate intellect. Into every conceivable channel or byway of work he contrived to divert and infuse this overflowing fervour of mind; the least bit of engraving, the poorest scrap or scratch of drawing or writing traceable to his hands, has on it the mark of passionate labour and enjoyment; but of all this devotion of laborious life, the only upshot visible to most of us consists in a heap of tumbled and tangled relics, verse and prose mainly inexplicable, paintings and engravings mainly unacceptable if not unendurable. And if certain popular theories of the just aims of life, duties of an earnest-minded man, and meritorious nature of practical deeds and material services only, are absolutely correct—in that case the work of this man's life is certainly a sample of deplorable waste and failure. A religion which has for Walhalla some factory of the Titans, some prison fitted with moral cranks and divine treadmills of all the virtues, can have no place among its heroes for the most energetic of mere artists. To him, as to others of his kind, all faith, all virtue, all moral duty or religious necessity, was not so much abrogated or superseded as summed up, included and involved, by the one matter of art. To him, as to other such workmen, it seemed better to do this well and let all the rest drift than to do incomparably well in all other things and dispense with this one. For this was the thing he had to do; and this once well done, he had the assurance of a certain faith that other things could not be wrong with him. As long as two such parties exist among men who think and act, it must always be some pleasure to deal with a man of either party who has no faith or hope in compromise. These middle-men, with some admirable self-sufficient theory of reconciliation between two directly opposite aims and forces, are fit for no great work on either side. If it be in the interest of facts really desirable that "the poor Fine Arts should take themselves away," let it be fairly avowed and preached in a distinct manner. That thesis, so delivered, is comprehensible, and deserves respect. One may add that if art can be destroyed it by all means ought to be. If for example the art of verse is not indispensable and indestructible, the sooner it is put out of the way the better. If anything can be done instead better worth doing than painting or poetry, let that preferable thing be done with all the might and haste that may be attainable. And if to live well be really better than to write or paint well, and a noble action more valuable than the greatest poem or most perfect picture, let us have done at once with the meaner things that stand in the way of the higher. For we cannot on any terms have everything; and assuredly no chief artist or poet has ever been fit to hold rank among the world's supreme benefactors in the way of doctrine, philanthropy, reform, guidance, or example : what is called the artistic faculty not being by any means the same thing as a general capacity for doing good work, diverted into this one strait or shallow in default of a better outlet. Even were this true for example of a man so imperfect as Burns, it would remain false of a man so perfect as Keats. The great men, on whichever side one finds them, are never found trying to take truce or patch up terms. Savonarola burnt Boccaccio ; Cromwell proscribed Shakespeare. The early Christians were not great at verse or sculpture. Men of immense capacity and energy who do seem to think or assert it possible to serve both masters—a Dante, a Shelley, a Hugo—poets whose work is mixed with and coloured by personal action or suffering for some cause moral or political—these even are no real exceptions. It is not as artists that they do or seem to do this. The work done may be, and in such high cases often must be, of supreme value to art ; but not the moral implied. Strip the sentiments and re-clothe them in bad verse, what residue will be left of the slightest importance to art ? Invert them, retaining the manner or form (supposing this feasible, which it might be), and art has lost nothing. Save the shape, and art will take care of the soul for you :* unless that is all right, she will refuse to run or start at all ; but the shape or style of workman- ship each artist is bound to look to, whether or no he may choose to trouble himself about the moral or other bear- ings of his work.   This principle, which makes the manner of doing a thing the essence of the thing done, the pur- pose or result of it the accident, thus reversing the prin- ciple of moral or material duty, must inevitably expose art to the condemnation of the other party—the party of those who (as aforesaid) regard what certain of their leaders call an earnest life or a great acted poem (that is, material virtue or the mere doing and saying of good or instructive deeds and words) as infinitely preferable to any possible feat of art.   Opinion is free, and the choice always open ; but if any man leaning on crutches of theory chooses to halt between the two camps, it shall be at his own peril—imminent peril of conviction as one unfit for service on either side.   For Puritanism is in this one thing absolutely right about art ; they cannot live and work together, or the one under the other.   All ages which were great enough to have space for both, to hold room for a fair fighting-field between them, have always accepted and acted upon this evident fact.   Take the Renaissance age for one example ; you must have Knox or Ronsard, Scotch or French ; not both at once ; there is no place under reformers for the singing of a "Pléiade." Take the mediæval period in its broadest sense ; not to speak of the notably heretical and immoral Albigeois with their

---

* Of course, there can be no question here of bad art : which indeed is a non- entity or contradiction in terms, as to speak of good art is to run into tautology. It is assumed, to begin with, that the artist has something to say or do worth doing or saying in an artistic form.

exquisite school of heathenish verse, or of that other rebellious gathering under the great emperor Frederick II., a poet and pagan, when eastern arts and ideas began to look up westward at one man's bidding and open out Saracenic prospects in the very face and teeth of the Church—look at home into familiar things, and see by such poems as Chaucer's *Court of Love*, absolutely one in tone and handling as it is with the old Albigensian *Aucassin* and all its paganism,* how the poets of the time, with their eager nascent worship of beautiful form

* Observe especially in Chaucer's most beautiful of young poems that appalling passage, where, turning the favourite edgetool of religious menace back with point inverted upon those who forged it, the poet represents men and women of religious habit or life as punished in the next world, beholding afar off with jealous regret the salvation and happiness of Venus and all her servants (converse of the Hörsel legend, which shows the religious or anti-Satanic view of the matter; though there too there is some pity or sympathy implied for the pagan side of things, revealing in the tradition the presence and touch of some poet) : expressly punished, these monks and nuns, for their continence and holiness of life, and compelled after death to an eternity of fruitless repentance for having wilfully missed of pleasure and made light of indulgence in this world ; which is perfect Albigeois. Compare the famous speech in *Aucassin et Nicolette*, where the typical hero weighs in a judicial manner the respective attractions of heaven and hell ; deciding of course dead against the former on account of the deplorably bad company kept there ; priests, hermits, saints, and such-like, in lieu of knights and ladies, painters and poets. One may remark also, the minute this pagan revival begins to get breathing-room, how there breaks at once into flower a most passionate and tender worship of nature, whether as shown in the bodily beauty of man and woman or in the outside loveliness of leaf and grass ; both Chaucer and his anonymous southern colleague being throughout careful to decorate their work with the most delicate and splendid studies of colour and form. Either of the two choice morsels of doctrinal morality cited above would have exquisitely suited the palate of Blake. He in his time, one need not doubt, was considerably worried and gibbered at by "monkeys in houses of brick," moral theorists, and "pantopragmatic" men of all sorts ; what can we suppose he would have said or done in an epoch given over to preachers (lay, clerical, and mixed) who assert without fear or shame that you may demand, nay are bound to demand, of a picture or poem what message it has for you, what may be its moral utility or material worth ? "Poetry must conform itself to" &c. ; "art must have a mission and meaning appreciable by earnest men in an age of work," and so forth. These be thy gods, O Philistia.

and external nature, dealt with established opinion and
the incarnate moralities of church or household. It is
easy to see why the Church on its own principle found
it (as in the Albigensian case) a matter of the gravest
necessity to have such schools of art and thought cut
down or burnt out. Priest and poet, all those times
through, were proverbially on terms of reciprocal biting
and striking. That magnificent invention of making
" Art the handmaid of Religion" had not been stumbled
upon in the darkness of those days. Neither minstrel nor
monk would have caught up the idea with any rapture.
As indeed they would have been unwise to do ; for the
thing is impossible. Art is not like fire or water, a good
servant and bad master ; rather the reverse. She will
help in nothing, of her own knowledge or freewill : upon
terms of service you will get worse than nothing out of
her. Handmaid of religion, exponent of duty, servant of
fact, pioneer of morality, she cannot in any way become ;
she would be none of these things though you were to
bray her in a mortar. All the battering in the world will
never hammer her into fitness for such an office as that.
It is at her peril, if she tries to do good : one might say,
borrowing terms from the other party, " she shall not try
that under penalty of death and damnation." Her business is not to do good on other grounds, but to be good
on her own : all is well with her while she sticks fast to
that. To ask help or furtherance from her in any extraneous good work is exactly as rational as to expect lyrical
beauty of form and flow in a logical treatise. The contingent result of having good art about you and living in
a time of noble writing or painting may no doubt be

this ; that the spirit and mind of men then living will receive on some points a certain exaltation and insight caught from the influence of such forms and colours of verse or painting ; will become for one thing incapable of tolerating bad work, and capable therefore of reasonably relishing the best ; which of course implies and draws with it many other advantages of a sort you may call moral or spiritual. But if the artist does his work with an eye to such results or for the sake of bringing about such improvements, he will too probably fail even of them. Art for art's sake first of all, and afterwards we may suppose all the rest shall be added to her (or if not she need hardly be overmuch concerned) ; but from the man who falls to artistic work with a moral purpose, shall be taken away even that which he has—whatever of capacity for doing well in either way he may have at starting. A living critic* of incomparably delicate insight and subtly good sense, himself "impeccable" as an artist, calls this

* I will not resist the temptation to write a brief word of comment on this passage. While my words of inadequate and now of joyless praise were in course of printing, I heard that a mortal illness had indeed stricken the illustrious poet, the faultless critic, the fearless artist ; that no more of fervent yet of perfect verse, no more of subtle yet of sensitive comment, will be granted us at the hands of Charles Baudelaire : that now for ever we must fall back upon what is left us. It is precious enough. We may see again as various a power as was his, may feel again as fiery a sympathy, may hear again as strange a murmur of revelation, as sad a whisper of knowledge, as mysterious a music of emotion ; we shall never find so keen, so delicate, so deep an unison of sense and spirit. What verse he could make, how he loved all fair and felt all strange things, with what infallible taste he knew at once the limit and the licence of his art, all may see at a glance. He could give beauty to the form, expression to the feeling, most horrible and most obscure to the senses or souls of lesser men. The chances of things parted us once and again ; the admiration of some years, at last in part expressed, brought me near him by way of written or transmitted word ; let it be an excuse for the insertion of this note, and for a desire, if so it must be, to repeat for once the immortal words which too often return upon our lips ;

" Ergo in perpetuum, frater, ave atque vale !"

"the heresy of instruction" (*l'hérésie de l'enseignement*): one might call it, for the sake of a shorter and more summary name, the great moral heresy. Nothing can be imagined more futile ; nothing so ruinous. Once let art humble herself, plead excuses, try at any compromise with the Puritan principle of doing good, and she is worse than dead. Once let her turn apologetic, and promise or imply that she really will now be "loyal to fact" and useful to men in general (say, by furthering their moral work or improving their moral nature), she is no longer of any human use or value. The one fact for her which is worth taking account of is simply mere excellence of verse or colour, which involves all manner of truth and loyalty necessary to her well-being. That is the important thing ; to have her work supremely well done, and to disregard all contingent consequences. You may extract out of Titian's work or Shakespeare's any moral or immoral inference you please ; it is none of their business to see after that. Good painting or writing, on any terms, is a thing quite sufficiently in accordance with fact and reality for them. Supplant art by all means if you can ; root it out and try to plant in its place something useful or at least safe, which at all events will not impede the noble moral labour and trammel the noble moral life of Puritanism. But in the name of sense and fact itself let us have done with all abject and ludicrous pretence of coupling the two in harness or grafting the one on the other's stock : let us hear no more of the moral mission of earnest art ; let us no longer be pestered with the frantic and flatulent assumptions of quasi-secular clericalism willing to think the best of all sides, and ready even, with consecrating hand, to lend meritorious art and poetry a timely pat or shove. Philistia had far better (always providing it be possible) crush art at once, hang or burn it out of the way, than think of plucking out its eyes and setting it to grind moral corn in the Philistine mills ; which it is certain not to do at all well. Once and again the time has been that there was no art worth speaking of afloat anywhere in the world ; but there never has been or can have been a time when art, or any kind of art worth having, took active service under Puritanism, or indulged for its part in the deleterious appetite of saving souls or helping humanity in general along the way of labour and progress.* Let no artist or poet listen to the bland bark of those porter dogs of the Puritan kingdom even when they fawn and flirt with tongue or tail. *Cave canem.* That Cerberus of the portals of Philistia will swallow your honey-cake to no purpose ; if he does not turn and rend you, his slaver as he licks your hand will leave it impotent and palsied for all good work.

Thus much it seemed useful to premise, by way of exposition rather than excursion, so as once for all to indicate beyond chance of mistake the real point of view taken during life by Blake, and necessary to be taken by those who would appreciate his labours and purposes. Error on this point would be ruinous to any student.

---

* There are exceptions, we are told from the first, to all rules ; and the sole exception to this one is great enough to do all but establish a rival rule. But, as I have tried already to say, the work—all the work—of Victor Hugo is in its essence artistic, in its accident alone philanthropic or moral. I call this the sole exception, not being aware that the written work of Dante or Shelley did ever tend to alter the material face of things ; though they may have desired that it should, and though their unwritten work may have done so. Accidentally of course a poet's work may tend towards some moral or actual result; that is beside the question.

No one again need be misled by the artist's eager incursions into grounds of faith or principle ; his design being merely to readjust all questions of such a kind by the light of art and law of imagination—to reduce all outlying provinces, and bring them under government of his own central empire—the "fourfold spiritual city" of his vision. Power of imaginative work and insight— "the Poetic Genius, as you now call it"—was in his mind, we shall soon have to see, "the first principle" of all things moral or material, "and all the others merely derivative;" a hazardous theory in its results and corollaries, but one which Blake at all events was always ready to push to its utmost consequences and defend at its extreme outworks. Against all pretensions on the part of science or experimental reasoning to assume this post he was especially given to rebel and recalcitrate. Whether or no he were actually prepared to fight science in earnest on its own pitched field—to dispute seriously the conquest of facts achieved by it—may be questionable ; I for one am inclined to disbelieve this, and to refer much of his verbal pugnacity on such matters to the strong irregular humour, rough and loose as that of children, and the half simple half scornful love of paradox, which were ingrained in the man. For argument and proof he had the contempt of a child or an evangelist. Not that he would have fallen back in preference upon the brute resource of thaumaturgy ; the coarse and cheap machinery of material miracle was wholly insufficient and despicable to him. No wonder-monger of the low sort need here have hoped for a pupil, a colleague, or an authority. This the biographer has acutely noted,

and taken well into account; as we must all do under
pain of waste time and dangerous error. Let this too
be taken note of; that to believe a thing is not neces-
sarily to heed or respect it; to despise a thing is not
the same as to disbelieve it. Those who argue against
the reality of the meaner forms of "spiritualism" in
disembodied life, on the ground apparently that whatever is not of the patent tangible flesh must be of high
imperishable importance, are merely acting on the old
ascetic assumption that the body is of its nature base
and the soul of its nature noble, and that between the
two there is a great gulf fixed, neither to be bridged
over nor filled up. Blake, as a mystic of the higher and
subtler kind, would have denied this superior separate
vitality of the spirit; but far from inferring thence that
the soul must expire with the body, would have main-
tained that the essence of the body must survive with
the essence of the soul: accepting thus (as we may have
to observe he did), in its most absolute and profound
sense, the doctrine of the Resurrection of the Flesh. As
a temporary blind and bar to the soul while dwelling
on earth, fit only (if so permitted) to impede the spiritual
vision and hamper the spiritual feet, he did indeed
appear to contemn the "vegetable" and sensual nature of
man; but on no ascetic grounds. Admitting once for
all that it was no fit or just judge of things spiritual,
he claimed for the body on its own ground an equal
honour and an equal freedom with the soul; denying the
river's channel leave to be called the river—refusing to
the senses the license claimed for them by materialism
to decide by means of bodily insight or sensation ques-

tions removed from the sphere of sensual evidence—and reserving always the absolute assurance and certain faith that things do exist of which the flesh can take no account, but only the spirit—he would grant to the physical nature the full right to every form of physical indulgence : would allow the largest liberty to all powers and capacities of pleasure proper to the pure bodily life. In a word, translated into crude practical language, his creed was about this : as long as a man believes all things he may do any thing ; scepticism (not sin) is alone damnable, being the one thing purely barren and negative ; do what you will with your body, as long as you refuse it leave to disprove or deny the life eternally inherent in your soul. That we believe is what people call or have called by some such name as "antinomian mysticism :" do anything but doubt, and you shall not in the end be utterly lost. Clearly enough it was Blake's faith ; and one assuredly grounded not on mere contempt of the body, but on an equal reverence for spirit and flesh as the two sides or halves of a completed creature : a faith which will allow to neither license to confute or control the other. The body shall not deny, and the spirit shall not restrain ; the one shall not prescribe doubt through reasoning ; the other shall not preach salvation through abstinence. A man holding such tenets sees no necessity to deny that the indulged soul may be in some men as ignoble as the indulged body in others may be noble ; and that a spirit ignoble while embodied need not become noble or noticeable by the process of getting disembodied ; in other words, that death or change need not be expected to equalize the unequal by raising or lowering spirits to one settled level. Much of the existing evidence as to baser spiritual matters, Blake, like other men of candid sense and insight, would we may suppose have accepted—and dropped with the due contempt into the mass of facts worth forgetting only, which the experience of every man must carry till his memory succeeds in letting go its hold of them. Nothing, he would doubtless have said, is worth disputing in disproof of, which if proved would not be worth giving thanks for. Let such things be or not be as the fates of small things please ; but will any one prove or disprove for me the things I hold by warrant of imaginative knowledge ? things impossible to discover, to analyze, to attest, to undervalue, to certify, or to doubt ?

This old war—not (as some would foolishly have it defined) a war between facts and fancies, reason and romance, poetry and good sense, but simply between the imagination which apprehends the spirit of a thing and the understanding which dissects the body of a fact —this strife which can never be decided or ended—was for Blake the most important question possible. He for one, madman or no madman, had the sense to see that the one thing utterly futile to attempt was a reconciliation between two sides of life and thought which have no community of work or aim imaginable. This is no question of reconciling contraries. Admit all the implied pretensions of art, they remain simply nothing to science ; accept all the actual deductions of science, they simply signify nothing to art. The eternal "Après ? " is answer enough for both in turn. "True, then, if

you will have it; but what have we to do with your good
or bad poetries and paintings?" "Undeniably; but
what are we to gain by your deductions and discoveries,
right or wrong?" The betrothal of art and science were
a thing harder to bring about and more profitless to proclaim than "the marriage of heaven and hell." It were
better not to fight, but to part in peace; but better certainly to fight than to temporize, where no reasonable
truce can be patched up. Poetry or art based on
loyalty to science is exactly as absurd (and no more)
as science guided by art or poetry. Neither in effect
can coalesce with the other and retain a right to exist.
Neither can or (while in its sober senses) need wish to
destroy the other; but they must go on their separate
ways, and in this life their ways can by no possibility
cross. Neither can or (unless in some fit of fugitive
insanity) need wish to become valuable or respectable to
the other: each must remain, on its own ground and
to its own followers, a thing of value and deserving
respect. To art, that is best which is most beautiful;
to science, that is best which is most accurate; to
morality, that is best which is most virtuous. Change
or quibble upon the simple and generally accepted
significance of these three words, "beautiful," "accurate," "virtuous," and you may easily (if you please, or
think it worth while) demonstrate that the aim of all
three is radically one and the same; but if any man be
correct in thinking this exercise of the mind worth the
expenditure of his time, that time must indeed be
worth very little. You can say (but had perhaps better
not say) that beauty is the truthfullest, accuracy the

most poetic, and virtue the most beautiful of things;
but a man of ordinary or decent insight will perceive
that you have merely reduced an affair of things to an
affair of words—shifted the body of one thing into the
clothes of another—and proved actually nothing.

To attest by word or work the identity of things
which never can become identical, was no part of
Blake's object in life. What work it fell to his lot to
do, that, having faith in the fates, he believed the best
work possible, and performed to admiration. It is in
consequence of this belief that, apart from all conjectural or problematic theory, the work he did is absolutely good. Intolerant he was by nature to a degree
noticeable even among freethinkers and prophets; but
the strange forms assumed by this intolerance are best
explicable by the singular facts of his training—his
perfect ignorance of well-known ordinary things and
imperfect quaint knowledge of much that lay well out
of the usual way. He retained always an excellent
arrogance and a wholly laudable self-reliance; being
incapable of weak-eyed doubts or any shuffling modesty. His great tenderness had a lining of contempt—
his fiery self-assertion a kernel of loyalty. No one, it is
evident, had ever a more intense and noble enjoyment
of good or great works in other men—took sharper or
deeper delight in the sense of a loyal admiration : being
of his nature noble, fearless, and fond of all things good;
a man made for believing. This royal temper of mind
goes properly with a keen relish of what excellence or
greatness a man may have in himself. Those must be
readiest to feel and to express unalloyed and lofty plea-

sure in the great powers and deeds of a neighbour, who,
while standing clear alike of reptile modesty and pretentious presumption, perceive and know in themselves such
qualities as give them a right to admire and a right to
applaud. If a man thinks meanly of himself, he can
hardly in reason think much of his judgment; if he
depreciates the value of his own work, he depreciates
also the value of his praise. Those are loyallest who
have most of a just self-esteem; and their applause is
best worth having. It is scarcely conceivable that a
man should take delight in the real greatness or merit
of his own work for so pitiful and barren a reason as
merely that it *is* his own; should be unable to pass with
a fresh and equal enjoyment from the study and relish
of his own capacities and achievements to the study and
relish of another man's. A timid jealousy, easily startled
into shrieks of hysterical malice and disloyal spite, is
(wherever you may fall in with it) the property of
base men and mean artists who, at sight of some
person or thing greater than themselves, are struck
sharply by unconscious self-contempt, and at once,
whether they know it or not, lose heart or faith in their
own applauded work. To recognize their equal, even
their better when he does come, must be the greatest
delight of great men. "All the gods," says a French
essayist, "delight in worship: is one lesser for the
other's godhead? Divine things give divine thanks for
companionship; the stars sang not one at once, but all
together." Like all men great enough to enjoy greatness, Blake was born with the gift of admiration; and
in his rapid and fervent nature it struck root and broke

into flower at the least glimpse or chance of favourable
weather. Therefore, if on no other ground, we may
allow him his curious outbreaks of passionate dispraise
and scorn against all such as seemed to stand in the way
of his art. Again, as we have noted, he had a faith of
his own, made out of art for art's sake, and worked by
means of art ; and whatever made against this faith was
as hateful to him as any heresy to any pietist. In a
rough and rapid way he chose to mass and sum up
under some one or two types, comprehensible at first
sight to few besides himself, the main elements of opposition which he conceived to exist. Thus for instance
the names of Locke and Newton, of Bacon and Voltaire,
recur with the most singular significance in his writings,
as emblems or incarnate symbols of the principles opposite to his own : and when the clue is once laid hold of,
and the ear once accustomed to the curious habit of
direct mythical metaphor or figure peculiar to Blake—his
custom of getting whole classes of men or opinions embodied, for purposes of swift irregular attack, in some one
representative individual—much is at once clear and
amenable to critical reason which seemed before mere
tempestuous incoherence and clamour of bodiless rhetoric.
There is also a certain half-serious perversity and wilful
personal humour in the choice and use of these representative names, which must be taken into account by a
startled reader unless he wishes to run off at a false tan-
gent. After all, it is perhaps impossible for any one not
specially qualified by nature for sympathy with such a
man's kind of work, to escape going wrong in his estimate
of Blake ; to such excesses of paradox did the poet-

painter push his favourite points, and in such singular attire did he bring forward his most serious opinions. But at least the principal and most evident chances of error may as well be indicated, by way of warning off the over-hasty critic from shoals on which otherwise he is all but certain to run.

It is a thing especially worth regretting that Balzac, in his Swedenborgian researches, could not have fallen in with Blake's "prophetic" works. Passed through the crucible of that supreme intellect—submitted to the test of that supple practical sense, that laborious apprehension, so delicate and so passionate at once, of all forms of thought or energy, which were the great latent gifts of the deepest and widest mind that ever worked within the limits of inventive prose—the strange floating forces of Blake's instinctive and imaginative work might have been explained and made applicable to direct ends in a way we cannot now hope for. The incomparable power of condensing apparent vapour into tangible and malleable form, of helping us to handle air and measure mist, which is so instantly perceptible whenever Balzac begins to open up any intricate point of physical or moral speculation, would here have been beyond price. He alone who could push analysis to the verge of creation, and with his marvellous clearness of eye and strength of hand turn discovery almost to invention ; he who was not "a prose Shakespeare" merely, but rather perhaps a Shakespeare complete in all but the lyrical faculty ; he alone could have brought a scale to weigh this water, a sieve to winnow this wind. That wonderful wisdom, never at fault on its own ground, which made him not simply the chief of dramatic story, but also the great master of morals,* would not have failed of foothold or eyesight even in this cloudy and noisy borderland of vision and of faith. Even to him too, the supreme student and interpreter of things, our impulsive prophet with his plea of mere direct inspiration might have been of infinite help and use : to'such an eye and brain as his, Blake might have made straight the ways which Swedenborg had left crooked, set right the problems which

* The reader who cares to remember that everything here set down is of immediate importance and necessity for the understanding of the matter in hand (namely, the life of Blake, and the faith and works which made that life what it was) may as well take here a word of comment. It will soon be necessary for even the very hack-writers and ingenious people of ready pens and wits who now babble about Balzac in English and French as a splendid specimen of their craft, fertile but faulty, and so forth—to understand that they have nothing to do with Balzac ; that he is not of their craft, nor of any but the common craft of all great men—the guild of godlike things and people ; that a shelf holding "all Balzac's novels—forty volumes long," is not "cabin-furniture" for any chance "passenger" to select or reject. Error and deficiency there may be in his work ; but none such as they can be aware of. Of poetic form, for example, we know that he knew nothing ; the error would be theirs who should think his kind of work the worse for that. Among men equally great, the distinctive supremacy of Balzac is this ; that whereas the great men who are pure artists (Shakespeare for instance) work by implication only, and hardly care about descending to the level of a preacher's or interpreter's work, he is the only man not of their kind who is great enough to supply their place in his own way—to be their correlative in a different class of workmen ; being from his personal point of view simply impeccable and infallible. The pure artist never asserts; he suggests, and therefore his meaning is totally lost upon moralists and sciolists—is indeed irreparably wasted upon the run of men who cannot work out suggestions. Balzac asserts ; and Balzac cannot blunder or lie. So profound and extensive a capacity of moral apprehension no other prose writer, no man of mere analytic faculty, ever had or can have. This assuredly, when men become (as they will have to become) capable of looking beyond the mere clothes and skin of his work, will be always, as we said, his great especial praise ; that he was, beyond any other man, the master of morals—the greatest direct expounder of actual moral fact. Once consent to forget or overlook the mere *entourage* and social habiliment of Balzac's intense and illimitable intellect, you cannot fail of seeing that he of all men was fittest to grapple with all strange things and words, and compel them by divine violence of spiritual rape to bring forth flowers and fruits good for food and available for use.

mesmerism had set wrong.   As however we cannot have this, we must do what share of interpreter's work falls to our lot as well as we can.

There are two points in the work of Blake which first claim notice and explanation ; two points connected, but not inseparable ; his mysticism and his mythology. This latter is in fact hardly more in its relation to the former, than the clothes to the body or the body to the soul.   To make either comprehensible, it is requisite above all things to get sight of the man in whom they became incarnate and active as forces or as opinions.   Now, to those who regard mysticism with distaste or contempt, as essentially in itself a vain or noxious thing—a sealed bag or bladder that can only be full either of wind or of poison—the man, being above all and beyond all a mystic in the most subtle yet most literal sense, must remain obscure and contemptible. Such readers—if indeed such men should choose or care to become readers at all—will be (for one thing) unable to understand that one may think it worth while to follow out and track to its root the peculiar faith or fancy of a mystic without being ready to accept his deductions and his assertions as absolute and durable facts.   Servility of extended hand or passive brain is the last quality that a mystic of the nobler kind will demand or desire in his auditors.   Councils and synods may put forth notes issued under their stamp, may exact of all recipients to play the part of clerks and indorse their paper with shut eyes : to the mystic such a way of doing spiritual business would seem the very frenzy of fatuity ; whatever else may be profitable, that (he would

say) is suicidal. And assuredly it is not to be expected
that Blake's mystical creed, when once made legible and
even partially coherent, should prove likely to win over
proselytes. Nor can this be the wish or the object of a
reasonable commentator, whose desire is merely to do
art a good turn in some small way, by explaining the
"faith and works" of a great artist. It is true that
whatever a good poet or a good painter has thought
worth representing by verse or design must probably be
worth considering before one deliver judgment on it.
But the office of an apostle of some new faith and the
business of a commentator on some new evangel are two
sufficiently diverse things. The present critic has not
(happily) to preach the gospel as delivered by Blake ; he
has merely, if possible, to make the text of that gospel
a little more readable. And this must be worth doing,
if it be worth while to touch on Blake's work at all.
What is true of all poets and artists worth judging is
especially true of him ; that critics who attempt to judge
him piecemeal do not in effect judge him at all, but
some one quite different from him, and some one (to any
serious student) probably more inexplicable than the
real man. For what are we to make of a man whose
work deserves crowning one day and hooting the next ?
If the " Songs" be so good, are not those who praise
them bound to examine and try what merit may be
latent in the " Prophecies "?—bound at least to explain
as best they may how the one comes to be worth so
much and the other worth nothing ? On this side
alone the biography appears to us emphatically deficient ; here only do we feel how much was lost, how

much impaired by the untimely death of the writer.
Those who had to complete his work have done their part
admirably well; but here they have not done enough.
We are not bound to accept Blake's mysticism; we
are bound to take some account of it. A disciple
must take his master's word for proof of the thing
preached. This it would be folly to expect of a biographer; even Boswell falls short of this, having courage on
some points to branch off from the strait pathway of
his teacher and strike into a small speculative track of
his own. But a biographer must be capable of expound-
ing the evangel (or, if such a word could be, "dys-
angel") of his hero, however far he may be from thinking
it worth acceptance. And this, one must admit, the
writers on Blake have upon the whole failed of doing.
Consequently their critical remarks on such specimens of
Blake's more speculative and subtle work as did find
favour in their sight have but a narrow range and a
limited value. Some clue to the main character of the
artist's habit of mind we may hope already to have put
into the reader's hands—some frayed and ravelled "end
of the golden string," which with due labour he may
"wind up into a ball." To pluck out the heart of
Blake's mystery is a task which every man must be left
to attempt for himself: for this prophet is certainly not
"easier to be played on than a pipe." Keeping fast in
hand what clue we have, we may nevertheless succeed in
making some further way among the clouds. One thing
is too certain; if we insist on having hard ground
under foot all the way we shall not get far. The land
lying before us, bright with fiery blossom and fruit,

musical with blowing branches and falling waters, is not to be seen or travelled in save by help of such light as lies upon dissolving dreams and dividing clouds. By moonrise, to the sound of wind at sunset, one may tread upon the limit of this land and gather as with muffled apprehension some soft remote sense of the singing of its birds and flowering of its fields.

This premised, we may start with a clear conscience. Of Blake's faith we have by this time endeavoured to give the reader some conception—if a faint one, yet at least not a false : of the form assumed by that faith (what we have called the mythology) we need not yet take cognizance. To follow out in full all his artistic and illustrative work, with a view to extract from each separate fruit of it some core of significance, would be an endless labour : and we are bound to consider what may be feasible rather than what, if it were feasible, might be worth doing. Therefore the purpose of this essay is in the main to deal with the artist's personal work in preference to what is merely illustrative and decorative. Designs, however admirable, made to order for the text of Blair, of Hayley, or of Young, are in comparison with the designer's original and spontaneous work mere extraneous by-play. These also are if anything better known than Blake's other labours. Again, the mass of his surviving designs is so enormous and as yet (except for the inestimable *Catalogue* in Vol. 2 of the *Life*) so utterly chaotic and unarrangeable that in such an element one can but work as it were by fits and plunges. Of these designs there must always be many which not having seen we cannot judge ; many too on which artists alone are finally competent to deliver sentence by authority. Moreover the supreme merits as well as the more noticeable qualities merely special and personal of Blake are best seen in his mixed work. Where both text and design are wholly his own, and the two forms or sides of his art so coalesce or overlap as to become inextricably interfused, we have the best chance of seeing and judging what the workman essentially was. In such an enterprise, we must be always duly grateful for any help or chance of help given us : and for one invaluable thing we have at starting to give due honour and thanks to the biographer. He has, one may rationally hope, finally beaten to powder the rickety and flaccid old theory of Blake's madness. Any one wishing to moot that question again will have to answer or otherwise get over the facts and inferences so excellently set out in Chap. xxxv. : to refute them we may fairly consider impossible. Here at least no funeral notice or obsequies will be bestowed on the unburied carcase of that forlorn fiction. Assuming as a reasonable ground for our present labour that Blake was superior to the run of men, we shall spend no minute of time in trying to prove that he was not inferior. Logic and sense alike warn us off such barren ground.

Of the editing of the present selections—a matter evidently of most delicate and infinite labour—we have here to say this only ; that as far as one can see it could not have been done better : and indeed that it could only have been done so well by the rarest of happy chances. Even with the already published poems there was enough work to get through ; for even these had

suffered much from the curiously reckless and helpless
neglect of form which was natural to Blake when his
main work was done and his interest in the matter pre-
maturely wound up. Those only who have dived after
the original copies can fully appreciate or apprehend
with what tenderness of justice and subtlety of sense
these tumbled folds have been gathered up and these
ragged edges smoothed off. As much power and labour
has gone to the perfect adjustment of these relics of
another man's work as a meaner man could have dreamed
only of expending on his own. Nor can any one thoroughly enter into the value and excellence of the thing
here achieved who has not in himself the impulsive
instinct of form—the exquisite desire of just and perfect
work. Alike to those who seem to be above it as to
those who are evidently below, such work must remain
always inappreciable and inexplicable. To the ingeni-
ously chaotic intellect, with its admirable aptitude for all
such feats of conjectural cleverness as are worked out
merely by strain and spasm, it will seem an offensive
waste of good work. But to all who relish work for
work's sake and art for art's it will appear, as it is,
simply invaluable—the one thing worth having yet not
to be had at any price or by any means, except when it
falls in your way by divine accident. True however as
all this is of the earlier and easier part of the editor's
task, it is incomparably more true of the arrangement
and selection of poems fit for publishing out of the
priceless but shapeless chaos of unmanageable MSS.
The good work here done and good help here given it is
not possible to over-estimate. Every light slight touch

of mere arrangement has the mark of a great art con-
summate in great things — the imprint of a sure and
strong hand, in which the thing to be done lies safe and
gathers faultless form. These great things too are so
small in mere size and separate place that they can never
get praised in due detail. They are great by dint of
the achievement implied and the forbearance involved.
Only a chief among lyric poets could so have praised
the songs of Blake ; only a leader among imaginative
painters could so have judged his designs ; only an
artist himself supreme at once in lordship of colour
and mastery of metre could so have spoken of Blake's
gifts and feats in metre and colour. Reading these notes,
one can rest with sufficient pleasure on the conviction
that, wherever else there may be failure in attaining the
right word of judgment or of praise, here certainly there
is none. Here there is more than (what all critics may
have) goodwill and desire to give just thanks ; for here
there is authority, and the right to seem right in deliver-
ing sentence.

But these notes, good as they are and altogether valuable, are the least part of the main work. To the beauty
and nobility of style, the exquisite strength of sifted
English, the keen vision and deep clearness of expression,
which characterize as well these brief prefaces as the
notes on *Job* and that critical summary in the final
chapter of the *Life*, one need hardly desire men's attention ; that splendid power of just language and gift of
grace in detail stand out at once distinguishable from the
surrounding work, praiseworthy as that also in the main
is ; neither from the matter nor the manner can any

careful critic mistake the exact moment and spot where
the editor of the poems has taken up any part of the
business, laid any finger on the mechanism of the book.
But this work, easier to praise, must have been also easier
to perform than the more immediate editorial labours
which were here found requisite. With care inappreciable and invaluable fidelity has the editing throughout
been done. The selection must of necessity have been
to a certain degree straitened and limited by many minor
and temporary considerations; publishers, tasters, and
such-like, must have fingered the work here and there,
snuffing at this and nibbling at that as their manner
is. For the work and workman have yet their way to
make in the judicious reading world; and so long as
they have, they are more or less in the lax limp clutch
of that "dieu ganache des bourgeois" who sits nodding
and ponderously dormant in the dust of publishing
offices, ready at any jog of the elbow to snarl and start—
a new Pan, feeding on the pastures of a fat and foggy
land his Arcadian herds of review or magazine :

$$\dot{\epsilon}\nu\tau\dot{\iota} \ \gamma\epsilon \ \pi\iota\kappa\rho\dot{o}s,$$
$$\kappa\alpha\dot{\iota} \ o\dot{\iota} \ \dot{\alpha}\epsilon\dot{\iota} \ \delta\rho\iota\mu\epsilon\hat{\iota}\alpha \ \chi o\lambda\dot{\alpha} \ \pi o\tau\dot{\iota} \ \dot{\rho}\iota\nu\dot{\iota} \ \kappa\dot{\alpha}\theta\eta\tau\alpha\iota.$$

Arcadian virtue and Bœotian brain, under the presi-
dency of such a stertorous and splenetic goat-god, given
to be sleepy in broadest noonday, are not the best
crucibles for art to be tried in. Then, again, thought
had to be taken for the poems themselves; not merely
how to expose them in most acceptable form for public
acceptance, but how at the same time to give them in
the main all possible fullness of fair play. This too by

dint of work and patience, still more by dint of pliable
sense and taste, has been duly accomplished. Future
editions may be, and in effect will have to be, altered
and enlarged : it is as well for people to be aware that
they have not yet a final edition of Blake ; that will
have to be some day completed on a due scale. But
for the great mass of his lyrical verse all there was to
do has been done here, and the ground-plan taken of a
larger building to come. These preliminaries stated, we
pass on to a rapid general review of those two great
divisions which may be taken as resuming for us the
ripe poetry of Blake's manhood. Two divisions, the one
already published and partially known, the other now
first brought into light and baptized with some legible
name ; the *Songs of Innocence and Experience*, and the
Ideas of Good and Evil. Under this latter head we will
class for purposes of readier reference as well the smaller
MS. volume of fairly transcribed verses as the great mass
of more disorderly writing in verse and prose to which
the name above given is attached in a dim broad scrawl
of the pencil evidently meant to serve as general title,
though set down only on the reverse page of the second
MS. leaf. This latter and larger book, extending in date
at least from 1789 to (August) 1811, but presumably
beyond the later date, is the great source and treasure-
house from which has been drawn out most of the fresh
verse and all of the fresh prose here given us : and is of
course among the most important relics left of Blake.

First then for the *Songs of Innocence and Experience.*
These at a first naming recall only that incomparable
charm of form in which they first came out clothed,

and hence vex the souls of men with regretful comparison. For here by hard necessity we miss the lovely
and luminous setting of designs, which makes the *Songs*
precious and pleasurable to those who know or care for
little else of the master's doing ; the infinite delight of
those drawings, sweeter to see than music to hear, where
herb and stem break into grace of shape and blossom of
form, and the branch-work is full of little flames and
flowers, catching as it were from the verse enclosed the
fragrant heat and delicate sound they seem to give back ;
where colour lapses into light and light assumes feature
in colour. If elsewhere the artist's strange strength of
thought and hand is more visible, nowhere is there such
pure sweetness and singleness of design in his work. All
the tremulous and tender splendour of spring is mixed
into the written word and coloured draught ; every page
has the smell of April. Over all things given, the sleep
of flocks and the growth of leaves, the laughter in dividing lips of flowers and the music at the moulded mouth
of the flute-player, there is cast a pure fine veil of
light, softer than sleep and keener than sunshine. The
sweetness of sky and leaf, of grass and water—the bright
light life of bird and child and beast—is so to speak kept
fresh by some graver sense of faithful and mysterious
love, explained and vivified by a conscience and purpose
in the artist's hand and mind. Such a fiery outbreak of
spring, such an insurrection of fierce floral life and radiant
riot of childish power and pleasure, no poet or painter
ever gave before : such lustre of green leaves and flushed
limbs, kindled cloud and fervent fleece, was never wrought
into speech or shape. Nevertheless this decorative

work is after all the mere husk and shell of the *Songs.*
These also, we may notice, have to some extent shared
the comparative popularity of the designs which serve as
framework to them. They have absolutely achieved the
dignity of a reprint ; have had a chance before now of
swimming for life ; whereas most of Blake's offspring
have been thrown into Lethe bound hand and foot, without hope of ever striking out in one fair effort. Perhaps
on some accounts this preference has been not unreasonable. What was written for children can hardly offend
men ; and the obscurities and audacities of the prophet
would here have been clearly out of place. It is indeed
some relief to a neophyte serving in the outer courts of such
an intricate and cloudy temple, to come upon this little
side-chapel set about with the simplest wreaths and
smelling of the fields rather than incense, where all the
singing is done by clear children's voices to the briefest
and least complex tunes. Not at first without a sense of
release does the human mind get quit for a little of the
clouds of Urizen, the fires of Orc, and all the Titanic
apparatus of prophecy. And these poems are really
unequalled in their kind. Such verse was never written
for children since verse-writing began. Only in a few of
those faultless fragments of childish rhyme which float
without name or form upon the memories of men shall
we find such a pure clear cadence of verse, such
rapid ring and flow of lyric laughter, such sweet and
direct choice of the just word and figure, such an impeccable simplicity ; nowhere but here such a tender wisdom
of holiness, such a light and perfume of innocence.
Nothing like this was ever written on that text of the

lion and the lamb ; no such heaven of sinless animal life
was ever conceived so intensely and sweetly.

> " And there the lion's ruddy eyes
>   Shall flow with tears of gold,
> And pitying the tender cries,
>   And walking round the fold,
> Saying *Wrath by His meekness*
> *And by His health sickness*
> *Is driven away*
> *From our immortal day.*
> *And now beside thee, bleating lamb,*
>   *I can lie down and sleep,*
> *Or think on Him who bore thy name,*
>   *Graze after thee, and weep.*"

The leap and fall of the verse is so perfect as to make it
a fit garment and covering for the profound tenderness
of faith and soft strength of innocent impulse embodied
in it. But the whole of this hymn of *Night* is wholly
beautiful ; being perhaps one of the two poems of loftiest
loveliness among all the *Songs of Innocence*. The other
is that called *The Little Black Boy ;* a poem especially
exquisite for its noble forbearance from vulgar pathos and
achievement of the highest and most poignant sweetness
of speech and sense ; in which the poet's mysticism is
baptized with pure water and taught to speak as from
faultless lips of children, to such effect as this.

> " And we are put on earth a little space
> *That we may learn to bear the beams of love ;*
> And these black bodies and this sunburnt face
> Are like a cloud and like a shady grove."

Other poems of a very perfect beauty are those of the
Piper, the Lamb, the Chimney-sweeper, and the two-days-
old baby ; all, for the music in them, more like the

notes of birds caught up and given back than the modu-
lated measure of human verse. One cannot say, being
so slight and seemingly wrong in metrical form, how
they come to be so absolutely right ; but right even in
point of verses and words they assuredly are. Add fuller
formal completion of rhyme and rhythm to that
song of *Infant Joy*, and you have broken up the soft
bird-like perfection of clear light sound which gives it
beauty ; the little bodily melody of soulless and painless
laughter.

Against all articulate authority we do however class
several of the *Songs of Experience* higher for the great
qualities of verse than anything in the earlier division
of these poems. If the *Songs of Innocence* have the
shape and smell of leaves or buds, these have in them
the light and sound of fire or the sea. Entering among
them, a fresher savour and a larger breath strikes one
upon the lips and forehead. In the first part we are
shown who they are who have or who deserve the gift
of spiritual sight : in the second, what things there are
for them to see when that gift has been given. Innocence, the quality of beasts and children, has the keenest
eyes ; and such eyes alone can discern and interpret
the actual mysteries of experience. It is natural that
this second part, dealing as it does with such things as
underlie the outer forms of the first part, should rise
higher and dive deeper in point of mere words. These
give the distilled perfume and extracted blood of the
veins in the rose-leaf, the sharp, liquid, intense spirit
crushed out of the broken kernel in the fruit. The last
of the *Songs of Innocence* is a prelude to these poems ;

in it the poet summons to judgment the young and
single-spirited, that by right of the natural impulse of
delight in them they may give sentence against the
preachers of convention and assumption ; and in the
first poem of the second series he, by the same "voice
of the bard," calls upon earth herself, the mother of all
these, to arise and become free : since upon her limbs
also are bound the fetters, and upon her forehead also
has fallen the shadow, of a jealous law : from which
nevertheless, by faithful following of instinct and
divine liberal impulse, earth and man shall obtain
deliverance.

> " Hear the voice of the bard !
> Who present, past, and future sees :
> Whose ears have heard
> The ancient Word
> That walked among the silent trees:
> Calling the lapsèd soul
> And weeping in the evening dew;
> That might control
> The starry pole
> And fallen fallen light renew! "

If they will hear the Word, earth and the dwellers
upon earth shall be made again as little children ; shall
regain the strong simplicity of eye and hand proper to
the pure and single of heart ; and for them inspiration
shall do the work of innocence ; let them but once
abjure the doctrine by which comes sin and the law by
which comes prohibition. Therefore must the appeal be
made ; that the blind may see and the deaf hear, and
the unity of body and spirit be made manifest in perfect freedom : and that to the innocent even the liberty
of "sin" may be conceded. For if the soul suffer by

the body's doing, are not both degraded? and if the
body be oppressed for the soul's sake, are not both the
losers?

> " O Earth, O Earth, return!
>   Arise from out the dewy grass!
> Night is worn,
> And the morn
>   Rises from the slumberous mass.
> Turn away no more;
>   Why wilt thou turn away?
> The starry shore,
> The watery floor,
>   Are given thee till the break of day."

For so long, during the night of law and oppression of
material form, the divine evidences hidden under sky
and sea are left her; even "till the break of day."
Will she not get quit of this spiritual bondage to the
heavy body of things, to the encumbrance of deaf clay
and blind vegetation, before the light comes that shall
redeem and reveal? But the earth, being yet in subjection to the creator of men, the jealous God who
divided nature against herself — father of woman and
man, legislator of sex and race—makes blind and bitter
answer as in sleep, "her locks covered with grey
despair."

> " Prisoned on this watery shore,
>   Starry Jealousy does keep my den;
> Cold and hoar,
> Weeping o'er,
>   I hear the father of the ancient men."

Thus, in the poet's mind, Nature and Religion are
the two fetters of life, one on the right wrist, the other
on the left; an obscure material force on this hand, and

on that a mournful imperious law : the law of divine
jealousy, the government of a God who weeps over his
creature and subject with unprofitable tears, and rules
by forbidding and dividing: the "Urizen" of the prophetic
books, clothed with the coldness and the grief of remote
sky and jealous cloud. Here as always, the cry is as
much for light as for license, the appeal not more against
prohibition than against obscurity.

> " Can the sower sow by night,
> Or the ploughman in darkness plough ? "

In the *Songs of Innocence* there is no such glory of
metre or sonorous beauty of lyrical work as here. No
possible effect of verse can be finer in a great brief way
than that given in the second and last stanzas of the first
part of this poem. It recals within one's ear the long
relapse of recoiling water and wash of the refluent wave ;
in the third and fourth lines sinking suppressed as with
equal pulses and soft sobbing noise of ebb, to climb again
in the fifth line with a rapid clamour of ripples and
strong ensuing strain of weightier sound, lifted with the
lift of the running and ringing sea.

Here also is that most famous of Blake's lyrics, *The
Tiger ;* a poem beyond praise for its fervent beauty and
vigour of music. It appears by the MS. that this was
written with some pains ; the cancels and various readings bear marks of frequent rehandling. One of the
latter is worth transcription for its own excellence and
also in proof of the artist's real care for details, which his
rapid instinctive way of work has induced some to
disbelieve in.

> " Burnt in distant deeps or skies
>   The cruel fire of thine eyes?
>   Could heart descend or wings aspire ? *
>   What the hand dare seize the fire ? "

Nor has Blake left us anything of more profound and perfect value than *The Human Abstract;* a little mythical vision of the growth of error ; through soft sophistries of pity and faith, subtle humility of abstinence and fear, under which the pure simple nature lies corrupted and

---

* Could God bring down his heart to the making of a thing so deadly and strong ? or could any lesser dæmonic force of nature take to itself wings and fly high enough to assume power equal to such a creation ? Could spiritual force so far descend or material force so far aspire ? Or, when the very stars, and all the armed children of heaven, the "helmed cherubim" that guide and the "sworded seraphim" that guard their several planets, wept for pity and fear at sight of this new force of monstrous matter seen in the deepest night as a fire of menace to man—

> " Did he smile his work to see?
>   Did he who made the lamb make thee ? "

We may add another cancelled reading to show how delicately the poem has been perfected ; although by an oversight of the writer's most copies hitherto have retained some trace of the rough first draught, neglecting in one line a change necessary to save the sense as well as to complete the sentence.

> " And when thy heart began to beat,
>   What dread hand and what dread feet
>
>   Could fetch it from the furnace deep
>   And in thy horrid ribs dare steep ?
>   In what clay and in what mould
>   Were thine eyes of fury rolled? "

Having cancelled this stanza or sketched ghost of a stanza, Blake in his hurry of rejection did not at once remember to alter the last line of the preceding one ; leaving thus a stone of some size and slipperiness for editorial feet to trip upon, until the recovery of that nobler reading—

> " What dread hand *framed thy* dread feet ? "

Nor was this little "rock of offence" cleared from the channel of the poem even by the editor of 1827, who was yet not afraid of laying hand upon the text. So grave a flaw in so short and so great a lyric was well worth the pains of removing and is yet worth the pains of accounting for ; on which ground this note must be of value to all who take in verse with eye and ear instead of touching it merely with eyelash and finger-tip in the manner of sand-blind students.

strangled ; through selfish loves which prepare a way
for cruelty, and cruelty that works by spiritual abase-
ment and awe.

> " Soon spreads the dismal shade
> Of Mystery over his head;
> And the caterpillar and fly
> Feed on the Mystery.
>
> And it bears the fruit of Deceit,
> Ruddy and sweet to eat ;
> And the raven his nest has made
> In the thickest shade."

Under the shadow of this tree of mystery,* rooted in
artificial belief, all the meaner kind of devouring things
take shelter and eat of the fruit of its branches ; the
sweet poison of false faith, painted on its outer husk
with the likeness of all things noble and desirable ; and
in the deepest implication of barren branch and deadly
leaf, the bird of death, with priests for worshippers (" the
priests of the raven of dawn," loud of lip and hoarse of
throat until the light of day have risen), finds house
and resting-place. Only in the "miscreative brain" of
fallen men can such a thing strike its tortuous root and
bring forth its fatal flower ; nowhere else in all nature
can the tyrants of divided matter and moral law,
"Gods of the earth and sea," find soil that will bear such
fruit.

Nowhere has Blake set forth his spiritual creed more
clearly and earnestly than in the last of the *Songs of*

---

* Compare the passage in *Ahania* where the growth of it is defined ; rooted in
the rock of separation, watered with the tears of a jealous God, shot up from
sparks and fallen germs of material seed ; being after all a growth of mere error,
and vegetable (not spiritual) life ; the topmost stem of it made into a cross
whereon to nail the dead redeemer and friend of men.

Experience. "Tirzah," in his mythology, represents the
mere separate and human nature, mother of the perishing
body and daughter of the "religion" which occupies
itself with laying down laws for the flesh ; which, while
pretending (and that in all good faith) to despise the
body and bring it into subjection as with control of bit
and bridle, does implicitly overrate its power upon the
soul for evil or good, and thus falls foul of fact on all
sides by assuming that spirit and flesh are twain, and
that things pleasant and good for the one can properly
be loathsome or poisonous to the other. This "religion"
or "moral law," the inexplicable prophet has chosen to
baptize under the singular type of "Rahab"—the "harlot
virgin-mother," impure by dint of chastity and forbearance from such things as are pure to the pure of heart :
for in this creed the one thing unclean is the belief in
uncleanness, the one thing forbidden is to believe in the
existence of forbidden things. Of this mystical mother
and her daughter we shall have to take some further
account when once fairly afloat on those windy waters of
prophecy through which all who would know Blake to
any purpose must be content to steer with such pilotage
as they can get. For the present it will be enough to
note how eager and how direct is the appeal here made
against any rule or reasoning based on reference to the
mere sexual and external nature of man—the nature
made for ephemeral life and speedy death, kept alive
"to work and weep" only through that mercy which
"changed death into sleep"; how intense the reliance on
redemption from such a law by the grace of imaginative
insight and spiritual freedom, typified in "the death of

Jesus."* Nor are any of these poems finer in structure or nobler in metrical form.

This present edition of the *Songs of Experience* is richer by one of Blake's most admirable poems of childhood—a division of his work always of especial value for its fresh and sweet strength of feeling and of words. In this newly recovered *Cradle Song* are perhaps the two loveliest lines of his writing :

> " Sleep, sleep : in thy sleep
> Little sorrows sit and weep."†

Before parting from this chief lyrical work of the poet's, we may notice (rather for its convenience as an explanation than its merit as a piece of verse) this

---

* Compare again in the *Vision of the Last Judgment* (v. 2, p. 163), that definition of the "Divine body of the Saviour, the true Vine of Eternity," as "the Human Imagination, who appeared to me as coming to judgment among his saints, and throwing off the Temporal that the Eternal might be established." The whole of that subtle and eloquent rhapsody is about the best commentary attainable on Blake's mystical writings and designs. It is impossible to overstate the debt of gratitude due from all students of Blake to the transcriber and editor of the *Vision*, whose indefatigable sense and patient taste have made it legible for all. To have extracted it piecemeal from the chaos of notes jotted down by Blake in the most inconceivable way, would have been a praiseworthy labour enough ; but without addition or omission to have constructed these abortive fragments into a whole so available and so admirable, is a labour beyond praise.

† This exquisite verse did not fall into its place by chance ; the poem has been more than once revised. Its opening stanza stood originally thus :—

> " Sleep, sleep; in thy sleep
> Thou wilt every secret keep ;
> Sleep, sleep, beauty bright,
> Thou shalt taste the joys of night."

Before recasting the whole, Blake altered the second line into—

> " Canst thou any secret keep ? "

The gist of the song is this ; the speaker, watching a girl newly-born, compares her innocuous infancy with the power that through beauty will one day be hers, her blameless wiles and undeveloped desires with the strong and subtle qualities now dormant which the years will assuredly awaken within her ; seeing as it were the whole woamn asleep in the child, he smells future fruit in the unblown bud. On retouching his work, Blake thus wound up the moral and tune of this song in a projected *Motto to the Songs of Innocence and of Experience,* which editors have left hitherto in manuscript :

> " The good are attracted by men's perceptions,
>   And think not for themselves
> Till Experience teaches them how to catch
>   And to cage the Fairies and Elves.
>
> And then the Knave begins to snarl,
>   And the Hypocrite to howl ;
> And all his* good friends show their private ends,
>   And the Eagle is known from the Owl."

Experience must do the work of innocence as soon as conscience begins to take the place of instinct, reflection of perception ; but the moment experience begins upon this work, men raise against her the conventional

stanza forming by its rhymes an exact antiphonal complement to the end of the first *Cradle Song.*

> " When thy little heart does wake,
> Then the dreadful lightnings break
> From thy cheek and from thine eye,
> O'er the youthful harvests nigh ;
> Infant wiles and infant smiles
> Heaven and earth of peace beguiles."

The epithet "infant" has supplanted that of "female," which was perhaps better : as to the grammatical licence, Blake followed in that the Elizabethan fashion which made the rule of sound predominate over all others. The song, if it loses simplicity, seems to gain significance by this expansion of the dim original idea ; and beauty by expression of the peril latent in a life whose smiles as yet breed no strife between friends, kindle no fire among the unripe shocks of growing corn ; but whose words shall hereafter be as very swords, and her eyes as lightning ; *teterrima belli causa.*

* "His," the good man's : this lax piece of grammar (shifting from singular to plural and back again without much tangible provocation) is not infrequent with Blake, and would hardly be worth righting if that were feasible. A remarkable instance is but too patent in the final "chorus" of the *Marriage of Heaven and Hell.* Such rough licence is given or taken by old poets ; and Blake's English is always beautiful enough to be pardonable where it slips or halts : especially as its errors are always those of a rapid lyrical style, never of a tortuous or verbose ingenuity : it stammers and slips occasionally, but never goes into convulsions like that of some later versifiers.

clamour of envy and stupidity. She teaches how to
entrap and retain such fugitive delights as children
and animals enjoy without seeking to catch or cage
them ; but this teaching the world calls sin, and
the law of material religion condemns : the face of
"Tirzah" is set against it, in the "shame and pride"
of sex.

> " Thou, mother of my mortal part,
> With cruelty didst mould my heart,
> And with false self-deceiving fears
> Didst bind my nostrils, eyes, and ears."

And thus those who live in subjection to the senses
would in their turn bring the senses into subjection ;
unable to see beyond the body, they find it worth while
to refuse the body its right to freedom.

In these hurried notes on the *Songs* an effort has
been made to get that done which is most absolutely
necessary—not that which might have been most facile or
most delightful. Analytic remark has been bestowed on
those poems only which really cannot dispense with it
in the eyes of most men. Many others need no herald
or interpreter, demand no usher or outrider : some of
these are among Blake's best, some again almost among
his worst.* Poems in which a doctrine or subject once

---

* Such we must consider, for instance, the second *Little Boy Lost*, which looks
at first more of a riddle and less worth solution than the haziest section of the
prophetic books. A cancelled reading taken from the rough copy in the *Ideas*
will at all events make one stanza more amenable to reason :

> " I love myself ; so does the bird
> That picks up crumbs around the door."

Blake was rather given to erase a comparatively reasonable reading and substitute something which cannot be confidently deciphered by the most daring
self-reliance of audacious ingenuity, until the reader has found some means of
pitching his fancy for a moment in the ordinary key of the prophet's. This un-

before nobly stated and illustrated is re-asserted in a
shallower way and exemplified in a feebler form,* require
at our hands no written or spoken signs of either assent
or dissent. Such poems, as the editor has well indicated,
have places here among their betters : none of them, it
may be added, without some shell of outward beauty or
seed of inward value. The simpler poems claim only
praise ; and of this they cannot fail from any reader
whose good word is in the least worth having. Those of

comfortable little poem is in effect merely an allegoric or fabulous appeal against
the oppression of formulas (or family "textualism" of the blind and unctuous
sort) which refuse to single and simple insight, to the outspoken innocence of a
child's laughing or confused analysis, a right to exist on any terms : just as the
companion poem is an appeal, so vague as to fall decidedly flat, against the
externals of moral fashion. Both, but especially the *Girl*, have some executive
merit : not overmuch. To the surprising final query, "Are such things done on
Albion's shore ?" one is provoked to respond, "On the whole, not, as far as we
can see ;" but the "Albion" of Blake's verse is never this weaving and spinning
country of our working days ; it is rather some inscrutable remote land of Titanic
visions, moated with silent white mist instead of solid and sonorous surf, and
peopled with vague pre-Adamite giants symbolic of more than we can safely
define or conceive. An inkling of the meaning may, if anything can, be extracted
from some parts of the *Jerusalem ;* but probably no one will try.

　* With more time and room to work in, we might have noticed in these less
dramatic and seemingly less original poems of the second series which take up
from the opposite point of view matters already handled to such splendid effect in
the *Songs of Innocence*, a depth and warmth of moral quality worth remark ;
infinite tenderness of heart and fiery pity for all that suffer wrong ; something of
Hugo's or Shelley's passionate compassion for those who lie open to "all the
oppression that is done under the sun" ; something of the anguish and labour, the
fever-heat of sleepless mercy and love incurable which is common to those two
great poets. The second *Holy Thursday* is doubtless far enough below the high
level of the first ; but the second *Chimney-sweeper* as certainly has a full share of
this passionate grace of pain and pity. Blake's love of children never wrung out
into his work a more pungent pathos or keener taste of tears than in the last verse
of this poem. It stood thus in the first draught :

　　　" And because I am happy and dance and sing
　　　　They think they have done me no injury,
　　　And are gone to praise God and his priest and king,
　　　　Who wrap themselves up in our misery."

　The quiet tremulous anger of that, its childish sorrow and contempt, are no less

a subtler kind (often, as must now be clear enough, the best worth study) claim more than this if they are to have fair play. It is pleasant enough to commend and to enjoy the palpable excellence of Blake's work; but another thing is simply and thoroughly requisite—to understand what the workman was after. First get well hold of the mystic, and you will then at once get a better view and comprehension of the painter and poet. And if through fear of tedium or offence a student refuses to be at such pains, he will find himself, while following Blake's trace as poet or painter, brought up sharply within a very short tether. "It is easy," says Blake himself in the *Jerusalem,* "to acknowledge a man to be great and good while we derogate from him in the trifles and small articles of that goodness; those alone are his friends who admire his minute powers."

Looking into the larger MS. volume of notes we seem to gain at once a clearer insight into the writer's daily habit of life and tone of thought, and a power of judging more justly the sort of work left us by way of result. Here, as by fits and flashes, one is enabled to look in upon that strange small household, so silent and simple on the outside, so content to live in the poorest domestic way, without any show of eccentric indulgence or erratic aspiration; husband and wife to all appearance the commonest citizens alive, satisfied with each other and with

---

true than subtle in effect. It recalls another floating fragment of verse on social wrongs which shall be rescued from the chaos of the *Ideas :*

> "There souls of men are bought and sold,
>   And milk-fed infancy, for gold;
>   And youths to slaughter-houses led,
>   And maidens, for a bit of bread."

their minute obscure world and straitened limits of living. No typical churchwarden or clerk of the parish could rub on in a more taciturn modest manner, or seem able to make himself happy with smaller things. It may be as well for us to hear his own account of the matter :

PRAYER.

I.

" I rose up at the dawn of day;
  ' Get thee away; get thee away!
  Pray'st thou for riches ? away, away!
  This is the throne of Mammon grey.'

II.

Said I, ' This sure is very odd ;
I took it to be the throne of God ;
For everything besides I have ;
It is only for riches that *I* can crave.

III.

' I have mental joys and mental health,
And mental friends and mental wealth ;
I've a wife I love and that loves me ;
I've all but riches bodily ;

IV.

' Then, if for riches I must not pray,
God knows I little of prayers need say ;
So, as a church is known by its steeple,
If I pray, it must be for other people.

V.

' I am in God's presence night and day,
And he never turns his face away ;
The accuser of sins by my side does stand,
And he holds my money-bag in his hand ;

VI.

' For my worldly things God makes him pay,
And he'd pay for more if to him I would pray ;
And so you may do the worst you can do,
Be assured, Mr. Devil, I won't pray to you.

VII.

' He says, if I do not worship him for a God,*
I shall eat coarser food and go worse shod ;
So, as I don't value such things as these,
You must do, Mr. Devil—just as God please.' "

One cannot doubt that to a man of this temper his life
was endurable enough. Faith in God and goodwill
towards men came naturally to him, being a mystic ; on
the one side he had all he wanted, and on the other he
wanted nothing. The praise and discipleship of men
might no doubt have added a kind of pleasure to his
way of life, but they could neither give nor take away
what he most desired to have ; and this he never failed
of having. His wife, of whose " goodness " to him he
has himself borne ample witness, was company enough
for all days. And indeed, by all the evidence left us,
it appears that this goodness of hers was beyond example.
Another woman of the better sort might have had equal
patience with his habit of speech and life, equal faith in
his great capacity and character ; but hardly in another
woman could such a man have found an equal strength
and sweetness of trust, an equal ardour of belief and
tenderness, an equal submission of soul and body for
love's sake ;—submission so perfect and so beautiful in
the manner of it, that the idea of sacrifice or a separate
will seems almost impossible. A man living with such
a wife might well believe in some immediate divine
presence and in visible faces like the face of an angel.

* This verse is of course to be read as one made up of rough but regular
anapæsts ; the heavier accents falling consequently upon every third syllable—
that is, upon the words *if, not,* and *him.* The next line is almost as rough, and
seems indeed to slip into the solid English iambic ; but may also be set right by
giving full attention to accent.

We have not now of course much chance of knowing at all what manner of angel she was ; but the few things we do know of her, no form of words can fitly express. To praise such people is merely to waste words in saying that divine things are praiseworthy. No doubt, if we knew how to praise them, they would deserve that we should try.*

The notes bearing in any way upon this daily life of Blake's are few and exceptional. In the mass of

---

* A strange and rather beautiful, if grotesque, evidence of the unity of faith and feeling to which Blake and his wife had come by dint of living and thinking so long together, is given by one of the stray notes in this same book : which we transcribe at full on account of its great biographical value as a study of character. Space might have been found for it in the Life, if only to prove once again how curiously the nature and spiritual habits of a great man leave their mark or dye upon the mind nearest to his own.

"SOUTH MOLTON STREET.

"*Sunday, August,* 1807.—My wife was told by a spirit to look for her fortune by opening by chance a book which she had in her hand ; it was Bysshe's ' Art Poetry.' She opened the following :—

' I saw 'em kindle with desire,
  While with soft sighs they blew the fire ;
  Saw the approches of their joy,
  He growing more fierce and she less coy ;
  Saw how they mingled melting rays,
  Exchanging love a thousand ways.
  Kind was the force on every side ;
  Her new desire she could not hide,
  Nor would the shepherd be denied.
  The blessed minute he pursued,
  Till she, transported in his arms,
  Yields to the conqueror all her charms.
  His panting breast to hers now joined,
  They feast on raptures unconfined,
  Vast and luxuriant ; such as prove
  The immortality of love.
  For who but a Divinity
  Could mingle souls to that degree
  And melt them into ecstasy ?

floating verse and prose there is absolutely no hint of
order whatever, save that, at one end of the MS., some

> Now like the Phœnix both expire,
> While from the ashes of their fire
> Springs up a new and soft desire.
> Like charmers, thrice they did invoke
> The God, and thrice new vigour took.'—*Behn.*

" I was so well pleased with her luck that I thought I would try my own, and
opened the following :—

> ' As when the winds their airy quarrel try,
> Jostling from every quarter of the sky,
> This way and that the mountain oak they bear,
> His boughs they scatter and his branches tear ;
> With leaves and falling mast they spread the ground ;
> The hollow valleys echo to the sound ;
> Unmoved, the royal plant their fury mocks,
> Or, shaken, clings more closely to the rocks :
> For as he shoots his towering head on high,
> So deep in earth his fixed foundations lie.'—*Dryden's Virgil.*"

Nothing is ever so cynical as innocence, whether it be a child's or a mystic's.
As a poet, Blake had some reason to be " well pleased" with his wife's curious
windfall ; for those verses of the illustrious Aphra's have some real energy and
beauty of form, visible to those who care to make allowance, first for the conventional English of the time, and secondly for the naked violence of manner
natural to that she-satyr, whose really great lyrical gifts are hopelessly overlaid
and encrusted by the rough repulsive husk of her incredible style of speech. Even
" Astræa" must however have fair play and fair praise ; and the simple truth is
that, when writing her best, this " unmentionable " poetess has a vigorous grace
and a noble sense of metre to be found in no other song-writer of her time. One
song, fished up by Mr. Dyce out of the weltering sewerage of Aphra's unreadable
and unutterable plays, has a splendid quality of verse, and even some degree of
sentiment not wholly porcine. Take four lines as a sample, and Blake's implied
approval will hardly seem unjustifiable :—

> " From thy bright eyes he took those fires
> Which round about in sport he hurled ;
> But 'twas from mine he took desires
> Enough to undo the amorous world."

The strong and subtle cadence of that magnificent fourth verse gives evidence of
so delicate an ear and such dexterous power of hand as no other poet between the
Restoration date and Blake's own time has left proof of in serious or tragic song.
Great as is Dryden's lyrical work in more ways than one, its main quality is mere
strength of intellect and solidity of handling—the forcible and imperial manner
of his satires ; and in pure literal song-writing, which (rather than any ' ode ' or

short poems are transcribed in a slightly more coherent form.   Among these and the other lyrics, strewn as from a liberal but too lax hand about the chaotic leaves of his note-book, are many of Blake's best things.   Some of the slight and scrawled designs, as noted in the *Catalogue* (pp. 242, 243), have also a merit and a power of their own ; but it is with the poet's lyrical work that we have to do at this point of our present notes ; and here we may most fitly wind up what remains to be said on that matter.

The inexhaustible equable gift of Blake for the writing of short sweet songs is perceptible at every turn we take in this labyrinth of lovely words, of strong and soft designs.   Considering how wide is the range of date from the earliest of these songs to the latest, they seem more excellently remote than ever from the day's verse and the day's habit.   They reach in point of time from the season of Mason to the season of Moore ; and never in any interval of work by any chance influence do these poems at their weakest lapse into likeness or tolerance of the accepted models.   From the era of plaster to the era of pinchbeck, Blake kept straight ahead of the times.   To the pseudo-Hellenic casts of the one school or the pseudo-Hibernian tunes of the other he was admirably deaf and blind.   While a grazing public straightened its bovine neck and steadied its flickering eyelids to look up between-

such-like mixed poem) may be taken as the absolute and final test of a poet's lyrical nature, he never came near this mark.   François Villon and Aphra Behn, the two most inexpressibly non-respectable of male or female Bohemians and poets, were alike in this as well ; that the supreme gift of each, in a time sufficiently barren of lyrical merit, was the gift of writing admirable songs ; and this, after all, has perhaps borne better fruit for us than any gift of moral excellence.

whiles, with the day's damp fodder drooping half-chewed
from its relaxed jaw, at some dim sick planet of the
Mason system, there was a poet, alive if obscure, who
had eyes to behold

> " the chambers of the East,
> The chambers of the sun, that now
> From ancient melody have ceased ; "

who had ears to hear and lips to reveal the music and
the splendour and the secret of the high places of verse.
Again, in a changed century, when the reading and
warbling world was fain to drop its daily tear and stretch
its daily throat at the bidding of some Irish melodist
—when the "female will" of "Albion" thought fit to
inhale with wide and thankful nostril the rancid flavour
of rotten dance-roses and mouldy musk, to feed "in
a feminine delusion" upon the sodden offal of perfumed
dog's-meat, and take it for the very eucharist of Apollo
—then too, while this worship of ape or beetle went so
noisily on, the same poet could let fall from lavish hand
or melodious mouth such grains of solid gold and flakes
of perfect honey as this :—

> " Silent, silent night,
> Quench the holy light
> Of thy torches bright;
>
> For possessed of day,
> Thousand spirits stray,
> That sweet joys betray.
>
> Why should love be sweet,
> Usèd with deceit,
> Nor with sorrows meet ? "

Verse more nearly faultless and of a more difficult perfection was never accomplished. The sweet facility of

being right, proper to great lyrical poets, was always an especial quality of Blake's. To go the right way and do the right thing, was in the nature of his metrical gift—a faculty mixed into the very flesh and blood of his verse.

There is in all these straying songs the freshness of clear wind and purity of blowing rain : here a perfume as of dew or grass against the sun, there a keener smell of sprinkled shingle and brine-bleached sand ; some growth or breath everywhere of blade or herb leaping into life under the green wet light of spring; some colour of shapely cloud or mound of moulded wave. The verse pauses and musters and falls always as a wave does, with the same patience of gathering form, and rounded glory of springing curve, and sharp sweet flash of dishevelled and flickering foam as it curls over, showing the sun through its soft heaving side in veins of gold that inscribe and jewels of green that inlay the quivering and sundering skirt or veil of thinner water, throwing upon the tremulous space of narrowing sea in front, like a reflection of lifted and vibrating hair, the windy shadow of its shaken spray. The actual page seems to take life, to assume sound and colour, under the hands that turn it and the lips that read ; we feel the falling of dew and have sight of the rising of stars. For the very sound of Blake's verse is no less remote from the sound of common things and days on earth than is the sense or the sentiment of it.

> " O what land is the land of dreams ?
> What are its mountains and what are its streams ?
> —O father, I saw my mother there,
> Among the lilies by waters fair.
>   .   .   .   .

> —Dear child, I also by pleasant streams
> Have wandered all night in the land of dreams ;
> But though calm and warm the waters wide
> I could not get to the other side."

We may say of Blake that he never got back from that other side—only came and stood sometimes, as Chapman said of Marlowe in his great plain fashion of verse, "up to the chin in that Pierian flood," and so sang half-way across the water.

Nothing in the *Songs of Innocence* is more beautiful as a study of childish music than the little poem from which we have quoted ; written in a metre which many expert persons have made hideous, and few could at any time manage as Blake did—a scheme in which the soft and loose iambics lapse into sudden irregular sound of full anapæsts, not without increase of grace and impulsive tenderness in the verse. Given a certain attainable average of intellect and culture, these points of workmanship, by dint of the infinite gifts or the infinite wants they imply, become the swiftest and surest means of testing a verse-writer's perfection of power, and what quality there may be in him to warrant his loftiest claim. By these you see whether a man can sing, as by his drawing and colouring whether he can paint. Another specimen of indefinable sweetness and significance we may take in this symbolic little piece of song ;

> " I walked abroad on a sunny day;
> I wooed the soft snow with me to play.
> She played and she melted in all her prime ;
> And the winter called it a dreadful crime." *

---

* Another version of this line, with less of pungent and brilliant effect, has

Against the "winter" of ascetic law and moral pre-
scription Blake never slackens in his fiery animosity;
never did a bright hot wind of March make such war
upon the cruel inertness of February. In his obscure
way he was always hurrying into the van of some forlorn
hope of ethics. Even Shelley, who as we said was no
less ready to serve in the same camp all his life long,
never shot keener or hotter shafts of lyrical speech into
the enemy's impregnable ground. Both poets seem to
have tried about alike, and with equally questionable
results, at a regular blockade of the steep central fortress
of "Urizen;" both after a little personal practice fell
back, not quite unscarred, upon light skirmishing and the
irregular work of chance guerilla campaigns. Moral
custom, " that twice-battered god of Palestine " round
which all Philistia rallies (specially strong in her British
brigade), seemed to suffer little from all their slings and
arrows. Being mere artists, they were perhaps at root
too innocent to do as much harm as they desired, or to
desire as much harm as they might have done. Blake
indeed never proposed to push matters quite to such a
verge as the other was content to stand on during his
Laon and Cythna period; from that inconceivable edge
of theory or sensation he would probably have drawn
back with some haste. But such sudden cries of melodious
revolt as this were not rare on his part.*

yet a touch of sound in it worth preserving : some may even prefer it in point of
simple lyrical sweetness :

> " She played and she melted in all her prime :
>   Ah ! that sweet love should be thought a crime."

* On closer inspection of Blake's rapid autograph I suspect that in the second
line those who please may read " the ruddy limbs and flowering hair," or perhaps

> " Abstinence sows sand all over
>   The ruddy limbs and flaming hair,
>   But desire gratified
>   Plants fruits of life and beauty there."

Assuredly he never made a more supremely noble and enjoyable effect of verse than that; the cadence of the first two lines is something hardly to be matched anywhere : the verse (to resume our old simile for a moment) turns over and falls in with the sudden weight and luminous motion of a strong long roller coming in with the-wind. So again, lying sad and sick under his marriage myrtle, even in a full rain of fragrant and brilliant blossoms that fall round him to waste, he must needs ask and answer the fatal final question.

> " Why should I be bound to thee,
>   O my lovely myrtle-tree ?
>   Love, free love, cannot be bound
>   To any tree that grows on ground."

Mixed with this fervour of desire for more perfect freedom, there appears at times an excess of pity (like Chaucer's in his early poems) for the women and men living under the law, trammelled in soul or body. For example, the poem called *Infant Sorrow*, in the *Songs of Experience*, ran at first to a greater length and through stranger places than it now overflows into ; and is worth giving here in its original form as extracted by cautious picking and sifting from a heap of tumbled readings.

I.
> " My mother groaned, my father wept ;
>   Into the dangerous world I leapt,

" flowery ;" but the type of flame is more familiar to Blake.   Compare further on " A Song of Liberty."

Helpless, naked, piping loud,
Like a fiend hid in a cloud.

II.

Struggling in my father's hands,
Striving against my swaddling bands,
Bound and weary, I thought best
To sulk upon my mother's breast.

III.

When I saw that rage was vain
And to sulk would nothing gain,
Twining many a trick and wile
I began to soothe and smile.

IV.

And I grew* day after day.
Till upon the ground I lay;
And I grew* night after night,
Seeking only for delight.

V.

And I saw before me shine
Clusters of the wandering vine;
And many a lovely flower and tree
Stretched their blossoms out to me.

VI.

But many a priest† with holy look,
In their hands a holy book,
Pronouncèd curses on his head
Who the fruit or blossoms shed.

---

* Other readings are "soothed" and "smiled"—readings adopted after the insertion of the preceding stanza. As the subject is a child not yet grown to standing and walking age, these readings are perhaps better, though less simple in sound, than the one I have retained.

† Here and throughout to the end, duly altering metre and grammar with a quite laudable care, Blake has substituted "my father" for the "priests;" not I think to the improvement of the poem, though probably with an eye to making the end cohere rather more closely with the beginning. This and the "Myrtle" are shoots of the same stock, and differ only in the second grafting. In the last-named poem the father's office was originally thus;

> "Oft my myrtle sighed in vain
> To behold my heavy chain:
> Oft my father saw us sigh,
> And laughed at our simplicity."

VII.

I beheld the priests by night;
They embraced the blossoms bright;
I beheld the priests by day;
Underneath the vines they lay.

VIII.

Like to serpents in the night,
They embraced my blossoms bright;
Like to holy men by day,
Underneath my vines they lay.

IX.

So I smote them, and their gore
Stained the roots my myrtle bore;
But the time of youth is fled,
And grey hairs are on my head."

Now not even the spilt blood of those who forbid and
betray shall quicken the dried root or flush the faded leaf
of love; the myrtle being past all comfort of soft rain or
helpful sun. So in the *Rose-Tree* (vol. ii. p. 60), when for
the sake of a barren material fidelity to his "rose" of marriage, he has passed over the offered flower " such as May
never bore," the rose herself " turns away with jealousy,"
and gives him thorns for thanks : nothing left of it for
hand or lip but collapsed blossom and implacable edges
of brier. Blake might have kept in mind the end of his
actual wild vine (vol. i. p. 100 of the *Life*), which ran
all to leaf and never brought a grape worth eating, for
fault of pruning-hooks and vine-dressers.

In all this there is a certain unmistakeable innocence
which accounts for the practical modesty and peaceable

Here too Blake had at first written, " Oft the priest beheld us sigh ; " he afterwards
cancelled the whole passage, perhaps on first remarking the rather too grotesque
confusion of a symbolic myrtle with a literal wife ; and the last stanza in either
form is identical. The simple subtle grace of both poems, and the singular care
of revision bestowed on them, are equally worth notice.

forbearance of the man's way of living. The material
shape of his speculations never goes beyond a sort of
boyish defiant complaint, a half-humorous revolt of the
will. Inconstancy with him is not rooted in satiety, but
in the freshness of pure pleasure ; he would never cast off
the old to put on the new. The chain once broken,
against which between sleeping and waking he chafes and
wrestles, he would lie for most hours of the day with
content enough in the old shade of wedded rose or myrtle
tree. Nor in leaping or reaching after the new flower
would he wilfully bruise or break the least bud of the
old. His desire is towards the freedom of the dawn of
things—not towards the " dark secret hour" that walks
under coverings of cloud.

> " Are not the joys of morning sweeter
> Than the joys of night? "

The sinless likeness of his seeming " sins "—mere
fancies as it appears they mostly were, mere soft light
aspirations of theory without body or flesh on them—has
something of the innocent immodesty of a birds' or babies'
paradise—of a fools' paradise, too, translated into the
practice and language of the untheoretic world. Shelley's
' Epipsychidion" scarcely preaches a more bodiless evangel
of bodily liberty. That famous and exquisitely written
passage beginning, "True love in this differs from gold
and clay," delivers in more daringly definite words the
exact message of Blake's belief.

Nowhere has the note of pity been more strongly
and sweetly struck than in those lovely opening verses

of the " Garden of Love," which must here be read once
again :—

> " I laid me down upon a bank
> Where Love lay sleeping:
> I heard among the rushes dank
> Weeping, weeping.
>
> Then I went to the heath and the wild,
> To the thistles and thorns of the waste ;
> And they told me how they were beguiled,
> Driven out, and compelled to be chaste."

The sharp and subtle change of metre here and at the
end of the poem has an audacity of beauty and a justice
of impulse proper only to the leaders of lyrical verse :
unfit alike for definition and for imitation, if any copyist
were to try his hand at it. The next song we transcribe
from the " Ideas " is lighter in tone than usual, and
admirable for humorous imagination; a light of laughter
shines and sounds through the words.

THE WILL AND THE WAY.

> " I asked a thief to steal me a peach ;
> He turned up his eyes ;
> I asked a lithe lady to lie her down
> Holy and meek, she cries.
>
> As soon as I went
> An angel came ;
> He winked at the thief
> And smiled at the dame ;
>
> And without one word spoke
> Had a peach from the tree ;
> And 'twixt earnest and joke
> Enjoyed the lady."*

---

* Those who insist on the tight lacing of grammatical stays upon the " painèd
loveliness " of a muse's over-pliant body may use if they please Blake's own
amended reading ; in which otherwise the main salt of the poem is considerably

A much better and more solid version of the same fancy than the one given in the "Selections" under the head of "Love's Secret;" which is rather weakly and lax in manner. Our present poem has on the other hand an exquisite "lithe" grace of limb and suppleness of step, suiting deliciously with the "light high laugh" in its tone : while for sweet and rapid daring, for angelically puerile impudence as it were, it may be matched against any song of its fantastic sort.

Less complete in a small way, but worth taking some care of, is this carol of a fairy, emblem of a man's light hard tyranny of will, calling upon the birds in the harness of Venus and the shafts in the hand of her son for help in setting up the kingdom of established and legal love : but caught himself in the very setting of his net.

THE MARRIAGE RING.

" ' Come hither, my sparrows,
　　My little arrows.
　　If a tear or a smile
　　Will a man beguile,
　　If an amorous delay
　　Clouds a sunshiny day,
　　If the step of a foot
　　Smites the heart to its root,
　　'Tis the marriage ring
　　Makes each fairy a king.'
　　So a fairy sang.
　　From the leaves I sprang;
　　He leaped from his spray
　　To flee away :

diluted as by tepid water : the angel (one might say) has his sting blunted and the best quill of his pinion pulled out.

" And without one word said
　　Had a peach from the tree ;
　　And still as a maid," &c.

> But in my hat caught,
> He soon shall be taught,
> Let him laugh, let him cry,
> He's my butterfly:
> For I've pulled out the sting
> Of the marriage ring."

It is not so easy to turn wasps to butterflies in the world of average things; but, as far as verses go, there are few of more supple sweetness than some of these. They recall the light lapse of measure found in the beautiful older germs of nursery rhyme ;* and the seeming retributive triumph of married lovers over unmarried, of wedlock over courtship, could not well be more gracefully translated than in the "Fairy's" call to his winged and feathered "arrows" —the lover's swift birds of prey, not without beak and claw. "If they do for a minute or so darken our days, dupe our fancies, prevail upon our nerves and blood, once well married we are kings of them at least." Pull out that sting of jealous reflective egotism, and your tamed "fairy"—the love that is in a man once set right—has no point or poison left it, but only rapid grace of wing and natural charm of colour.

Throughout the "Ideas" one or two other favourite

---

* We may find place here for another fairy song, quaint in shape and faint in colour, but with the signet of Blake upon it; copied from a loose scrap of paper on the back of which is a pencilled sketch of Hercules throttling the serpents, whose twisted limbs make a sort of spiral cradle around and above the child's triumphant figure: an attendant, naked, falls back in terror with sharp recoil of drawn-up limbs ; Alcmena and Amphitryon watch the struggle in silence, he grasping her hand.

> " A fairy leapt upon my knee
> Singing and dancing merrily ;
> I said, 'Thou thing of patches, rings,
> Pins, necklaces, and such-like things,

points of faith and feeling are incessantly thrown out in new fugitive forms; such as the last (rejected) stanza of "Cupid," which, though the song may well dispense with it and even gain by such a loss in the qualities of shape or sound, must be saved if only as a specimen of the persistent way in which Blake assumed the Greek and Roman habits of mind or art to be typical of "war" and restraint; an iron frame of mind good to fight in and not good for love to grow under.

> " 'Twas the Greek love of war
>   That turned Love into a boy *
> And woman into a statue of stone ;
>   And away fled every joy."

More frequent and more delightful is the recurrence of such loving views of love as that taken in the last lines of " William Bond ;" a poem full of strange and soft hints, of mist that allures and music that lulls; typical in the

> Disgracer of the female form,
> Thou paltry gilded poisonous worm ! '
> Weeping, he fell upon my thigh,
> And thus in tears did soft reply :
> ' Knowest thou not, O fairies' lord,
> How much by us contemned, abhorred,
> Whatever hides the female form
> That cannot bear the mortal storm ?
> Therefore in pity still we give
> Our lives to make the female live ;
> And what would turn into disease
> We turn to what will joy and please.' "

Even so dim and slight a sketch as this may be of worth as indicating Blake's views of the apparent and the substantial form of things, the primary and the derivative life ; also as a sample of his roughest and readiest work.

* Lest the kingdom of love left under the type of a woman should be over powerful for a nation of hard fighters and reasoners, such as Blake conceived the "ancients" to be. Compare for his general style of fancies on classic matters the prologue to "Milton" and the Sibylline Leaves on Homer and Virgil. To his half-trained apprehension Rome seemed mere violence and Greece mere philosophy.

main of the embodied struggle between selfish and sacri-
ficial passion, between the immediate impulse that brings
at least the direct profit of delight, and the law of
religious or rational submission that reaps mere loss and
late regret after a life of blind prudence and sorrowful
forbearance—the "black cloud" of sickness, malady of
spirit and body inflicted by the church-keeping "angels of
Providence" who have driven away the loving train of
spirits that live by innate impulse : not the bulk of
Caliban but the soul of Angelo being the deadliest direct
enemy of Ariel. "Providence" divine or human, prepense
moral or spiritual "foresight," was a thing in the excellence
of which our prophet of divine instinct and inspired flesh
could not consistently believe. His evangel could dispense with that, in favour of such faith in good things as
came naturally to him.

> "I thought Love lived in the hot sunshine,
> But oh, he lives in the moony light;
> I thought to find Love in the heat of day,
> But sweet Love is the comforter of night.
>
> "Seek Love in the pity of others' woe,
> In the gentle relief of another's care ;
> In the darkness of night and the winter's snow,
> In the naked and outcast, seek Love there."

The infinite and most tender beauty of such words
is but one among many evidences how thoroughly and
delicately the lawless fervour and passionate liberty of
desire were tempered in Blake by an exquisite goodness,
of sense rather than of thought, which as it were made
the pain or pleasure, the well-being or the suffering, of
another press naturally and sharply on his own nerves of
feeling. Deeply as his thought and fancy had struck into

strange paths and veins of spiritual life, he had never found or felt out any way to the debateable land where simple and tender pleasures become complex and cruel, and the roses gathered are redder at root than in leaf.

Another poem, slight of texture and dim of feature, but full of a cloudy beauty, is *The Angel:* a new allegory of love, blindly rejected or blindly accepted as a thing of course ; foiled and made profitless in either case : then lost, with all the sorrow it brings and all the comfort it gives : and the ways are barred against it by armed mistrust and jealousy, and its place knows it no more : but this immunity from the joys and sorrows of love is bought at the bitter price of untimely age. (I offer these somewhat verbose and wiredrawn attempts at commentary, only where the poem seems at once to require analysis and to admit such as I give ; how difficult it is to make such notes clear and full, yet not to stumble into confusion or slide into prolixity, those can estimate who will try their hand at such work.)

Frequent slips and hitches of grammar, it may be added, are common to Blake's rough studies and finished writings, and are therefore not always things to be weeded out. Little learning and much reading of old books made him more really inaccurate than were their writers, whose apparent liberties he might perhaps have pleaded in defence of his own hardly defensible licences.

None of these poems are worthier, for the delight they give, of the selected praise and most thankful study than *The Two Songs* and *The Golden Net:* a pair of perfect things, their feet taken in the deep places of thought, and their heads made lovely with the open light of lyric speech. Between the former of these* and *The Human Abstract* there is a certain difference : here, the moral point of the poem is, that innocence is wholly ignorant, and sees no deeper than the shell of form ; experience is mainly malignant, and sees the root of evil and seed of pain under the leaf of good and blossom of pleasant things :† there, the vision is the poet's own, and deals with that evil neither actually nor seemingly inherent in the system or scheme of created nature, but watered into life by the error and fed into luxuriance by the act of " the human brain" alone ; two widely unlike themes for verse. As to execution, here doubtless there is more of that swift fresh quality peculiar to Blake's simpler style ; but the *Abstract* again has more weight of verse and magnificence of symbol.

* Let the reader take another instance of the culture given to these songs—a gift which has happily been bequeathed by Blake to his editor. This one was at first divided into five equal stanzas ; the last two running thus :—

> " ' And pity no more would be
> If all were happy as we ; '
> At his curse the sun went down,
> And the heavens gave a frown.

> " Down poured the heavy rain
> Over the new-reaped grain ;
> And Misery's increase
> Is Mercy, Pity, Peace."

Thus one might say is the curse confuted ; for if, as the " grievous devil " will have it, the root of the sweetest goodness is in material evil, then may the other side answer that even by his own showing the flower or " increase " from that root is not evil, but good : a soft final point of comfort missed by the change which gives otherwise fresher colour to this poem.

† But as above shewn the vision of the wise man or poet is wider than both ; sees beyond the angel's blind innocent enjoyment to a deeper faith than his simple nature can grasp or include ; sees also past the truth of the devil's sad ingenious " analytics " to the broader sense of things, seen by which, " Good and Evil are no more."

Akin to *The Golden Net* is the form and manner of *Broken Love;* which, whatever taste may lie in the actual kernel of it, is visibly one of the poet's noblest studies of language. The grandeur of the growing metre and heat of passionate pulses felt through the throbbing body of its verse can escape no ear. In our notes on *Jerusalem* we shall have, like the "devil" of *The Two Songs*, to look at it from the inverse side and pass upon it a more laborious and less thankworthy comment.

Of the longest and gravest poem in the "Ideas of Good and Evil" we are bound to take some careful account. This is *The Everlasting Gospel,* a semi-dramatic exposition of faith on the writer's part; full of subtleties and paradoxes which might well straighten the stiffest hairs of orthodoxy and bewilder the sharpest brain of speculation. Blake has here stated once for all the why and the how of his Christian faith ; for Christian he averred that it was, and we may let his word pass for it. Readers must be recommended for the present to look at these things as much as possible from what we will call their artistic or poetic side, and bring no pulpit logic to get chopped or minced on the altar of this prophet's vision. His worst heresy, they may be assured, "will not bite." In effect one may hope (or fear, as the case may be) that there is much less of heresy underlying these daring forms of speech than seems to overlay their outer skirt : schism or division of body rather than of spirit from less wilful and outspoken forms of faith.

Let the student of this "Gospel" of inverted belief and intensified paradox lay hold of and cling fast to the clue given by the "Vision of the Last Judgment." There for one thing the prophet has laid down this rule : "Moral virtues do not exist ; they are allegories and dissimulations." For "moral allegory" we are therefore not to look here; we are in the house of pure vision, outside of which allegory halts blindly across the shifting sand of moral qualities, her right hand leaning on the staff of virtue, her left hand propped on the crutch of vice. Conscious unimpulsive "virtue," measured by the praise or judged by the laws of men, was to Blake always Pharisaic : a legal God none other than a magnified and divine Pharisee. Thus far have other (even European) mystics often enough pushed their inference ; but this time the mystic was a poet ; and therefore always, where it was possible, prone to prefer tangible form and given to beat out into human shape even the most indefinite features of his vision. Assuming Christ as the direct and absolute divine type (divine in the essential not in the clerical sense— divine to the spiritual not the technical reason) he was therefore obliged to set to work and strip that type of the incongruous garment of "moral virtues" cast over it by the law of religious form : to prove, as he elsewhere said, that Christ "was all virtue," not by the possession of these "allegoric" qualities called human virtues or abstinence from those others called human sins or vices : such abstinence or such possession cannot conceivably suffice for the final type of goodness or absolute incarnation of a thing unalterably divine. Virtues are no more predicable of the perfect virtue than vices of the perfect vice. As the supreme sin cannot be said to commit human faults, so neither can the supreme holiness obey the principles of human sanctity. "Deistical virtue" is

as the embroidery on the ephod of Caiaphas or the stain
left upon the water by the purified hands of Pilate. It
is the property of "the heathen schools"; a bitted and
bridled virtue, led by the nose and tied by the neck;
made of men's hands and subject to men's laws. Can
you make a God worth worship out of that? To say
that God is wise, chaste, humble, philanthropic, gentle, or
just; in one word, that he is "good" after the human
sense; is to lower your image of God not less than if you
had predicated of him the exactly reverse qualities, by
reason of which these exist, even as they by reason of
these. How much of all this Blake had fished up out of
his studies of Behmen, Swedenborg, or such others, his
present critic has not the means of deciding; but is
assured of one thing ; that where others dealt by induc-
tive rule and law, Blake dealt by assumptive preaching
and intuition ; that he found form of his own for the
body of thought, and body of his own for the spirit of
speculation, supplied by others ; playing Prometheus to
their Epimetheus, doing poet's or evangelist's work where
they did philosophic business ; not fumbling in the box
of Pandora for things flown or fugitive, but bringing from
extreme heaven the immediate fire in the hollow of his
reed or pen.

Such is the radical "idea" of the poem ; and as to
details, we are to remember that "modesty" with Blake
means a timid and tacit prurience, and "humility" a
mistrustful and mendacious cowardice : he puts these
terms to such uses in his swift fierce way, just as, in his
detestation of deism and its "impersonal God," he must
needs embody his vision of a deity or more perfect

humanity in the personal Christian type : a purely
poetical tendency, which if justly apprehended will serve
to account for the wildest bodily forms in which he drew
forth his visions from the mould of prophecy.

Thus much by way of prologue may suffice for the
moral side of this "Gospel"; the mythological or tech-
nically religious side is not much easier to deal with, and
indeed cannot well be made out except by such misty
light as may be won from the prophetic books. It seems
evident that Blake, at least for purposes of evangelism,
was content to regard the " Creator" of the mere bodily
man as one with the "legal" or " Pharisaic " God of the
churches : even as the "mother of his mortal part"—of
the flesh taken for the moment simply, and separated (for
reasoning purposes) from the inseparable spirit—is " Tirzah." This vision of a creator divided against his own
creation and having to be subdued by his own creatures
will appear more directly and demand more distinct remark
when we come to deal with its symbolic form in the great
myth of "Urizen;" where also it will be possible to follow
it out with less likelihood of offensive misconstruction.
One is compelled here to desire from those who care to
follow Blake at all, the keenest ardour of attention possible ; they will blunder helplessly if they once fail to
connect this present minute of his work with the past
and the future of it : if they once let slip the thinnest
thread of analogy, the whole prophetic or evangelic web
collapses for them into a chaos of gossamer, a tangle of
unclean and flaccid fibres, the ravelled woof of an insane
and impotent Arachne, who should be retransmuted with
all haste into a palpable spider by the spell of reason.

Here, as in all swift "inspired" writing, there are on the outside infinite and indefinable anomalies, contradictions, incompatibilities enough of all sorts ; open for any Paine or Paley to impugn or to defend. But let no one dream that there is here either madness or mendacity : the heart or sense thus hidden away is sound enough for a mystic.

The greatest passage of this poem is also the simplest ; that division which deals with the virtue of " chastity," and uses for its text the story of "the woman taken in adultery :" who is identified with Mary Magdalene. We give it here in full ; hoping it may now be comprehensible to all who care to understand, and may bear fruit of its noble and almost faultless verse for all but those who prefer to take the sterility of their fig-tree on trust rather than be at the pains of lifting a single leaf.

> " Was Jesus *chaste?* or did he
> Give any lessons of chastity ?
> The morning blushed fiery red ;
> Mary was found in adulterous bed.
> Earth groaned beneath, and heaven above
> Trembled at discovery of love.
> Jesus was sitting in Moses' chair ;
> They brought the trembling woman there.
> Moses commands she be stoned to death :
> What was the sound of Jesus' breath ?
> He laid his hand on Moses' law ;
> The ancient heavens, in silent awe,
> Writ with curses from pole to pole,
> All away began to roll ;
> The earth trembling and naked lay
> In secret bed of mortal clay—
> On Sinai felt the hand Divine
> Pulling* back the bloody shrine—

* Query " Putting ?"　This whole poem is jotted down in a close rough hand-writing, not often easy to follow with confidence.

And she heard the breath of God
As she heard by Eden's flood :
' Good and Evil are no more ;
Sinai's trumpets, cease to roar ;
Cease, finger of God, to write
The heavens are not clean in thy sight.
Thou art good, and thou alone ;
Nor may the sinner cast one stone.
To be good only, is to be
A God, or else a Pharisee.
Thou Angel of the Presence Divine,
That didst create this body of mine,
Wherefore has thou writ these laws
And created hell's dark jaws ?
My Presence I will take from thee ;
A cold leper thou shalt be.
Though thou wast so pure and bright
That heaven was impure in thy sight,
Though thine oath turned heaven pale,
Though thy covenant built hell's gaol,
Though thou didst all to chaos roll
With the serpent for its soul,
Still the breath Divine does move—
And the breath Divine is love.
Mary, fear not. Let me see
The seven devils that torment thee.
Hide not from my sight thy sin,
That forgiveness thou mayst win.
Hath no man condemnèd thee ? '
' No man, Lord.'   ' Then what is he
Who shall accuse thee ?   Come ye forth,
Fallen fiends of heavenly birth
That have forgot your ancient love
And driven away my trembling dove ;
You shall bow before her feet ;
You shall lick the dust for meat ;
And though you cannot love, but hate,
Shall be beggars at love's gate.
—What was thy love ?   Let me see't ;
Was it love or dark deceit ? '
' Love too long from me has fled ;
'Twas dark deceit, to earn my bread ;
'Twas covet, or 'twas custom, or
Some trifle not worth caring for :

That they may call a shame and sin
Love's temple that God dwelleth in,
And hide in secret hidden shrine
The naked human form divine,
And render that a lawless thing
On which the soul expands her wing.
But this, O Lord, this was my sin—
When first I let these devils in,
In dark pretence to chastity
Blaspheming love, blaspheming thee.
Thence rose secret adulteries,
And thence did covet also rise.
My sin thou hast forgiven me;
Canst thou forgive my blasphemy ?
Canst thou return to this dark hell
And in my burning bosom dwell ?
And canst thou die that I may live ?
And canst thou pity and forgive ? ' "

In no second poem shall we find such a sustained passage as that; such light of thought and thunder of verse; such sudden splendour of fire seen across a strange land and among waste places beyond the receded landmarks of the day or above the glimmering lintels of the night. The passionate glory of its rapid and profound music fills the sense with too deep and sharp a delight to leave breathing-space for any thought of analytic or apologetic work. But the spirit of the verse is not less great than the body of it is beautiful. " Divide from the divine glory the softness and warmth of human colour— subtract from the divine the human presence—subdue all refraction to the white absolute light—and that light is no longer as the sun's is, warm with sweet heat of life and liberal of good gifts; but foul with overmuch purity, sick with disease of excellence, unclean through exceeding cleanness, like the skin of a leper 'as white as snow.' " For the divine nature is not greater than the human ; (they are

one from eternity, sundered by the separative creation or
fall, severed into type and antitype by bodily generation,
but to be made one again when life and death shall both
have died ;) not greater than the human nature, but
greater than the qualities which the human nature assumes
upon earth. God is man, and man God ; as neither of
himself the greater, so neither of himself the less : but
as God is the unfallen part of man, man the fallen part
of God, God must needs be (not more than man, but
assuredly) more than the qualities of man. Thus the
mystic can consistently deny that man's moral goodness
or badness can be predicable of God, while at the same
time he affirms man's intrinsic divinity and God's intrinsic humanity. Man can only possess abstract qualities
—"allegoric virtues"—by reason of that side of his
nature which he has *not* in common with God : God, not
partaking of the "generative nature," cannot partake of
qualities which exist only by right of that nature. The
other "God"* or "Angel of the Presence" who created
the sexual and separate body of man did but cleave in
twain the "divine humanity," which becoming reunited
shall redeem man without price and without covenant
and without law ; he meantime, the Creator,† is a divine

* In the line "A God or else a Pharisee," Blake with a pencil-scratch has
turned "a God" to "a devil" ; as if the words were admittedly or admissibly
interchangeable ! A prophet so wonderfully loose-tongued may well be the
despair of his faithfullest commentators : but as it happens the pencil-scratch
should here be of some help and significance to us : following this small clue, we
may come to distinguish the God of his belief from this demon-god of the created
" mundane shell "—the God of Pharisaic religion and moral law.

† The creator by division, father of men and women, fashioner of evil and
good ; literally in the deepest sense " the God of this world," who " does not
know the garment from the man ; " cannot see beyond the two halves which
he has made by violence of separation ; would have the body perishable, yet the

dæmon, liable to error, subduable by and through this very created nature of his invention, which he for the present imprisons and torments. *His* law is the law of Moses, which according to the Manichean heresy Christ came to reverse as diabolic. This singular (and presumably "Pantheistic") creed of Blake's has a sort of Asiatic flavour about it, but seems harder and more personal in its mythology than an eastern philosopher's; has also a distinct western type and Christian touch in it; being wrought as it were of Persian lotus-leaves hardened into the consistency of English oak-timber. The most wonderful part of his belief or theory is this: "That after Christ's death he became Jehovah:" * which may mean simply that through Christ the law of liberty came to supplant the bondage of law, so that where Jehovah was Christ is; or may typify the change of evangel into law, of full-grown Christianity into a fresh type of "Judaism," of the Gospel or good news of freedom into the Church

qualities of the bodily life permanent: thus inverting order and reversing fact. Parallel passages might be brought in by the dozen on all hands, after a little dipping into mystic books; but I want to make no more room here for all this than is matter of bare necessity.

* We shall see this presently. I conceive however that Blake, to save time and contract the space of his preaching, uses the consecrated Hebrew name to design now the giver of the Mosaic law, now that other and opposite Divinity which after the "body of clay" had been "devoured" was the residue or disembodied victorious spirit of the human Saviour. Mysticism need not of necessity be either inaccurate or incoherent: neither need it give offence by its forms and expressions of faith: but a mystic is but human after all, and with the best intentions may slip somewhere, especially a mystic so little in *training* as Blake, and so much of a poet or artist; who is not accustomed to any careful feeling of his way among words, except with an eye to the perfection of their bodily beauty. Indeed, as appears by Mr. Crabb Robinson's notes of his conversation, Blake affirmed that according to scripture itself the world was created by "the Elohim," not by Jehovah; whose covenant he elsewhere asserted was simply "forgiveness of sins." Thus even according to this heretical creed the God of the Jews would seem to be ranged on the same side with Christ against "the God of this world."

or dogmatic body of faith ; or may imply that the
two forces, after that supreme sacrifice, coalesced and
became one, all absolute Deity, being absorbed into the
Divine Humanity; or, as a practical public would suggest,
may mean or typify nothing. It is certain that Blake
appears so far to have accepted the " Catholic tradition "
as to regard this death or sacrifice as tending somehow
not merely to the redemption of man (which would be no
more than the sequel or outcome of his mystic faith in
the salvation of man by man, the deliverance or redemption of the accident through the essence), but also to the
union of the divine crucified man with the creative
governing power. Somehow ; but the prophet must explain for himself the exact means. We are now fairly up
to the ears in mysticism, and cannot afford to strike out at
random, for fear of being carried right off our feet by the
ground-swell and drifted into waters where swimming
will be yet tougher work.

The belief in " holy insurrection" must be almost as
old as the oldest religions or philosophies afloat or articulate. In the most various creeds this feature of faith
stands out sharply with a sort of tangible human appeal.
Earlier heretics than the author of *Jerusalem* have taken
this to be the radical significance of Christianity ; a
divine revolt against divine law ; an evidence that man
must become as God only by resistance to God—" the
God of this world ;" that if Prometheus cannot, Zeus
will not deliver us : and that man, if saved at all, must
indeed be saved " so as by fire "—by ardour of rebellion
and strenuous battle against the God of nature : who
as of old must yet feed upon his children, and will no

longer take stone for flesh though never so well wrapped
up; who must have the organ of destruction and division,
by which alone he lives* and has ability to beget, cut

* Compare this fragment of a paraphrase or "excursus" on a lay sermon by a
modern pagan philosopher of more material tendencies ; but given to such tragic
indulgence in huge Titanic dithyrambs. "Nature averse to crime? I tell you,
nature lives and breathes by it ; hungers at all her pores for bloodshed, aches in
all her nerves for the help of sin, yearns with all her heart for the furtherance of
cruelty. Nature forbid that thing or this? Nay, the best or worst of you will
never go so far as she would have you ; no criminal will come up to the measure
of her crimes, no destruction seem to her destructive enough. We, when we
would do evil, can disorganise a little matter, shed a little blood, quench a little
breath at the door, of a perishable body ; this we can do, and can call it crime.
Unnatural is it ? Good friend, it is by criminal things and deeds unnatural that
nature works and moves and has her being ; what subsides through inert virtue, she
quickens through active crime ; out of death she kindles life ; she uses the dust
of man to strike her light upon ; she feeds with fresh blood the innumerable
insatiable mouths suckled at her milkless breast ; she takes the pain of the whole
world to sharpen the sense of vital pleasure in her limitless veins : she stabs and
poisons, crushes and corrodes, yet cannot live and sin fast enough for the cruelty
of her great desire. Behold, the ages of men are dead at her feet ; the blood of
the world is on her hands ; and her desire is continually toward evil, that she
may see the end of things which she hath made. Friends, if we would be one
with nature, let us continually do evil with our might. But what evil is here for
us to do, where the whole body of things is evil ? The day's spider kills the
day's fly, and calls it a crime ? Nay, could we thwart nature, then might crime
become possible and sin an actual thing. Could but a man do this ; could he cross
the courses of the stars, and put back the times of the sea ; could he change the
ways of the world and find out the house of life to destroy it ; could he go into
heaven to defile it and into hell to deliver it from subjection ; could he draw
down the sun to consume the earth, and bid the moon shed poison or fire upon
the air ; could he kill the fruit in the seed and corrode the child's mouth with
the mother's milk ; then had he sinned and done evil against nature. Nay, and
not then : for nature would fain have it so, that she might create a world of new
things ; for she is weary of the ancient life : her eyes are sick of seeing and her
ears are heavy with hearing ; with the lust of creation she is burnt up, and rent
in twain with travail until she bring forth change ; she would fain create afresh,
and cannot, except it be by destroying : in all her energies she is athirst for
mortal food, and with all her forces she labours in desire of death. And what
are the worst sins we can do—we who live for a day and die in a night ? a few
murders, a few "——we need not run over the not so wholly insignificant roll-
call ; but it is curious to observe how the mystical evangelist and the material
humourist meet in the reading of mere nature and join hands in their interpretation of the laws ruling the outer body of life: a vision of ghastly glory, without
pity or help possible.

off from him with the sharpest edge of flint that rebellious hands can whet. In these galliambics of Blake's we see the flint of Atys whetted for such work ; made ready against the priests of Nature and her God, though by an alien hand that will cast no incense upon the altar of Cybele ; no Phrygian's, who would spend his own blood to moisten and brighten the high places of her worship : but one ready, with what fire he can get, to burn down the groves and melt down the cymbals of Dindymus.

Returning now to the residue of the immediate matter in hand, we may duly notice in this excursive and all but shapeless poem many of Blake's strong points put forth with all his strength : curiously crossed and inter-mixed with rough skirmishing attacks on the opposite faction, clerical or sceptical, by way of interlude. "You would have Christ act according to what you call a rational or a philanthropic habit of mind—set the actual God to reason, to elevate, to convince or convert after the fashion in which you would set about it? redeem, not the spiritual man by inspiration of his spirit, but the bodily man by application of his arguments ? make him as 'Bacon and Newton'" (Blake's usual types of the mere understanding) ?

> "For thus the Gospel St. Isaac confutes :
>   'God can only be known by his attributes ;
>   And as to the indwelling of the Holy Ghost
>   Or of Christ and the Father, it's all a boast
>   And pride and vanity of imagination
>   That did wrong to follow this world's fashion.'
>   To teach doubt and experiment
>   Certainly was not what Christ meant."

Certainly also no doggrel can be rougher, looser, heavier-weighted about the wrists and ankles, than this ;

which indeed it was perhaps hardly fair to transcribe ;
for take out the one great excerpt already given, and the
whole poem is a mass of huddled notes jotted down in
a series of hints, on stray sides and corners of leaves,
crammed into holes and byways out of sight or reach.
So perfect a poet is not to be judged by the scrawls and
sketches of his note-book ; but as we cannot have his
revision of the present piece of work, and are not here to
make any revision of our own, we must either let drop
the chance of insight thus afforded, or make shift with
the rough and ragged remnants allowed us by the sparing
fingers of a close-handed fate. And this chance of insight
is not to be lightly let go, if we mean to look at all into
Blake's creed and mind. "Experiment" to the mystic
seems not insufficient merely, but irrational. "Reason
says *miracle;* Newton says *doubt;*" as Blake in another
place expounds to such disciples as he may get. On this
point also his "Vision of Christ" is other than the Christian public's.

> "Thine is the friend of all mankind ;
> Mine speaks in parables to the blind."

His Christ cared no more to convince "the blind" by
plain speech than to save "the world"—the form or flesh
of the world, not that imperishable body or complement
of the soul which if a man "keep under and bring into
subjection" he transgresses against himself; but the mere
"sexual" shell which only exists (as we said) by error and
by division and by right of temporal appearance.

Keeping in mind the utter roughness and formal in-
completion of these notes—which in effect are the mere
broken shell or bruised husk of a poem yet unfledged

and unembodied—we may put to some present use the ensuing crude and loose fragments.

> " What was he doing all that time
> From twelve years old to manly prime ?
> Was he then idle, or the less
> About his Father's business ?
> If he had been Antichrist aping* Jesus,
> He'd have done anything to please us ;
> Gone sneaking into synagogues
> And not used the elders and priests like dogs ;
> But humble as a lamb or ass
> Obeyed himself to Caiaphas.
> God wants not man to humble himself.
> That is the trick of the ancient Elf.
> This is the race that Jesus ran :
> Humble to God, haughty to man ;
> Cursing the rulers before the people
> Even to the temple's highest steeple ;
> And when he humbled himself to God,
> Then descended the cruel rod."

(This noticeable heresy is elsewhere insisted on. Its root seems to be in that doctrine that nothing is divine which is not human—has not in it the essence of completed manhood, clear of accident or attribute ; servility therefore to a divine ruler is one with servility to a human ruler. More orthodox men have registered as fervent a protest against the degradation involved in base forms of worship ; but this singular mythological form seems peculiar to Blake, who was bent on finding in the sacred text warrant or illustration for all his creed.)

> " ' If thou humblest thyself thou humblest me :
> Thou also dwell'st in eternity.

---

* Blake had first written "the creeping," then cancelled "the" and interlined the word "Antichrist": I have no doubt intending some such alteration as that in the text of "creeping" to "aping"; but as far as we can now know the day for rewriting his fair copy never came.

> Thou art a man; God is no more;
> Thine own humanity learn to adore,
> For that is my spirit of life.
> Awake: arise to spiritual strife;
> And thy revenge abroad display
> In terror at the Last Judgment Day.' "

(Another special point of faith. "Redemption by forgiveness of sins? yes: but the power of redeeming or
forgiving must come by strife. A gospel is no mere
spiritual essence of boiled milk and rose-water. There
are the energies of nature to fight and beat—unforgivable
enemies, embodied in Melitus or Annas, Caiaphas or Lycon.
Sin is pardonable; but these things, in the body or out
of it, are not pardonable. Revenge also is divine; whatever you may think or say while in the body, there is a
part of nature not forgivable, an element in the world
not redeemable, which in the end must be cast out and
tormented." To the priests of Pharisaic morals or Satanic
religion—those who crucify the great "human" nature
and "scourge sin instead of forgiving it"—to these the
Redeemer must be the tormentor.)

> " ' God's mercy and long-suffering
> Are but the sinner to justice to bring.
> Thou on the cross for them shalt pray—
> And take revenge at the last day.'
> Jesus replied, and thunders hurled:
> ' I never will pray for the world.
> Once I did so when I prayed in the garden;
> I wished to take with me a bodily pardon.' "

These few lines, interpolated by way of comfortable
exposition, are more likely to increase the offence and
perplexity: but assuredly no irreverent brutality of paradox was here in the man's mind. Even the "divine
humanity" of his quasi-Pantheistic worship must give up

(he says) the desire of redeeming the unredeemable
"world"—the quality subject to law and technical religion. No "bodily pardon" for that, whatever the divine
pity may have hoped, while as yet full-grown in love
only, not in knowledge—seraphic fire without' cherubic
light; before, that is, it had perfect insight into the brute
nature or sham body of things. That must be put off—
changed as a vesture—by the risen and reunited body
and soul. What is it that has to be saved? What is
it that can be?

> " Can that which was of woman born
> In the absence of the morn,
> While the soul fell into sleep
> And (? heard) archangels round it weep,
> Shooting out against the light
> Fibres of a deadly night,
> Reasoning upon its own dark fiction,
> In doubt which is self-contradiction,"

can that reason itself into redemption? The absolute
body and essential soul, as we have said, are with all their
energies, passive and active powers and pleasures, natural
properties and liberties, of an imperishable and vital holiness; but their appended qualities, their form and law,
their morals and philosophies, their reason and religion,
these are perishable and damnable. The "holy reasoning
power," in whose "holiness is closed the abomination of
desolation," must be annihilated. "Rational Truth, root
of Evil and Good," must be plucked up and burnt with
fire. You cannot, save in an empirical sense, walk by
sight and not by faith : you cannot "walk by faith
and not by sight," for there is no sight except faith.
(Compare generally the *Gates of Paradise*, for illustra-

tions of all these intricate and intense conceptions.)
Doubt then, being one of the perishable qualities which
depend on externals, is mere impotence and error : now
let us hear further :—

> " Humility is only doubt
> And does the sun and moon blot out,
> Roofing over with thorns and stems
> The buried soul and all its gems.
> This life's dim window of the soul
> Distorts the heavens from pole to pole
> And leads you to believe a lie
> When you see with, not through, the eye,
> That was born in a night, to perish in a night,
> When the soul slept in the beams of light."

Part of this reappears with no less vigour of evangelic
assertion in the *Auguries of Innocence,* but stripped of
the repellent haze of mythological form. That poem, full
as it is of delicate power and clear sweetness of thought,
does not however reproduce in full the emblematic
beauty of our last extract : nor does it throw so much
light of a fitful flame-like sort upon or over the subtlest
profundities of Blake's faith.

Elsewhere, reverting with fresh spirit to the same
charge, he demands (or his spectre for him—"This was
spoken by my spectre to Voltaire, Bacon, &c.") :—

> " Did Jesus teach doubt ? or did he
> Give any lessons of philosophy ?
> Charge visionaries with deceiving ?
> Or call men wise for not believing ? "

Unhappily the respective answers from Verulam and
Cirey have not been registered by a too contemptuous
prophet ; they would have been worth reading.

The dogma of " Christian humility " is totally indi-

gestible to Blake ; he batters upon it with the heaviest
artillery of his "gospel."

> " Was Jesus humble ? or did he
> Give any proofs of humility ?
> Boast of high things with humble tone,
> And give with charity a stone ? "

Again ;

> " When the rich learned Pharisee
> Came to consult him secretly,
> Upon his heart with iron pen
> He wrote ' Ye must be born again.'
> He was too proud to take a bribe :
> He spoke with authority, not like a Scribe."

Nor can the love of enemies be accepted literally as an
endurable doctrine ; for "he who loves his enemies hates
his friends," in the mind of the too ardent and candid
poet, who proceeds to insist that the divine teacher
"must mean the mere *love* of civility" (*amour de conve-
nance*); "and so he must mean concerning humility" : for
the willing acceptance of death cannot humiliate, and is
therefore no test of "humility"* in Blake's sense ; self-

---

* There are (says the mystic) two forms of "humility" : detestable both, and
condemnable. By one, the extrinsic form, a man cringes and submits, doubts
himself and gives in to others ; becomes in effect impotent, a sceptic and a
coward ; by the other or intrinsic form, he conceives too meanly of his own soul,
and comes to believe himself less than God—of course, to a pure Pantheist, the
one radical and ruinous error which throws up on all sides a crop of lies and mis-
conceptions, rank and ready ; as base a thing to believe as an act of bodily
"humility" were base to do : consequently any mere external worship is by
this law heathenish, heretical and idolatrous. This heathenish or idolatrous
heresy of spiritual humility comes merely of too much reliance on the reasoning
power ; man is undivine as to his mere understanding, and by using that as an
eye instead of an eyeglass "distorts" all which he does not obliterate. "Pride
of reason " is a foolish thing for any clerical defender of the "faith" to impugn ;
such pride is essentially humility. To be proud of having an empty eye-socket
implies that you would be ashamed of having eyesight ; then you are proud on
the wrong side, and humble there exactly where humility is a mere blundering

sacrifice in effect implies an "honest triumphant pride."
(Here of course the writer drops for a moment the religious view and divine meaning of the Passion, and looks
towards Calvary from the simply human side as it
appeared to casual bystanders; for here he has only to
deal with what he conceives to be errors in the human
conception of Christ's human character.   "You the
orthodox, and you the reasoners, assert through the
mouths of your churches or philosophies that purely
human virtues are actually predicable of Christ, and
appeal for evidence to his life and death.   Well and good;
we will, to gain ground for argument with you, forget that
the Passion is not, and admit that it is, what you would
call a purely human transaction.   Are then these virtues
predicable of it even as such?")   A good man who incurs
risk of death by his goodness, is too "proud" to abjure
that goodness and live; here is none of that you

suicide's cut at his own throat; if you are *not* of your nature heavenly, how shall
any alien celestial quality be sewn or stuck on to you? in whose cast clothes will
you crawl into heaven by rational or religious cross-roads?   "Imputed righteousness" will not much help your case; if you "impute" a wrong quality to any
imaginable substance, does your imputation change the substance?   What it had
not before, it has not now; your tongue has not the power of turning truth to a
lie or a lie to truth; the fact gives your assertion a straight blow in the face.
The mystic who says that man is God has some logical cause for pride; but the
sceptic has no more than the cleric—he who asserts that reason, which is finite,
can be final, is essentially as "humble" as he who admits that he can be "saved"
by accepting as a gift some "imputed" goodness which is not in any sense his.
For reason—the "spectre" of the *Jerusalem*—is no matter for pride; if you
make out that to be the best faculty about you, you give proof of the stupidest
modesty and hatefullest humility.   Look across the lower animal reason, and over
the dim lying limit of tangible and changeable flesh; and be humble if you can
or dare, then; for if what you apprehend of yourself beyond is not God, there is
none—except in that sad sense of a dæmon or natural force, strong only to create
and to divide and to destroy and to govern by reason or religion the material
scheme of things.   *Extra hominem nulla salus.*   "God is no more than man;
because man is no less than God:" there is Blake's Pantheistic Iliad in a nut-
shell.

call "humility." Such a man need not have died;
"Caiaphas would forgive" if one "died with Christian
ease asking pardon" after your "humble" fashion :—

> "He had only to say that God was the devil
> And the devil was God, like a Christian civil;
> Mild Christian regrets to the devil confess
> For affronting him thrice in the wilderness;"

and such an one might have become a very Cæsar's
minion, or Cæsar himself. Though of course mainly
made up of violent quibbling and perversities of passionate humour, which falls to work in this vehement
way upon words as some personal relief (a relief easily
conceivable in Blake's case by any student of his life),
all this has also its value in helping us to measure
according to what light we may have in us the stronger
and weaker, the worse and better, the graver and lighter
sides of the man. It belongs evidently to the period when
he painted portraits of the dead and transcribed *Jerusalem*
from spiritual dictation. "This," he lets us know by
way of prelude or opening note, "is what Joseph of
Arimathæa said to my Fairy," or natural spiritual part
by which he conversed with spirits. Next in his defiant
doggrel he calls on "Pliny and Trajan"—heathen learning and heathen power or goodness—to "come before
Joseph of Arimathæa" and "listen patient." "What,
are you here?" he asks as if in the direct surprise of
vision. (I will not give these roughest notes in the perfection of their pure doggrel. As verse, serious or
humorous, they are irreclaimable and intolerable; what
empirical value they may have must be wrung out of
them with all haste.)

We may now as well look into a later division of the
poem, where Christ is tempted of Satan to obey.

> " ' John for disobedience bled ;
> But you can turn the stones to bread.
> God's high king and God's high priest
> Shall plant their glories in your breast
> If Caiaphas you will obey,
> If Herod you with bloody prey
> Feed with the sacrifice* and be
> Obedient, fall down, worship me.'
> Thunder and lightning broke around
> And Jesus' voice in thunder's sound ;
> ' Thus I seize the spiritual prey ;
> Ye smiters with disease, make way.
> I come your King and God to seize ;
> Is God a smiter with disease ? ' "

This divine revolt and deliverance of the spiritual
human " prey " out of the hands of law and fangs of religion is made matter of accusation against him by the
" unredeemable part of the world " of which we spoke--
using here as its mouthpiece the " shadowy man " or
phantasmal shell of man, which " rolled away " when the
times were full " from the limbs of Jesus, to make them
his prey " :—

> " Crying ' Crucify this cause of distress
> Who don't keep the secrets of holiness.
> All mental powers by diseases we bind :
> But he heals the deaf and the dumb and the blind,
> Whom God has afflicted for secret ends ;
> He comforts and heals and calls them friends.' "

But Christ, instead of becoming a prey to it, himself
makes his prey of this unclean shadow or ghastly ghost

---

* An ugly specimen of ready-writing ; meaning of course " with the sacrifice
of bloody prey :" but doubtless even Blake would not have let this stand, though
we cannot safely alter it : and the passage did upon the whole appear worth citing.

of the bodily life now divided from him—this pestilent nature in bondage to the dæmonic deity, which thought to consume *him* by dint of death :

> " An ever-devouring appetite
> Glittering with festering venoms bright; "*

puts it off and devours it in three nights; even as now also he feeds upon it to consume it ; being made perfect in pride, that he may overcome the body by spiritual and " galling pride :" eat what " never was made for man to eat," the body of dust and clay, the meal's meat of the old serpent : as " the white parts or lights " of a plate are " eaten away with aqua-fortis or other acid, leaving prominent " the spiritual " outline " (*Life*, v. 1, ch. ix., p. 89). This symbol, taken from Blake's own artistic

---

* This is so like Blake's style of design that one can scarcely help fancying he must somewhere have translated it into colours perhaps more comprehensible than his words : have given somewhere in painter's types the likeness of that bodily appetite, serpentine food of the serpent, a lithe and strenuous body of clay, fair with luminous flakes of eruptive poison, foul with cold and coloured scales as the scales of a leper in grain ; with green pallor of straining mouth and bloodlike expansion of fiery throat; teeth and claws convulsed with the painful lust of pain, eyelids cloven in sunder with a dull flame of desire, the visible venom of its breath shot sharp against the face and eyes of the divine human soul : he, disembodied yet incarnate in the eternal body, stripped of accidental and clothed with essential flesh, naked of attribute that he may be girdled with substance, wrestling silent with fair great limbs, but with calm hair and brows blanched as in fire, with light of lordship in the " sunclear joyful eyes " that already absorb and devour by sweet strength of radiance the relapsing reluctant bulk of body, that foulest ravenous birth begotten of accident or error upon time; eyes beautiful with the after-light of ancient tears, that shall not weep again for ever : " for the former things are passed away" : and by that light of theirs shall all men see light. Behind these two, an intense and tremulous night stricken through with stars and fire ; and overhead the dividing roof and underfoot the sundering floor-work of the grave ; a waste place beyond, full of risen bones that gather flesh and springing roots that strike out or catch at light flying flames of life. Decidedly the design must exist somewhere; and presumably in " Golgonooza." We have the artist's prophetic authority for believing that his works written and painted before he came upon earth do in effect fill whole chambers in heaven, and are " the delight and study of archangels :" an apocalyptic fact not unnaturally unacceptable and inconceivable to the cleverest of Scotch stonemasons.

work of engraving—from the process through which we have with us the Songs and Prophecies—will give with some precision the exact point indicated, and might have been allowed of by himself, as not unacceptable or inapposite.

This final absorption of the destructible body, consumption of "the serpent's meat," is but the upshot of a life of divine rebellion and "spiritual war," not of barren physical qualities and temporal virtues :—

> " The God of this world raged in vain ;
> He bound old Satan in his chain :
> Throughout the land he took his course,
> And traced diseases to their source :
> He cursed the Scribe and Pharisee,
> Trampling down hypocrisy."

His wrath was made as it were a chariot of fire ; at the wheels of it was dragged the God of this world, over-thrown and howling aloud :—

> " Where'er his chariot took its way
> Those gates of death let in the day ; "

every chain and bar broken down from them, and the staples of the doors loosed ; his voice was heard from Zion above the clamour of axle and wheel,

> " And in his hand the scourge shone bright ;
> He scourged the merchant Canaanite
> From out the temple of his mind,
> And in his body tight does bind
> Satan and all his hellish crew ;
> And thus with wrath he did subdue
> The serpent bulk of nature's dross
> Till he had nailed it to the cross.
> He put on sin in the Virgin's womb,
> And put it off on the cross and tomb
> To be worshipped by the Church of Rome : "

not to speak of other churches. One may notice how to the Pantheist the Catholic's worship is a worship of sin, even as his own is to the Catholic. "You adore as divine the fallen nature and sinful energies of man:" "you, again, the cast-off body wherein Satan and sin were shut up, that he who assumed it might crucify them." Sin or false faith or "hypocrisy" was scourged out of the mind into the body, and the separate animal body then delivered over to death with the sins thereof—all the sins of the world garnered up in it to be purged away with fire: and of this body you make your God. The expressed gird at the "Church of Rome" is an interpolation; at first Blake had merely written "And on the cross he sealed its doom" in place of our two last-quoted lines. Akin to this view of the "body of sin" is his curious heresy of the Conception; reminding one of that Christian sect which would needs worship Judas as the necessary gateway of salvation: for without his sin how could redemption have come about?

> " Was Jesus born of a virgin pure
> With narrow soul and looks demure ?
> If he intended to take on sin,
> His mother should an harlot (have) been :
> Just such a one as Magdalen,
> With seven devils in her pen.
> Or were Jew virgins still more cursed,
> And more sucking devils nursed ? "

(This ingenious solution, worthy of any mediæval heresiarch of the wilder sort in a time of leprosy, is also an afterthought. From the sudden anti-Judaic rapture of grotesque faith or humour into which Blake suddenly dips hereabouts, one might imagine he had been lately bitten

or stung by some dealer or other such dangerous craftsman of the Hebrew kind ; for that any mortal Jew—or
for that matter any conceivable Gentile—would have
credited him to the amount of a penny sterling, no one
will imagine.   Let the reader meanwhile endure him a
little further, suppressing if he is wise any comment on
Blake's "insanity" or "blasphemous doggrel"; for he should
now at least understand that this literal violence of manner, these light or grave audacities of mere form, imply
no offensive purpose or significance, except insomuch as
offence is inseparable from any strange kind of earnestly
heretical belief.   Neither is Blake here busied in fetch-
ing milk to feed his babes and sucklings.   This he could
do incomparably well on occasion, with such milk as a
nursing-goddess gave to the son of Metaneira ; but here
he carves meat for men—of a strange quality, tough and
crude : but not without savour or sustenance if eaten
with the right sauce and prefaced with a proper grace.)

> " Or what was it that he took on
>   That he might bring salvation ?
>   A body subject to be tempted,
>   From neither pain nor grief exempted,
>   Or such a body as could not feel
>   The passions that with sinners deal ?
>   Yes : but they say he never fell.
>   Ask Caiaphas : for he can tell."

Here follow as given by Caiaphas the old charges of
Sabbath-breach, blasphemy and strange doctrine; given
again almost word for word, but with a nobler frame of
context, in the *Marriage of Heaven and Hell*, where, and
not here, we will prefer to read them.   One charge will
be allowed to pass as new coin, having Blake's image and
superscription in lieu of Cæsar's.

> " He turned the devils into swine
> That he might tempt the Jews to dine ;
> Since when, a pig has got a look
> That for a Jew may be mistook.
> ' Obey your parents ' ? What says he ?
> ' Woman, what have I to do with thee ?
> No earthly parents I confess :
> I am doing my Father's business.'
> He scorned earth's parents, scorned earth's God,
> And mocked the one and the other's rod ;
> His seventy disciples sent*
> Against religion and government,"

and caused his followers to die by the sword of justice as rebels and blasphemers of this world's God and his law : overturned " the tent of secret sins and its God," with all

---

* Compare Hugo's admirable poem in the *Châtiments* (vii. 11. p. 319-321) — "'Paroles d'un conservateur à propos d'un perturbateur :"—where, speaking through the mouth of " Elizab, a scribe," the chief poet of our time gives in his great swift manner a dramatic summary of the view taken by priests and elders of Christ. It is worth looking to trace out how nearly the same historical points of objection are selected and the same lines of inference struck into by the two poets; one aiming straight at present politics, one indirectly at mystic doctrine.

> "Cet homme était de ceux qui n'ont rien de sacré,
> Il ne respectait rien de tout ce qu'on respecte.
> Pour leur inoculer sa doctrine suspecte,
> Il allait ramassant dans les plus méchants lieux
> Des bouviers, des pêcheurs, des drôles bilieux,
> D'immondes va-nu-pieds n'ayant ni sou ni maille :
> Il faisait son cénacle avec cette canaille.
> *   *   *   *   *
> L'honnête homme indigné rentrait dans sa maison
> Quand ce jongleur passait avec cette sequelle.
> *   *   *   *   *
> Il traînait à sa suite une espèce de fille.
> Il allait pérorant, ébranlant la famille,
> Et la religion et la société.
> Il sapait la morale et la propriété.
> *   *   *   *   *
>   Quant aux prêtres,
> Il les déchirait ; bref, il blasphémait.   Cela
> Dans la rue.   Il contait toutes ces horreurs-là
> Aux premiers gueux venus, sans cape et sans semelles.
> Il fallait en finir, les lois étaient formelles,
> On l'a crucifié."

the cords of his weaving, prisons of his building and snares of his setting; overthrew the "bloody shrine of war," the holy place of the God of battles, whose cruel light and fire of wrath was poured forth upon the world till it reached "from star to star"; thus casting down all things of "church and state as by law established," camps and shrines, temples and prisons,

> "Halls of justice, hating vice,
> Where the devil combs his lice."

Upon all these, to the great grief of Caiaphas and the grievous detriment of the God of this world, he sent "not peace but a sword": lived as a vagrant upon other men's labour, kept company by preference with publicans and harlots.

> "And from the adulteress turned away
> God's righteous law, that lost its prey."

So we end as we began, at that great practical point of revolt: and finally, with deep fervour of satisfaction, and the sense of a really undeniable achievement, the new evangelist jots down this couplet by way of epilogue:

> "I'm sure this Jesus will not do
> Either for Englishman or Jew."

Scarcely, as far as one sees: we may surely allow him that. And yet, having somehow steered right through this chaotic evangel, we may as surely admit that none but a great man with a great gift of belief could have conceived or wrought it out even as roughly as it is here set down. There is more absolute worship implied in it than in most works of art that pass muster as religious;

a more perfect power of noble adoration, an intenser faculty of faith and capacity of love, keen as flame and soft as light; a more uncontrollable desire for right and lust after justice, a more inexhaustible grace of pity for all evil and sorrow that is not of itself pitiless, a more deliberate sweetness of mercy towards all that are cast out and trodden under. This "vision of Christ," though it be to all seeming the "greatest enemy" of other men's visions, can hardly be regarded as the least significant or beautiful that the religious world has yet been brought into contact with. It is at least not effeminate, not unmerciful, not ignoble, and not incomprehensible: other "visions" have before now been any or all of these. Thus much it is at least; the "vision" of a perfectly brave, tender, subtle and faithful spirit; in which there was no fear and no guile, nothing false and nothing base. Of the technical theology or "spiritualism" each man who cares to try will judge as it may please him; it goes at least high and deep enough to draw down or pluck up matter for absolution or condemnation. It is no part of our affair further to vindicate, to excuse, or to account for the singular gospel here preached.*

* In a briefer and less important fragment of verse Blake as earnestly incul- cates this faith of his : that all mere virtues and vices were known before Christ; of right and wrong Plato and Cicero, men uninspired, were competent to speak as well as he ; but until his advent "the moral virtues in their pride" held rule over the world, and among them as they rode clothed with war and sacrifice, driving souls to hell before them, shone "upon the rivers and the streams" the face of the Accuser, holy God of this Pharisaic world. Then arose Christ and said to man "Thy sins are all forgiven thee;" and the "moral virtues," in terror lest their reign of war and accusation should now draw to an end, cried out "Crucify him," and formed with their own hands the cross and the nails and the spear : and the Accuser spoke to them saying :—

"Am I not Lucifer the great
And ye my daughters, in great state,

Space may be made here (before we pass on to larger
things if not greater) for another stray note or two on
separate poems. *The Crystal Cabinet,* one of the com-
pletest short poems by Blake which are not to be called
songs, is an example of the somewhat jarring and
confused mixture of apparent " allegory " with actual
" vision" which is the great source of trouble and error
to rapid readers of his verse or students of his designs.
The " cabinet " is either passionate or poetic vision—a
spiritual gift, which may soon and easily become a
spiritual bondage ; wherein a man is locked up, with keys
of gold indeed, yet is he a prisoner all the same : his
prison built by his love or his art, with a view open
beyond of exquisite limited loveliness, soft quiet and
light of dew or moon, and a whole fresh world to rest
in or look into, but intangible and simply reflective ; all
present pleasure or power trebled in it, until you try
at too much and attempt to turn spiritual to physical
reality—" to seize the inmost form " with " hands of
flame " laid upon things of the spirit which will endure
no such ardent handling—to translate eternal existence

> The fruit of my mysterious tree
> Of Good and Evil and Misery ? "

If, the preacher adds, moral virtue was Christianity, Christ's pretensions were
madness, "and Caiaphas and Pilate men praiseworthy ;" and the lion's den a
fitter emblem of heaven than the sheepfold. " The moral Christian is the cause
of the unbeliever ;" and Antichrist is incarnate in those who close heaven
against sinners

> " With iron bars in virtuous state
> And Rhadamanthus at the gate."

But men have so long allowed the heathen virtues, whose element is war and
whose essence retaliation, to "take Jesus' and Jehovah's name" that the Accuser,
Antichrist and Lucifer though he be, is now worshipped by those holy names over
all the world : and the era called Christian is the era of his reign. For the rest,
this new relic has no special merit, although it may be allowed some share of
interest as a supplement or illustration to the larger poem or sermon.

into temporal, essential into accidental, substantial into
attributive ; when at once the whole framework, which
was meant otherwise to last out your present life, breaks
up and leaves you stranded or cast out, feeble and
sightless "like a weeping babe;" so that whereas at
first you were full of light natural pleasure, "dancing
merrily" in "the wild" of animal or childish life, you
are now a child again, but unhappy instead of happy—
less than a child, thrown back on the crying first stage
of babyhood—having had the larger vision, and lost your
hold of it by too great pressure of impatience or desire—
unfit for the old pleasure and deprived of the new; and
the maiden-mother of your spiritual life, your art or
your love, is become wan and tearful as you, "pale
reclined" in the barren blowing air which cannot again
be filled with the fire and the luminous life of vision.
In *Mary* we come again upon the main points of inner
contact between Blake's mind and Shelley's. This frank
acceptance of pleasure, this avowal without blushing or
doubting "that sweet love and beauty are worthy our
care," was as beautiful a thing to Shelley as to Blake : he
has preached the excellence of it in *Rosalind and Helen*
and often elsewhere : touching also, as Blake does here,
on the persecution of it by all "who *amant miserè*":—

> "Some said she was proud, some called her a whore,
> And some when she passed by shut to the door ; "

for in their sight the tender and outspoken purity of
instinct and innocence becomes confounded with base
desire or vanity. This rather than genius or mere beauty
seems to be the thing whose persecution by the world is
here symbolized.

Many others of these brief poems are not less excellent; the slightest among them have the grace of form and heat of life which are indivisible in all higher works of poetry. One, *The Mental Traveller*, is full of sweet and vigorous verses turned loose upon a somewhat arid and thorny pasture. By a miracle of patient ingenuity this poem has been compelled to utter some connected message ; but it may perhaps be doubted whether the message be not too articulate and coherent for Blake. Thus limited and clarified, the broad chafing current of mysticism seems almost too pure and too strait to issue from such a source : a well-head of living speech that bursts up with sudden froth and steam through more outlets than one at once. To have contrived such an elaborate allegory, so welded link by sequent link together, seems an exercise of logical patience to which Blake would hardly have submitted his passionate genius, his overstrained and wayward will. Separate stanzas may be retraced wellnigh through every word in other books. The latter part seems again to record, as in two preceding poems, the perversion of love ; which having annihilated all else, falls at last to feed upon itself, to seek out strange things and barren ways, to invent new loves and invert the old, to fill the emptied heart and flush the subsiding veins with perverse passion. Alone in the desert it has made, beguiled to second youth by the incessant diet of joy, fear comes upon love ; fear, and seeming hate, and weariness and cunning ; fruits of the second graft of love, not native to the simple stock : till reduced at last to the likeness of the two extremes of life, age and infancy, love can be no further abused or consumed. These stages of

love, once seen or heard of, allure lovers to eat of the
strange fruits and herd with the strange flocks of trans-
forming or transformed desire; the visible world, destroyed at the first advent of love and absorbed into
the soul by a single passion, is again felt nearer; the
trees bring forth their pleasure, and the planets lavish
their light. For the second love, in its wayward and
strange delights, is a thing half material; not alien at
least from material forms, as was the first simple and
spiritual ardour of equal love. Passionate and perverse
emotion touches all things with some fervent colour of its
own, mixes into all water and all wine some savour of
the dubious honey gathered from its foreign flowers. Pure
first love will not coexist with outward things, burns up
with white fire all tangible form, and so, an unfed lamp,
must at last burn itself down to the stage of life and
sensation which breeds those latter loves. The babe that
is " born a boy," often painfully begot and joyfully brought
forth, I take to signify human genius or intellect, which
none can touch and not be consumed except the " woman
old," faith or fear : all weaker things, pain and pleasure,
hatred and love, fly with shrieking averted faces from
before it. The grey and cruel nurse, custom or religion,
crucifies and torments the child, feeding herself upon his
agony to false fresh youth ; an allegory not even literally
inapt. Grown older, and seeing her made fair with his
blood and strong by his suffering, he weds her, and con-
strains her to do him service, and turns her to use ;
custom, the daily life of men, once married to the fresh
intellect, bears fruit to him of profit and pleasure, and
becomes through him nobler than she was ; but through

such union he grows old the sooner, soon can but wander round and look over his finished work and gathered treasure, the tragic passions and splendid achievements of his spirit, kept fresh in verse or colour ; which he deals to all men alike, giving to the poorest of this divine meat and drink, the body and the blood of genius, caught in golden vessels of art and rhyme, that sight and hearing may be fed. This, the supreme and most excellent delight possible to man, is the fruit of his pain; of his suffering at the hands of life, of his union with her as with a bride. The "female* babe" sprung from the fire that burns always on his hearth, is the issue or result of genius, which, being too strong for the father, flows into new channels and follows after fresh ways ; the thing which he has brought forth knows him no more, but must choose its own mate or living form of expression, and expel the former nature—casting off (as theologians say) the old man. The outcast intellect can then be vivified only by a new love, or by a new aim of which love is the type; a bride unlike the first, who was old at root and in substance, young only in seeming and fair only through cruel theft of his own life and strength ; unlike also the art which has now in its ultimate expression turned against him ; love which can change the face of former

---

* The words "female" and "reflex" are synonymous in all Blake's writings. What is feminine in its material symbol is derivative in its spiritual significance ; "there is no such thing in eternity as a female will ;" for in eternity substances lose their shadows, and essence puts off accident. The "frowning babe" of the last stanzas is of course the same or such another as the one whose birth is first spoken of ; not the latter female growth born in the earthly house of art, but genius itself, whose likeness is terrible and unlovely at first sight to the run of men, filling them with affright and scandal, with wonder and the repellent sense that a new and strange thing is brought into the world.

things and scatter in sunder the gatherings of former friends; love which masters the senses and transfigures the creatures of the earthly life, leaving no light or sustenance but what comes of itself. Then follow the stages of love, and the phases of action and passion bred from either stage; of these we have already taken account. If this view of the poem be wholly or partially correct, then we may roughly sum up the problem by saying that its real obscurity arises in the main from a verbal confusion between the passion of art and the passion of love. These are always spoken of by Blake in terms which prove that in his nature the two feelings had actually grown into each other; had become interfused past all chance of mutual extrication. Art was to him as a lust of the body; appetite as an emotion of the soul. This saying, true as to some extent it must be of all great men, was never so exclusively and finally true of any other man as of this one. It is no bad sample of Blake's hurried manner of speech, that having sustained halfway through his poem an allegory of intellect in its relations to art and to common life, he should suddenly stumble over a type of his own setting up, and be led off into a new allegory of love which might better have made a separate poem. As it is, the two symbols are welded together not without strength and cunning of hand.

Some further and final notice may here be taken of the manifold designs scattered about the MS. pages which we have found so prodigal of verse. Among the most curious of these we rank a series of drawings not quite so roughly pencilled as the rest, each inscribed with a

brief text or metrical motto.   Many of these have been
wrought up into the "Gates of Paradise"; many more
remain to speak and shift for themselves as they may.*
Published as it stands here, the series would exceed in
length the whole of that little book : and there is evidently some thread of intended connexion between all,
worn thin and all but broken.   They are numbered in
a different order from that in which they stand, which is
indeed plainly a matter of chance.   Several have great
grace and beauty ; one in especial, where Daphne passes
into the laurel ; her feet are roots already and grasp
the ground with strong writhing fibres ; her lifted arms
and wrestling body struggle into branch and stem,
with strange labour of the supple limbs, with agony
of convulsed and loosening hair.   One of the larger
designs seems to be a rough full-length study for Adam
and Eve, with these lines opposite by way of suggested
epigraph :

> " What is it men in women do require ?
> The lineaments of gratified desire.
> What is it women do in men require ?
> The lineaments of gratified desire."

These are barely to be recognised in the crude sketch :
the faces are merely serious and rather grim : though
designed to reproduce the sweet silence of beauty, filling
features made fair with soft natural pleasure and a clear
calm of soul and body.   There is however a certain grace
and nobility of form in the straight limbs and flowing

---

* It seems not impossible that this series may have been intended, in its complete form, to bear the title of *Ideas of Good and Evil*, which we find loosely
attached to the general MS.   When the designer broke it up into different sets,
this name would naturally have been abandoned.

hair, not unworthy the typical man and woman. Another design which deserves remark is a fine sketch after the manner of the illustrations to Blake's prophecies, in which a figure caught in the fierce slanting current of a whirl-wind is drifted sideways like a drowning swimmer under sea, below the orbit of three mingling suns or planets seen above thick drifts of tempestuous air. Other and better notices than ours, of various studies hidden away in the chaos of this MS., the reader will find on reference to that admirable Catalogue which will remain always the great witness for Blake's genius before the eyes of all who read his life.

We have done now with the lyrical side of this poet's work,* and pass on to things of less direct attraction. Those who have found any in the record of his life and character, the study of his qualities and abilities, may safely follow him further. The perfect sweetness and sufficiency of his best lyrics and his best designs, we

---

* Of Blake's prose other samples are extant besides the notes on art published in the second volume of the *Life and Selections*. These strays are for the most part, as far as I have seen, mere waifs of weed and barren drift. One fragment, not without some grace and thoughtfulness curiously used up and thrown away, is an allegory of "the Gods which came from Fear," of Shame born of the "poisonous seed" of pride, and such things; written much in the manner of those early Ossianic studies which dilate and deform the volume of *Poetical Sketches:* perhaps composed (though properly never composed at all) about the same time. Another, a sort of satire on critics and "philosophers," seems to emulate the style of Sterne in his intervals of lax and dull writing; in execution it is some depths below the baby stories of little Malkin, whose ghost might well have blushed rejection of the authorship. The fragment on *Laocoon* is a mere cento of stray notes on art which reaffirm in a chaotic and spluttering manner Blake's theories that the only real prayer is study of art, the only real praise, its practice; that excellence of art, not moral virtue, is the aim and the essence of Christianity; and much more of the same sort. These notes, crammed into every blank space and corner of the engraved page, burst out as it were and boil over, disconnected but irrepressible, in a feverish watery style. All really good or even passable prose of Blake's seems to be given in the volume of *Selections*.

may not find ; of these we take now farewell, with thanks and final praise such as we have to give ; but we shall not fail to find the traces of a great art and an exalted spirit, to feel about us the clear air of a great man's presence.

III.—THE PROPHETIC BOOKS.

BEFORE entering upon any system of remark or comment on the Prophetic Books, we may set down in as few and distinct words as possible the reasons which make this a thing seriously worth doing ; nay, even requisite to be done, if we would know rather the actual facts of the man's nature than the circumstances and accidents of his life. Now, first of all, we are to recollect that Blake himself regarded these works as his greatest, and as containing the sum of his achieved ambitions and fulfilled desires : as in effect inspired matter, of absolute imaginative truth and eternal import. We shall not again pause to rebut the familiar cry of response, to the effect that he was mad and not accountable for the uttermost madness of error. It must be enough to reply here that he was by no means mad, in any sense that would authorise us in rejecting his own judgment of his own aims and powers on a plea which would be held insufficient in another man's case. Let all readers and all critics get rid of that notion for good—clear their minds of it utterly and with all haste ; let them know and remember, having once been told it, that in these strangest of all written

books there is purpose as well as power, meaning as well
as mystery.   Doubtless, nothing quite like them was
ever pitched out headlong into the world as they were.
The confusion, the clamour, the jar of words that half
suffice and thoughts that half exist—all these and other
more absolutely offensive qualities—audacity, monotony,
bombast, obscure play of licence and tortuous growth of
fancy—cannot quench or even wholly conceal the living
purport and the imperishable beauty which are here
latent.

And secondly we are to recollect this ; that these books
are not each a set of designs with a text made by order to
match, but are each a poem composed for its own sake
and with its own aim, having illustrations arranged by
way of frame or appended by way of ornament.   On all
grounds, therefore, and for all serious purpose, such notices
as some of those given in this biography are actually
worse than worthless.   Better have done nothing than
have done this and no more.   All the criticism included
as to the illustrative parts merely, is final and faultless,
nothing missed and nothing wrong ; this could not have
been otherwise, the work having fallen under hands and
eyes of practical taste and trained to actual knowledge,
and the assertions being therefore issued by authority.
So much otherwise has it fared with the books themselves,
that (we are compelled in this case to say it) the clothes
are all right and the body is all wrong.   Passing from
some phrase of high and accurate eulogy to the raw ragged
extracts here torn away and held up with the unhealed
scars of mutilation fresh and red upon them, what is any
human student to think of the poet or his praisers ? what,

of the assertion of his vindicated sanity with such appalling counterproof thrust under one's eyes ? In a word, it must be said of these notices of Blake's prophetic books* (except perhaps that insufficient but painstaking and well-meant chapter on the *Marriage of Heaven and Hell*) that what has been done should not have been done, and what should have been done has not been done.

Not that the thing was easy to do. If any one would realize to himself for ever a material notion of chaos, let him take a blind header into the midst of the whirling foam and rolling weed of this sea of words. Indeed the sound and savour of these prophecies constantly recall some such idea or some such memory. This poetry has the huge various monotonies, the fervent and fluent colours, the vast limits, the fresh sonorous strength, the certain confusion and tumultuous law, the sense of windy and weltering space, the intense refraction of shadow or light, the crowded life and inanimate intricacy, the patience and the passion of the sea. By no manner of argument or analysis will one be made able to look back or forward with pure confidence and comprehension. Only there are laws, strange as it must sound, by which

---

* It should not be overlooked that this part of his work was left unfinished, all but untouched, by the author of the *Life*. Without as long a study and as deep a sympathy as his, it would seem to any follower, however able and zealous, the most toilsome as well as the most sterile part of the task in hand. The fault therefore lies with chance or fate alone. Less than I have said above could not here be said ; and more need not be. I was bound at starting to register my protest against the contempt and condemnation which these books have incurred, thinking them as I do not unworthy the trouble of commentary ; but no word was designed to depreciate the careful and admirable labour which has completed a monument cut short with the life of the sculptor, joined now in death to the dead whom he honoured.

the work is done and against which it never sins. The biographer once attempts to settle the matter by asserting that Blake was given to contradict himself, by mere impulse if not by brute instinct, to such an extent that consistency is in no sense to be sought for or believed in throughout these works of his : and quotes, by way of ratifying this quite false notion, a noble sentence from the *Proverbs of Hell,* aimed by Blake with all his force against that obstinate adherence to one external opinion which closes and hardens the spirit against all further message from the new-grown feelings or inspiration from the altering circumstances of a man. Never was there an error more grave or more complete than this. The expression shifts perpetually, the types blunder into new forms, the meaning tumbles into new types ; the purpose remains, and the faith keeps its hold.

There are certain errors and eccentricities of manner and matter alike common to nearly all these books, and distinctly referable to the character and training of the man. Not educated in any regular or rational way, and by nature of an eagerly susceptible and intensely adhesive mind, in which the lyrical faculty had gained and kept a preponderance over all others visible in every scrap of his work, he had saturated his thoughts and kindled his senses with a passionate study of the forms of the Bible as translated into English, till his fancy caught a feverish contagion and his ear derived a delirious excitement from the mere sound and shape of the written words and verses. Hence the quaint and fervent imita-tion of style, the reproduction of peculiarities which to most men are meaningless when divested of their old

sense or invested with a new. Hence the bewildering
catalogues, genealogies, and divisions which (especially in
such later books as the *Jerusalem*) seem at first invented
only to strike any miserable reader with furious or la-
chrymose lunacy. Hence, though heaven knows by no
fault of the originals, the insane cosmogony, blatant
mythology, and sonorous aberration of thoughts and
theories. Hence also much of the special force and
supreme occasional loveliness or grandeur in expression.
Conceive a man incomparably gifted as to the spiritual
side of art, prone beyond all measure to the lyrical form
of work, incredibly contemptuous of all things and
people dissimilar to himself, of an intensely sensitive
imagination and intolerant habit of faith, with a passionate power of peculiar belief, taking with all his might
of mental nerve and strain of excitable spirit to a perusal
and reperusal of such books as Job and Ezekiel. Observe
too that his tone of mind was as far from being critical
as from being orthodox. Thus his ecstacy of study was
neither on the one side tempered and watered down by
faith in established forms and external creeds, nor on the
other side modified and directed by analytic judgment
and the lust of facts. To Blake either form of mind
was alike hateful. Like the Moses of Rabbinical tradition, he was "drunken with the kisses of the lips of
God." Rational deism and clerical religion were to him
two equally abhorrent incarnations of the same evil
spirit, appearing now as negation and now as restriction.
He wanted supremacy of freedom with intensity of faith.
Hence he was properly neither Christian nor infidel: he
was emphatically a heretic. Such men, according to the

temper of the times, are burnt as demoniacs or pitied as lunatics. He believed in redemption by Christ, and in the incarnation of Satan as Jehovah. He believed that by self-sacrifice the soul should attain freedom and victorious deliverance from bodily bondage and sexual servitude ; and also that the extremest fullness of indulgence in such desire and such delight as the senses can aim at or attain was absolutely good, eternally just, and universally requisite. These opinions, and stranger than these, he put forth in the cloudiest style, the wilfullest humour, and the stormiest excitement. No wonder the world let his books drift without caring to inquire what gold or jewels might be washed up as waifs from the dregs of churned foam and subsiding surf. He was the very man for fire and faggot ; a mediæval inquisitor would have had no more doubt about him than a materialist or " theophilanthropist " of his own day or of ours.

A wish is expressed in the *Life* that we could accompany the old man who appears entering an open door, star in hand, at the beginning of the *Jerusalem*, and thread by his light those infinite dark passages and labyrinthine catacombs of invention or thought. In default of that desirable possibility, let us make such way as we can for ourselves into this submarine world, along its slippery and unpaven ways, under its roof of hollow sound and tumbling storm.

> " We shall see, while above us
> The waves roar and whirl,
> A ceiling of amber,
> A pavement of pearl."

At the entrance of the labyrinth we are met by huge

mythologic figures, created of fire and cloud. Titans of monstrous form and yet more monstrous name obstruct the ways; sickness or sleep never formed such savage abstractions, such fierce vanities of vision as these : office and speech they seem at first to have none: but to strike or clutch at the void of air with feeble fingers, to babble with vast lax lips a dialect barren of all but noise, loud and loose as the wind. Slowly they grow into something of shape, assume some foggy feature and indefinite colour: word by word the fluctuating noise condenses into music, the floating music divides into audible notes and scales. The sound which at first was as the mere collision of cloud with cloud is now the recognizable voice of god or demon. Chaos is cloven into separate elements; air divides from water, and earth releases fire. Upon each of these the prophet, as it were, lays hand, compelling the thing into shape and speech, constraining the abstract to do service as a man might. These and such as these make up the personal staff or executive body of his prophecies. But it would be waste of time to conjecture how or why he came to inflict upon them such incredible names. These hapless energies and agencies are not simply cast into the house of allegoric bondage, and set to make bricks without straw, to construct symbols without reason ; but find themselves baptized with muddy water and fitful fire, by names inconceivable, into a church full of storm and vapour; regenerated with a vengeance, but disembodied and disfigured in their resurrection. Space fell into sleep, and awoke as Enitharmon : Time suffered eclipse, and came forth as Los. The Christ or Prometheus of this faith is Orc or Fuzon ;

Urizen takes the place of "Jehovah, Jove, or Lord."
Hardly in such chaotic sounds can one discern the
slightest element of reason gone mad, the narrowest
channel of derivation run dry. In this last word, one of
incessant recurrence, there seems to flicker a thin reminiscence of such names as Uranus, Uriel, and perhaps
Urien; for the deity has a diabolic savour in him, and
Blake was not incapable of mixing the Hellenic, the
Miltonic, and the Celtic mythologies into one drugged and
adulterated compound. He had read much and blindly;
he had no leaning to verbal accuracy, and never acquired
any faculty of comparison. Any sound that in the
dimmest way suggested to him a notion of hell or heaven,
of passion or power, was significant enough to adopt and
register. Commentary was impossible to him: if his
work could not be apprehended or enjoyed by an instinct
of inspiration like his own, it was lost labour to dissect or
expound; and here, if ever, translation would have been
treason. He took the visions as they came; he let the
words lie as they fell. These barbarous and blundering
names are not always without a certain kind of melody
and an uncertain sort of meaning. Such as they are,
they must be endured; or the whole affair must be tossed
aside and thrown up. Over these clamorous kingdoms
of speech and dream some few ruling forces of supreme
discord preside: and chiefly the lord of the world of man;
Urizen, God of cloud and star, "Father of jealousy,"
clothed with a splendour of shadow, strong and sad and
cruel; his planet faintly glimmers and slowly revolves, a
horror in heaven; the night is a part of his thought,
rain and wind are in the passage of his feet; sorrow is

in all his works ; he is the maker of mortal things, of the
elements and sexes ; in him are incarnate that jealousy
which the Hebrews acknowledged and that envy which
the Greeks recognized in the divine nature ; in his worship faith remains one with fear. Star and cloud, the
types of mystery and distance, of cold alienation and
heavenly jealousy, belong of right to the God who
grudges and forbids : even as the spirit of revolt is made
manifest in fiery incarnation—pure prolific fire, " the cold
loins of Urizen dividing." These two symbols of " cruel
fear " or " starry jealousy " in the divine tyrant, of ardent
love or creative lust in the rebellious saviour of man,
pervade the mystical writings of Blake. Orc, the man-
child, with hair and flesh like fire, son of Space and Time,
a terror and a wonder from the hour of his birth, containing within himself the likeness of all passions and
appetites of men, is cast out from before the face of
heaven ; and falling upon earth, a stronger Vulcan or
Satan, fills with his fire the narrowed foreheads and the
darkened eyes of all that dwell thereon ; imprisoned
often and fed from vessels of iron with barren food and
bitter drink,* a wanderer or a captive upon earth, he

* Something like this may be found in a passage of Werner translated by Mr.
Carlyle, but mixed with much of meaner matter, and debased by a feebleness and
a certain spiritual petulance proper to a man so much inferior. The German
mystic, though ingenious and laborious, is also tepid, pretentious, insecure ; half
terrified at his own timid audacities, half choked by the fumes of his own alembic.
He labours within a limit, not fixed indeed, but never expansive ; narrowing
always at one point as it widens at another : his work is weak in the head and
the spine ; he ventures with half a heart and strikes with half a hand ; throughout his myth of Phosphorus he goes halting and hinting ; not ungracefully, nay
with a real sense of beauty, but never like a man braced up for the work requisite ;
he labours under a dull devotion and a cloudy capacity. Above all, he can neither
speak nor do well, being no artist or prophet ; and so makes but a poor preacher
or essayist. The light he shows is thick and weak ; Blake's light, be it meteor
or star, rises with the heat and radiance of fire of the morning.

shall rise again when his fire has spread through all
lands to inflame and to infect with a strong contagion the
spirit and the sense of man, and shall prevail against the
law and the commandments of his enemy. This endless myth of oppression and redemption, of revelation
and revolt, runs through many forms and spills itself
by strange straits and byways among the sands and
shallows of prophetic speech. But in these books there
is not the substantial coherence of form and reasonable
unity of principle which bring within scope of apprehension even the wildest myths grown out of unconscious idealism and impulsive tradition. A single man's
work, however exclusively he may look to inspiration for
motive and material, must always want the breadth and
variety of meaning, the supple beauty of symbol, the
infectious intensity of satisfied belief, which grow out of
creeds and fables native to the spirit of a nation, yet
peculiar to no man or sect, common yet sacred, not
invented or constructed, but found growing and kept
fresh with faith. But for all the dimness and violence of
expression which pervert and darken the mythology of
these attempts at gospel, they have qualities great enough
to be worth finding out. Only let none conceive that
each separate figure in the swarming and noisy life of
this populous dæmonic creation has individual meaning
and vitality. Blake was often taken off his feet by the
strong currents of fancy, and indulged, like a child
during its first humour of invention, in wild byplay and
erratic excesses of simple sound ; often lost his way in a
maze of wind-music, and transcribed as it were with eyes
closed and open ears the notes caught by chance as they

drifted across the dream of his subdued senses. Alternating between lyrical invention and gigantic allegory, it is hard to catch and hold him down to any form or plan. At one time we have mere music, chains of ringing names, scattered jewels of sound without a thread, tortuous network of harmonies without a clue; and again we have passages, not always unworthy of an Æschylean chorus, full of fate and fear; words that are strained wellnigh in sunder by strong significance and earnest passion; words that deal greatly with great things, that strike deep and hold fast; each inclusive of some fierce apocalypse or suggestive of some obscure evangel. Now the matter in hand is touched with something of an epic style; the narrative and characters lose half their hidden sense, and the reciter passes from the prophetic tripod to the seat of a common singer; mere names, perhaps not even musical to other ears than his, allure and divert him; he plays with stately cadences, and lets the wind of swift or slow declamation steer him whither it will. Now again he falls with renewed might of will to his purpose; and his grand lyrical gift becomes an instrument not sonorous merely but vocal and articulate. To readers who can but once take their stand for a minute on the writer's footing, look for a little with his eyes and listen with his ears, even the more incoherent cadences will become not undelightful; something of his pleasure, with something of his perception, will pass into them; and understanding once the main gist of the whole fitful and high-strung tune, they will tolerate, where they cannot enjoy, the strange diversities and discords which intervene.

Among many notable eccentricities we have touched upon but two as yet ; the huge windy mythology of elemental dæmons, and the capricious passion for catalogues of random names, which make obscure and hideous so much of these books. Akin to these is the habit of seeing or assuming in things inanimate or in the several limbs and divisions of one thing, separate forms of active and symbolic life. This, like many other of Blake's habits, grows and swells enormously by progressive indulgence. At first, as in *Thel,* clouds and flowers, clods and creeping things, are given speech and sense ; the degree of symbolism is already excessive, owing to the strength of expression and directness of dramatic vision peculiar to Blake ; but in later books everything is given a soul to feel and a tongue to speak ; the very members of the body become spirits, each a type of some spiritual state. Again, in the prophecies of *Europe* and *America,* there is more fable and less allegory, more overflow of lyrical invention, more of the divine babble which sometimes takes the place of earthly speech or sense, more vague emotion with less of reducible and amenable quality than in almost any of these poems. In others, a habit of mapping out and marking down the lines of his chaotic and Titanic scenery has added to Blake's other singularities of manner this above all, that side by side with the jumbled worlds of Tharmas and Urthona, the whirling skies and plunging planets of Ololon and Beulah, the breathless student of prophecy encounters places and names absurdly familiar ; London streets and suburbs make up part of the mystic antediluvian world ; Fulham and Lambeth, Kentish Town and Poland Street, cross the courses and break the metres of the stars. This apparent madness of final absurdity has also its root in the deepest and soundest part of Blake's mind and faith. In the meanest place as in the meanest man he beheld the hidden spirit and significance of which the flesh or the building is but a type. If continents have a soul, shall suburbs or lanes have less? where life is, shall not the spirit of life be there also? Europe and America are vital and significant; we mean by all names somewhat more than we know of; for where there is anything visible or conceivable, there is also some invisible and inconceivable thing. This is but the rough grotesque result of the tenet that matter apart from spirit is non-existent. Launched once upon that theory, Blake never thought it worth while to shorten sail or tack about for fear of any rock or shoal. It is inadequate and even inaccurate to say that he allotted to each place as to each world a presiding dæmon or deity. He averred implicitly or directly, that each had a soul or spirit, the quintessence of its natural life, capable of change but not of death; and that of this soul the visible externals, though a native and actual part, were only a part, inseparable as yet but incomplete. Thus whenever, to his misfortune and ours, he stumbles upon the proper names of terrene men and things, he uses these names as signifying not the sensual form or body but the spirit which he supposed to animate these, to speak in them and work through them. In *America* the names of liberators, in *Jerusalem* the names of provinces, have no separate local or mundane sense whatever; throughout the prophecies "Albion" is the mythical and typical fatherland of human

life, much what the East might seem to other men : and
by way of making this type actual and prominent
enough, Blake seizes upon all possible divisions of the
modern visible England in town or country, and turns
them in his loose symbolic way into minor powers and
serving spirits. That he was wholly unconscious of the
intolerably laughable effect we need not believe. He had
all the delight in laying snares and giving offence, which
is proper to his kind. He had all the confidence in his
own power and right to do such things and to get over the
doing of them which accompanies in such men the subtle
humour of scandalizing. And unfortunately he had not
by training, perhaps not by nature, the conscience which
would have reminded him that whether or not an artist
may allowably play with all other things in heaven and
earth, one thing he must certainly not play with ; the
material forms of art : that levity and violence are here
prohibited under grave penalties. Allowing however
for this, we may notice that in the wildest passages of
these books Blake merely carries into strange places or
throws into strange shapes such final theories as in the
dialect of calmer and smaller men have been accounted
not unreasonable.

Further preface or help, however loudly the subject
might seem to call for it, we have not in this place to
give ; and indeed more words would possibly not bring
with them more light. What was explicable we have
endeavoured to explain ; to suggest where a hint was
profitable ; to prepare where preparation was feasible :
but many voices might be heard crying in this wilderness
before the paths were made straight. The pursuivant

would grow hoarse and the outrider saddle-sick long before the great man's advent ; and for these offices we have no further taste or ability.   Those who will may now, with what furtherance they have here, follow us through some brief revision of each book in its order.*

* A word in passing may here be spared to the singular MS. of *Tiriel*. This little poem or mythical episode is evidently a growth of the crude Ossianic period ; in style it is somewhat weak and inadequate to any grave or subtle expression of thought : a few noticeable lines intervene, but the general execution is heavy, faint, and rough even for a sketch.   Here however (if I am not incorrect in referring it to a date earlier than the earliest of the prophetic books) we may see the dull dawn of a day full of fiery presage, of the light and vapour of tempestuous revelation.   The name of Tiriel king of the West, father of a rebellious race of children who perish by his curse, hardly reappears once as "Thiriel" the cloud-born son of Urizen ; Har and Heva, the gentler father and mother of the great eastern family, who in the *Song of Los* are seen flying before the windy flames of a broad-blown sunset, chased over Asia with fire and sword by the divine tyrant and his tributary kings, are here seen forsaken of their sons in extreme and childish age, but tended by "Mutha" their mother ; "they are holy and forgiving, filled with loving mercy, forgetting the offences of their most rebellious children."   Into the story or subject-matter we need not go far ; but it is worth notice that the series of twelve designs classified in the catalogue, section B., No. 156, pp. 253-4 of vol. 2, must evidently (as is there half suggested) be a set of illustrations to this *Tiriel*.   In one of these any reader will recognize the serpentine hair which at her father's imprecation rose and hissed around the brows of "Hela" (*Tiriel*, ch. 6) ; but these designs have as evidently fallen out of order ; thus the one lettered (*k*) appears to illustrate the very first lines of the poem ; and others seem equally misarranged.   In this faint allegory of the blind discrowned king with his two brothers, the mad invulnerable giant of the woods and the fettered dotard dwelling in caves, some fresh incomplete symbol is discernible of tyranny and error, of strength made insane or perverse and weakness made cruel or imbecile by oppression of the spirit or the flesh ; the "eloquent" outcast oppressor might then be the uninspired intellect, against whose errors and tyrannies its own children revolt, and perish by the curse of their perishing father and mother, blind reason and powerless faith : but from such shallow and sandy soil the conjectural Muse of commentary can reap little worth her pains to garner, and at every sweep of her sickle must risk being blinded by the sand blown into her eyes.   Some stray verses might be gathered up, perhaps worth a place in the gleaner's loose sheaf; such as these :

> "And aged Tiriel stood and said : Where does the thunder sleep ?
> Where doth he hide his terrible head ? and his swift and fiery daughters,
> Where do they shroud their fiery wings and the terrors of their hair ?"

Anything better worth citation than such crude sonorous snatches of lyric style I

The Book of Thel, first in date and simplest in tone of
the prophecies, requires less comment than the others.
This poem is as the one sister, feeblest if also fairest,
among that Titanic brotherhood of books. It has the
clearness and sweetness of spring-water; they have in
their lips the speech, in their limbs the pulses of the sea.
In this book, as in the illustrations to Blair, the poet
attempts to comfort life through death; to assuage by
spiritual hope the fleshly fear of man. The "shining
woman," youngest and mortal daughter of the angels of
God, leaving her sisters to tend the flocks and close the
folds of the stars, fills herself with the images of perishable things; she feeds upon the sorrow that comes of
beauty, the heathen weariness of heart, that is sick of
life because death will come, seeing how " our little life is
rounded with a sleep." Let all these things go, for they
are mortal; but if I die with the flowers, let me also die
as they die. This is the end of all things, to sleep; but
let me fall asleep softly, not without the lulling sound of

have not found here, except in chap. vii., where the dying Tiriel lays his final
curse on Har — "weak mistaken father of a lawless race," whose "laws and
Tiriel's wisdom end together in a curse." Here, in words afterwards variously
repeated and enlarged, he appeals against the laws of mere animal life, the
narrowed senses and material bondage of men upon earth; against unnatural
training and abstinence through which " milk is cut off from the weeping mouth
with difficulty and pain," when first "the little lids are lifted and the little
nostrils opened ;" against " hypocrisy, the idiot's wisdom and the wise man's
folly," by which men are "compelled to pray repugnant and to handle the
immortal spirit" till like Tiriel they become as subtle serpents in a paradise which
they consume fruit by fruit and flower by flower till at its fall they themselves
are left desolate. Thus too he inveighs against faith in matter and "respect of
persons" under their perishable and finite forms: "Can wisdom be put in a
silver rod or love in a golden bowl? is the son of a king warmed without wool?
or does he cry with a voice of thunder? does he look upon the sun and laugh, or
stretch his little hands into the depths of the sea?" Much of this has been half
erased, probably with a view to remoulding the whole : for here alone does anything in tone or thought recall the nobler mysticism of Blake's later writings.

God's voice audible in my ears. The flower makes answer; does God not care for the least of these? they shall not die, they shall all be changed. She answers again; the flower is serviceable to God's creatures, giving food to the pasturing lambs and flavour to the honey of the gleaning bees: but her beauty is barren as a lighted cloud's; wherefore should she live? She is bidden to seek counsel then of the cloud; and of him she asks the secret of his glad ephemeral life; for she, not less ephemeral, has no such joy of her life. Here again she is shown that life and permanence are twain; the cloud has drunk at the springs of the sun, whence all hours are renewed; and shall not die though he pass away; for his falling drops find out the living flowers, and are wedded to the dew in these; and they are made one before the sun, and kept alive to feed other flowers: and all these are as women and men, having souls and senses, capable of love and prayer. But she answers, that of her fair body no cloud or bird gets food, but the worm only; why should anything survive of her who has been helpful to nothing? The worm therefore is called to witness; and appears in an infant's likeness, inarticulate, naked, weeping; but upon it too the divine earth has mercy, and the clay finds a voice to speak for it; this likewise is not the sad unprofitable thing it seems; for the very earth, baser and liker death than the least thing bred of it, is the bride of God, a fruitful mother of all his children. "We live not for ourselves;" else indeed were earth and the worm of earth things mournful and fruitless. The secret of creation is sacrifice; the very act of growth is a sacrament: and through this eternal generation in which one life is given for another and shed into new veins of existence, each thing is redeemed from perpetual death by perpetual change. This secret once made evident to Thel, her fear is in a measure removed ; for the very deathbed of earth in which she must lie is now revealed as a mother's bosom, warm and giving warmth, living and prodigal of life. That God would care for the least thing he made she knew always ; but now knows also that in the least thing there is something of God's life infused, which makes it substantially imperishable. So far one may say the poem is as fluent and translucent as the merest sermon on faith, hope, and charity could well be : and not less inoffensive. The earth, who has overheard and gathered up all the flitting sighs of this unwedded Eve, now unveils to her the mysteries of the body, bred in the grave whither all sorrows tend and whence all tears arise. The forces of material nature give way before her ; passing to her own grave, she hears thence a voice lamenting over the nature of all the senses, their sweet perilous gifts and strange limits, and all their offices which fill and discolour the days of mortal life. To this, the question lying at the root of life and under the shadow of death, nothing makes answer ; as though no word spoken upon earth or under could explain the marvel of the flesh, the infinite beauty and delight of it, the infinite subtlety and danger ; its prodigalities and powers, its wide capacity and utter weakness. Set face to face with this bodily mystery, and affrighted at the sudden nakedness of natural life, the soul recoils ; and Thel regains the common air and quiet light of earth. Such, cut short and melted down, is the

purport of this poem : a prophecy as literally as any
other of Blake's, being professedly an inspired exposition
of material things; for none of course pretend to be
prophecies in the inaccurate and vulgar sense of predic-
tion. It is full of small sweet details, bright and soft as
summer grass, regular to monotony in its cadence until
the last division, where the tone suddenly strengthens and
deepens. There and not for the last time the strong
imagination of Blake wrestles with the great questions of
physical life, constraining the mute rebellious flesh as in a
fervent and strenuous grasp of spirit, if perchance it will
yield up the heart of its mystery. Throughout the book
his extreme and feminine tenderness of faith speaks more
softly and shows a simpler face than elsewhere. One
might almost say that *Thel* had overmuch of this gracious
and delicate beauty ; that the intense faith and compassion which thus animate all matter give a touch of almost
dubious and effeminate sweetness to the thought and
style. Not however justly ; for there is a firm body of
significance in the poem, and the soft light leaves in
which the fruit lies wrapped are solid as well as sweet.

It is well worth while to compare any average copy of
Thel with the smaller volume of designs now in the
British Museum, which reproduces among others the main
illustrations of this book. The clear, sweet, pallid colour
of the fainter version will then serve to throw into full
effect the splendour of the more finished work. Especially in the separate copy of the frontispiece, the sove-
reignty of colour and glorious grace of workmanship
double and treble its original beauty ; give new light and
new charm to the fervent heaven, to the bowing figure of

the girl, to the broad cloven blossoms whose flickering and
sundering petals release the bright leaping forms of loving
spirits, raindrop and dewdrop wedded before the sun ;
and again, where Thel sees the worm in likeness of a new-
born child, the colours of tree and leaf and sky are of a
more excellent and lordly beauty than in any copy known
to me of the book itself ; though in all good copies these
designs appear full of great and gracious qualities. Of
the book of designs here referred to more must not now
be said ; not even of the twelfth plate where the mother-
goddess and her fiery first-born child exult with flying
wingless limbs through splendid spaces of the infinite
morning, coloured here like opening flowers and there like
climbing fire, where all the light and all the wind of
heaven seem to unite in fierce gladness as of a supreme
embrace and exultation ; for to these better praise than
ours has been already given at p. 374 of the *Life,* in
words of choice and incomparable sufficiency, not less
bright and sweet, significant and subtle, than the most
tender or perfect of the designs described.

In 1790 Blake produced the greatest of all his books ;
a work indeed which we rank as about the greatest produced by the eighteenth century in the line of high
poetry and spiritual speculation. *The Marriage of
Heaven and Hell* gives us the high-water mark of his
intellect. None of his lyrical writings show the same
sustained strength and radiance of mind ; none of his
other works in verse or prose give more than a hint here
and a trace there of the same harmonious and humorous
power, of the same choice of eloquent words, the same
noble command and liberal music of thought ; small

things he could often do perfectly, and great things often imperfectly ; here for once he has written a book as perfect as his most faultless song, as great as his most imperfect rhapsody. His fire of spirit fills it from end to end; but never deforms the body, never singes the surface of the work, as too often in the still noble books of his later life. Across the flicker of flame, under the roll and roar of water, which seem to flash and to resound throughout the poem, a stately music, shrill now as laughter and now again sonorous as a psalm, is audible through shifting notes and fitful metres of sound. The book swarms with heresies and eccentricities ; every sentence bristles with some paradox, every page seethes with blind foam and surf of stormy doctrine ; the humour is of that fierce grave sort, whose cool insanity of manner is more horrible and more obscure to the Philistine than any sharp edge of burlesque or glitter of irony ; it is huge, swift, inexplicable ; hardly laughable through its enormity of laughter, hardly significant through its condensation of meaning ; but as true and thoughtful as the greatest humourist's. The variety and audacity of thoughts and words are incomparable : not less so their fervour and beauty. "No bird soars too high if he soars with his own wings." This proverb might serve as motto to the book : it is one of many " Proverbs of Hell," as forcible and as finished.

It was part of Blake's humour to challenge misconception, conscious as he was of power to grapple with it : to blow dust in their eyes who were already sandblind, to strew thorns under their feet who were already lame. Those whom the book in its present shape would perplex

and repel he knew it would not in any form have attracted ; and how such readers may fare is no concern
of such writers ; nor in effect need it be.   Aware that he
must at best offend a little, he did not fear to offend
much.   To measure the exact space of safety, to lay
down the precise limits of offence, was an office neither
to his taste nor within his power.   Those who try to clip
or melt themselves down to the standard of current feeling,
to sauce and spice their natural fruits of mind with such
condiments as may take the palate of common opinion,
deserve to disgust themselves and others alike.   It is
hopeless to reckon how far the timid, the perverse, or the
malignant irrelevance of human remarks will go ; to set
bounds to the incompetence or devise landmarks for the
imbecility of men.   Blake's way was not the worst ; to
indulge his impulse to the full and write what fell to his
hand, making sure at least of his own genius and natural
instinct.   In this his greatest book he has at once given
himself freer play and set himself to harder labour than
elsewhere : the two secrets of great work.   Passion and
humour are mixed in his writing like mist and light ;
whom the light may scorch or the mist confuse it is not
his part to consider.

In the prologue Blake puts forth, not without grandeur
if also with an admixture of rant and wind, a chief tenet
of his moral creed.   Once the ways of good and evil
were clear, not yet confused by laws and religions ; then
humility and benevolence, the endurance of peril and
the fruitful labour of love, were the just man's proper
apanage ; behind his feet the desert blossomed ; by his
toil and danger, by his sweat and blood, the desolate

places were made rich and the dead bones clothed with
flesh as the flesh of Adam.   Now the hypocrite has come
to reap the fruits, to divide and gather and eat; to drive
forth the just man and to dwell in the paths which he
found perilous and barren, but left safe and fertile.
Churches have cast out apostles ; creeds have rooted out
faith.   Henceforth anger and loneliness, the divine indignation of spiritual exile, the salt bread of scorn and the
bitter wine of wrath, are the portion of the just man ;
he walks with lions in the waste places, not worth making
fertile that others may reap and feed.   "Rintrah," the
spirit presiding over this period, is a spirit of fire and
storm ; darkness and famine, wrath and want, divide the
kingdoms of the world.   "Prisons are built with stones
of Law ; brothels with bricks of Religion."   "As the
caterpillar chooses the fairest leaves to lay her eggs on, so
the priest lays his curse on the fairest joys."   In a third
proverb the view given of prayer is no less heretical ;
"As the plough follows words, so God rewards prayers."
This was but the outcome or corollary of his main
doctrine ; as what we have called his "evangel of bodily
liberty" was but the fruit of his belief in the identity of
body with soul.   The fear which restrains and the faith
which refuses were things as ignoble as the hypocrisy
which assumes or the humility which resigns.   Veils and
chains must be lifted and broken.   "Folly is the cloak of
knavery ; shame is pride's cloak."   Again ; "He who
desires but acts not breeds pestilence."   "Sooner murder
an infant in its cradle than nurse unacted desires."   The
doctrine of freedom could hardly run further or faster.
Translated into rough practice, and planted in a less pure

soil than that of the writer's mind, this philosophy might
bring forth a strange harvest.   Together with such width
of moral pantheism as will hardly admit a " tender curb,"
leave " a little curtain of flesh on the bed of our desire,"
there is a vehemence of faith in divine wrath, in the
excellence of righteous anger and revenge, to be outdone
by no prophet or Puritan.   " A dead body revenges not
injuries."   Sincerity and plain dealing at least are virtues
not to be thrown over ; Blake indeed could not conceive
an impulse to mendacity, a tortuous habit of mind, a soul
born crooked.   This one quality of falsehood remains
damnable in his sight, to be consumed with all that comes
of it.   In man or beast or any other part of God he found
no native taint or birthmark of this.   Upon all else the
divine breath and the divine hand are sensible and visible.

> " The pride of the peacock is the glory of God ;
> The lust of the goat is the bounty of God ;
> The wrath of the lion is the wisdom of God ;
> The nakedness of woman is the work of God."

All form and all instinct is sacred ; but no invention or
device of man's.   All crafts and creeds of theirs are " the
serpent's meat :" and that a man should be born cruel
and false is barely imaginable.   " If the lion was advised
by the fox he would be cunning."   Such counsel was
always wasted on the high clear spirit and stainless intellect of Blake.

   We have given some of the most subtle and venturous
" Proverbs of Hell "—samples of their depth of doctrine
and plainness of speech.   But even here Blake rarely
indulges in such excess and exposure.   There are jewels
in this treasure-house neither set so roughly nor so sharply

cut as these ; they may be seen in the *Life*, taken out and reset, so as to offend no customer. And these sayings must themselves be read by the light of Blake's life and weighed against others of his words not less weighty than they. Apology shall now and always remain as far from us as it was in life from Blake himself ; to excuse and to explain are different offices. To plead for his acquittal on the base and foolish ground that he meant no harm, knew not what he did, had no design or desire to afflict or offend, is no office for his counsel ; who must strive at least to speak not less frankly and clearly than did Blake when he could speak in his own cause. Neither have we to approve or condemn ; but only to endeavour that we may see the right and deliver the truth as to this man and his life. " That I cannot live," he says, in the Butts correspondence, " without doing my duty to lay up treasures in heaven, is certain and determined, and to this I have long made up my mind. And why this should be made an objection to me, while drunkenness, lewdness, gluttony, and even idleness itself does not hurt other men, let Satan himself explain. The thing I have most at heart—more than life, or all that seems to make life comfortable without (it)—is the interest of true religion and science." His one fear is to " omit any duty to my station as a soldier of Christ ; " a fear that "gives him the greatest torments ;" for " if our footsteps slide in clay, how can we do otherwise than fear and tremble ? " And such books as these were part of his spiritual taskwork. From whencesoever the inspiration of them came, inspiration it was and no invention. He is content with that knowledge ; and if it please the hearer to call it diabolic, diabolic it shall be. If he has a devil, he will make the most and the best of him. If these things come from hell, let us look to it and hold them fast, that we may see what it is that divides hell from heaven.

"As a new heaven is begun, and it is now thirty-three years since its advent: the Eternal Hell revives. And lo! Swedenborg is the Angel sitting at the tomb : his writings are the linen clothes folded up. Now is the dominion of Edom, and the return of Adam into Paradise; see Isaiah xxxiv. and xxxv. chap.

"Without Contraries is no progression. Attraction and Repulsion, Reason and Energy, Love and Hate, are necessary to Human existence.

"From these Contraries spring what the religious call Good and Evil. Good is the passive that obeys Reason.

"Evil is the active springing from Energy.

"*Good is Heaven. Evil is Hell.*

"THE VOICE OF THE DEVIL.

"All Bibles or sacred codes have been the causes of the following Errors.

"1. That man has two real existing principles—viz., a Body and a Soul.

"2. That Energy, called Evil, is alone from the Body ; and that Reason, called Good, is alone from the Soul.

"3. That God will torment Man in Eternity for following his Energies.

"But the following contraries to these are True.

"1. Man has no Body distinct from his Soul, for that called Body is a portion of Soul discerned by the five Senses, the chief inlets of Soul in this age.

"2. Energy is the only life, and is from the Body ; and Reason is the bound or outward circumference of Energy.

"3. Energy is Eternal Delight.

"Those who restrain desire to do so because theirs is weak enough to be restrained ; and the restrainer, or reason, usurps its place and governs the unwilling.

"And being restrained it by degrees becomes passive, till it is only the shadow of desire.

"The history of this is written in 'Paradise Lost,' and the Governor, or Reason, is called Messiah.

"And the original Archangel, or possessor of the command of the heavenly host, is called the Devil or Satan, and his children are called Sin and Death.

" But in the Book of Job Milton's Messiah is called Satan.

" For this history has been adopted by both parties.

"It indeed appeared to Reason as if Desire was cast out; but the Devil's account is, that the Messiah fell, and formed a heaven of what he stole from the Abyss.

" This is shewn in the Gospel, where he prays to the Father to send the comforter or Desire, that Reason may have Ideas to build on, the Jehovah of the Bible being no other than he who dwells in flaming fire. Know that after Christ's death, he became Jehovah.

" But in Milton the Father is Destiny, the Son a Ratio of the five Senses, and the Holy Ghost, Vacuum.

" NOTE.—The reason Milton wrote in fetters when he wrote of Angels and God, and at liberty when of Devils and Hell, is because he was a true Poet, and of the Devil's party without knowing it."

Something of these high matters we have seen before, and should now be able to allow for the subtle intricate fashion in which Blake labours to invert the weapons of his antagonists upon themselves. Neither can the banns of marriage be published between heaven and hell with the voice of a parish clerk. This prophet came to do what Swedenborg his precursor had left undone, being but the watchman by the empty sepulchre, and his writings as the grave-clothes cast off by the risen Christ. Blake's estimate of Swedenborg, right or wrong, was, as we shall see, distinct and consistent; to this effect; that his inspiration was limited and timid, superficial and derivative; that he was content with leaves and husks, and had not the courage to examine the root and the kernel of things; that he clove to the heaven and shrank from the hell of other men; whereas, to men in whom " a new heaven is begun," the one must not be terrible nor the other desirable. To them the " flaming fire " wherein dwells a God whom men call devil, must seem a purer element of life than the starry and cloudy space wherein dwells a devil whom they call God. It must be remembered that Blake uses the current terms of religion, now as types of his own peculiar faith, now in the sense of ordinary preachers : impugning therefore at one time what at another he will seem to vindicate. Vague and violent as this overture may appear, it must be followed with care, that the writer's intensity of spiritual faith may be hereafter kept in sight. The senses, "the chief inlets of soul in this age" of brute doubt and brute belief, are worthy only as parts of the soul. This, it cannot be too much repeated and insisted on, this and no prurience of porcine appetite for rotten apples, no vulgarity of porcine adoration for unctuous wash, is what lies at the root of Blake's sensual doctrine. Let no reader now or ever forget, that while others will admit nothing beyond the body, the mystic will admit nothing outside the soul. That the two extremes, if reduced to hard practice, might run round and meet, not without lamentably curious consequences, those may assert who will ; it is none of our business to decide. Even granting that the result will be about equivalent if one man does for his soul's sake all that another would do for his body's sake, we might plead that the difference of thought and eye between these two would remain great and important. Indulgence bracketed to faith and vivified by that vigorous contact with things divine is not (we might say) the same, whether seen from the actual side of life or from the speculative, as indulgence cut loose and left to decompose. But these pleas we will leave the mystic to advance, if it please him, on his own behalf.

"A Memorable Fancy.

"As I was walking among the fires of hell, delighted with the enjoyments of Genius, which to Angels look like torment and insanity, I collected some of their Proverbs: thinking that as the sayings used in a nation mark its character, so the Proverbs of Hell show the nature of the Infernal wisdom better than any description of buildings or garments. When I came home, on the abyss of the five senses, where a flat-sided steep frowns over the present world, I saw a mighty Devil folded in black clouds, hovering on the sides of the rock; with corroding fires he wrote the following sentence, now perceived by the minds of men, and read by them on earth:—

"'How do you know but ev'ry Bird that cuts the airy way
Is an immense world of delight, clos'd by your senses five?'"

Here follow the " Proverbs of Hell," which give us the quintessence and the most fine gold of Blake's alembic. Each, whether earnest or satirical, slight or great in manner, is full of that passionate wisdom and bright rapid strength proper to the step and speech of gods. The simplest give us a measure of his energy, as this :— "Think in the morning, act in the noon, eat in the evening, sleep in the night." The highest have a light and resonance about them, as though in effect from above or beneath ; a spirit which lifts thought upon the high levels of verse.

From the ensuing divisions of the book we shall give full extracts ; for these detached sections have a grace and coherence which we shall not always find in Blake ; and the crude excerpts given in the *Life* are inadequate to help the reader much towards a clear comprehension of the main scheme.

"The ancient Poets animated all sensible objects with Gods or Geniuses, calling them by the names and adorning them with the properties of

woods, rivers, mountains, lakes, cities, nations, and whatever their
enlarged and numerous senses could perceive.

" And, particularly, they studied the genius of each city and country,
placing it under its mental deity.

" Till a system was formed, which some took advantage of and enslaved
the vulgar by attempting to realize or abstract the mental deities from
their objects : thus began Priesthood,

" Choosing forms of worship from poetic tales ;

"And at length they pronounced that the Gods had ordered such things.

" Thus men forgot that All deities reside in the human breast."

From this we pass to higher tones of exposition.
The next passage is one of the clearest and keenest in
the book, full of faith and sacred humour, none the less
sincere for its dramatic form. The subtle simplicity of
expression is excellently subservient to the intricate force
of thought.

" A MEMORABLE FANCY.

" The Prophets Isaiah and Ezekiel dined with me, and I asked them
how they dared so roundly to assert that God spoke to them ; and whether they did not think at the time that they would be misunderstood,
and so be the cause of imposition.

" Isaiah answered, ' I saw no God, nor heard any, in a finite or orga-
nical perception; but my senses discovered the infinite in everything,
and as I was then persuaded, I remain confirmed, that the voice of
honest indignation is the voice of God. I cared not for consequences, but
wrote.'

" Then I asked, ' Does a firm persuasion that a thing is so, make
it so ? '

" He replied, ' All poets believe that it does, and in ages of imagination
this firm persuasion removed mountains. But many are not capable of
a firm persuasion of anything.'

" Then Ezekiel said, ' The philosophy of the East taught the first principles of human perception. Some nations held one principle for the
origin and some another. We of Israel taught that the Poetic Genius (as
you now call it) was the first principle, and all the others merely derivative, which was the cause of our despising the Priests and Philosophers
of other countries, and prophesying that all Gods would at last be
proved to originate in ours, and to be the tributaries of the Poetic Genius.
It was this that our great poet King David desired so fervently and in-
vokes so pathetically, saying by this he conquers enemies and governs

kingdoms; and we so loved our God, that we cursed in his name all the deities of surrounding nations, and asserted that they had rebelled; from these opinions the vulgar came to think that all nations would at last be subject to the Jews.

" 'This,' said he, 'like all firm persuasions, is come to pass, for all nations believe the Jews' code and worship the Jews' God, and what greater subjection can be ?'

"I heard this with some wonder, and must confess my own conviction. After dinner, I asked Isaiah to favour the world with his lost works. He said none of equal value was lost.

" Ezekiel said the same of his.

"I also asked Isaiah what made him go naked and barefoot three years ? He answered, the same that made our friend Diogenes the Grecian.

"I then asked Ezekiel, why he eat dung, and lay so long on his right and left side ? he answered, the desire of raising other men into a perception of the infinite. This the North American tribes practise; and is he honest who resists his genius or conscience, only for the sake of present ease or gratification ?"

The doctrine of perception through not with the senses, beyond not in the organs, as also of the absolute existence of things thus apprehended, is again directly enforced in our next excerpt ; in praise of which we will say nothing, but leave the words to burn their way in as they may.

"The ancient tradition that the world will be consumed in fire at the end of six thousand years is true, as I have heard from Hell.

" For the cherub with his flaming sword is hereby commanded to leave his guard at the tree of life; and when he does, the whole creation will be consumed, and appear infinite and holy, whereas it now appears finite and corrupt.

"This will come to pass by an improvement of sensual enjoyment.

" But first the notion that man has a body distinct from his soul is to be expunged; this I shall do, by printing in the infernal method, by corrosives, which in Hell are salutary and medicinal, melting apparent surfaces away and displaying the infinite which was hid.

" If the doors of perception were cleansed, everything would appear to man as it is, infinite.

" For man has closed himself up, till he sees all things through narrow chinks of his cavern."

After which corrosive touch of revelation there follows a vision of knowledge; first, the human nature is cleansed and widened into shape, then decorated, then enlarged and built about with stately buildings for guest-chambers and treasure-houses; then the purged metal of knowledge, melted into form with divine violence, is made fluid and vital, that it may percolate and permeate the whole man through every pore of his spirit; then the metal is cast forth and put to use. All forms and forces of the world, viper and lion, half-human things and nameless natures, serve to help in this work; all manner of aspiration and inspiration, wrath and faith, love and labour, do good service here.

" The Giants who formed this world into its sensual existence, and now seem to live in it in chains, are in truth the causes of its life and the sources of all activity; but the chains are, the cunning of weak and tame minds, which have power to resist energy; according to the proverb, the weak in courage is strong in cunning.

" Thus one portion of being is the Prolific, the other, the Devouring; to the devourer it seems as if the producer was in his chains; but it is not so; he only takes portions of existence and fancies that the whole.

" But the Prolific would cease to be Prolific, unless the Devourer as a sea received the excess of his delights.

"Some will say, Is not God alone the Prolific ?

" I answer, God only Acts and Is in existing beings or Men.

" These two classes of men are always upon earth, and they should be enemies; whoever tries to reconcile them, seeks to destroy existence.

" Religion is an endeavour to reconcile the two.

" NOTE.—Jesus Christ did not wish to unite but to separate them, as in the Parable of sheep and goats! and he says I came not to send Peace but a Sword.

" Messiah or Satan or Tempter was formerly thought to be one of the Antediluvians who are our Energies."

These are hard sayings ; who can hear them ? At first sight also, as we were forewarned, this passage seems at direct variance with that other in the overture, where our prophet appears at first sight, and only appears, to speak of the fallen " Messiah " as the same with the Christ of his belief. Verbally coherent we cannot hope to make the two passages ; but it must be remarked and remembered that the very root or kernel of this creed is not the assumed humanity of God, but the achieved divinity of Man ; not incarnation from without, but development from within ; not a miraculous passage into flesh, but a natural growth into godhead. Christ, as the type or sample of manhood, thus becomes after death the true Jehovah ; not, as he seems to the vulgar, the extraneous and empirical God of creeds and churches, human in no necessary or absolute sense, the false and fallen phantom of his enemy, Zeus in the mask of Prometheus. We are careful to note and as far as may be to correct any apparent slips or shortcomings in expression, only because if left without a touch of commentary they may seem to make worse confusion than they do actually make. Subtle, trenchant and profound as is this philosophy, there is no radical flaw in the book, no positive incongruity, no inherent contradiction. A single consistent principle keeps alive the large relaxed limbs, makes significant the dim great features of this strange faith. It is but at the opening that the words are even partially inadequate and obscure. Revision alone could have righted and straightened them ; and revision the author would not give. Impatient of their insufficiency, and incapable of any labour that implies rest, he shook them together and flung them out in an irritated hurried manner, regardless who might gather them up or let them lie.

In the next and longest division of the book, direct allegory and imaginative vision are indivisibly mixed into each other. The stable and mill, the twisted root and inverted fungus, are transparent symbols enough : the splendid and stormy apocalypse of the abyss is a chapter of pure vision or poetic invention. Why "Swedenborg's volumes" are the weights used to sink the travellers from the "glorious clime" to the passive and iron void between the fixed stars and the coldest of the remote planets, will be conceivable in due time.

"A MEMORABLE FANCY.

"An Angel came to me and said, 'O pitiable foolish young man! O horrible! O dreadful state! Consider the hot burning dungeon thou art preparing for thyself to all eternity, to which thou art going in such career.'

"I said, 'Perhaps you will be willing to show me my eternal lot and we will contemplate upon it and see whether your lot or mine is most desirable.'

"So he took me through a stable and through a church and down into the church vault at the end of which was a mill; through the mill we went, and came to a cave; down the winding cavern we groped our tedious way, till a void, boundless as a nether sky, appeared beneath us, and we held by the roots of trees and hung over this immensity ; but I said, 'If you please, we will commit ourselves to this void, and see whether Providence is here also; if you will not, I will.'

"But he answered, 'Do not presume, O young man, but as we here remain, behold thy lot, which will soon appear when the darkness passes away.'

"So I remained with him, sitting in the twisted root of an oak; he was suspended in a fungus, which hung with the head downward into the deep.

"By degrees we beheld the infinite Abyss, fiery as the smoke of a burning city ; beneath us at an immense distance was the sun, black but shining ; round it were fiery tracks on which revolved vast spiders, crawling after their prey; which flew or rather swam in the infinite deep, in the most terrific shapes of animals sprung from corruption; and the air was full of them, and seemed composed of them; these are Devils, and are called Powers of the air. I now asked my companion which was my eternal lot? he said, between the black and white spiders.

"But now, from between the black and white spiders a cloud and fire burst and rolled through the deep blackening all beneath, so that the nether deep grew black as a sea and rolled with a terrible noise: beneath us was nothing now to be seen but a black tempest, till looking east between the clouds and the waves, we saw a cataract of blood mixed with fire, and not many stones' throw from us appeared and sunk again the scaly fold of a monstrous serpent; at last, to the east, distant about three degrees, appeared a fiery crest above the waves; slowly it reared, like a ridge of golden rocks, till we discovered two globes of crimson fire, from which the sea fled away in clouds of smoke: and now we saw it was the head of Leviathan; his forehead was divided into streaks of green and purple, like those on a tiger's forehead: soon we saw his mouth and red gills hang just above the raging foam, tinging the black deep with beams of blood, advancing toward us with all the fury of a spiritual existence.

"My friend the Angel climbed up from his station into the mill; I remained alone, and then this appearance was no more; but I found myself sitting on a pleasant bank beside a river by moonlight, hearing a harper who sung to the harp, and his theme was, The man who never alters his opinion is like standing water, and breeds reptiles of the mind.

"But I arose, and sought for the mill, and there I found my Angel, who, surprised, asked me how I escaped?

"I answered, 'All that we saw was owing to your metaphysics: for when you ran away, I found myself on a bank by moonlight hearing a harper. But now we have seen my eternal lot, shall I show you yours?' He laughed at my proposal: but I by force suddenly caught him in my arms, and flew westerly through the night, till we were elevated above the earth's shadow: then I flung myself with him directly into the body of the sun; here I clothed myself in white, and taking in my hand Swedenborg's volumes, sunk from the glorious clime, and passed all the planets till we came to Saturn: here I staid to rest, and then leaped into the void, between Saturn and the fixed stars.

"'Here,' said I, 'is your lot, in this space, if space it may be called.' Soon we saw the stable and the church, and I took him to the altar and opened the Bible, and lo! it was a deep pit, into which I descended, driving the Angel before me; soon we saw seven houses of brick; one we entered; in it were a number of monkeys, baboons, and all of that species chained by the middle, grinning and snatching at one another, but withheld by the shortness of their chains; however, I saw that they sometimes grew numerous, and then the weak were caught by the strong and, with a grinning aspect, first coupled with and then devoured, by plucking off first one limb and then another, till the body was left a helpless trunk; this, after grinning and kissing it with seeming kindness, they devoured too ; and here and there I saw one savourily picking the flesh off of his own tail. As the stench terribly annoyed us both, we went into the mill, and I in my hand brought the skeleton of a body, which in the mill was Aristotle's ' Analytics.'

"So the Angel said ; 'Thy phantasy has imposed upon me, and thou oughtest to be ashamed.'

" I answered; 'We impose on one another, and it is but lost time to converse with you, whose works are only Analytics.' "

The " seven houses of brick " we may take to be a reminiscence of the seven churches of St. John ; as indeed the traces of former evangelists and prophets are never long wanting when we track the steps of this one. Lest however we be found unawares on the side of these hapless angels and baboons, we will abstain with all due care from any not indispensable analysis. It is evident that between pure " phantasy " and mere " analytics " the great gulf must remain fixed, and either party appear to the other deceptive and deceived. That impulsive energy and energetic faith are the only means, whether used as tools of peace or as weapons of war, to pave or to fight our way toward the realities of things, was plainly the creed of Blake ; as also that these realities, once well in sight, will reverse appearance and overthrow tradition : hell will appear as heaven, and heaven as hell. The abyss once entered with due trust and courage appears a place of green pastures and gracious springs : the paradise of resignation once beheld with undisturbed eyes appears a place of emptiness or bondage, delusion or cruelty. On the humorous beauty and vigour of these symbols we need not expatiate ; in these qualities Rabelais and Dante together could hardly have excelled Blake at his best. What his meaning is should by this time be as clear as the meaning of a mystic need be ; it is but partially expressible by words, as (to borrow Blake's own symbol) the inseparable soul is yet but incompletely expressible through the body. Whether it be right or wrong, foolish or wise, we will neither inquire nor assert : the autocercophagous monkeys of the mill may be left to settle that for themselves with " Urizen."

We come now to a chapter of comments, intercalated between two sufficiently memorable " fancies."

" I have always found that Angels have the vanity to speak of themselves as the only wise; this they do with a confident insolence sprouting from systematic reasoning.

" Thus Swedenborg boasts that what he writes is new, though it is only the Contents or Index of already published books.

" A man carried a monkey about for a show, and because he was a little wiser than the monkey, grew vain, and conceived himself as much wiser than seven men. It is so with Swedenborg: he shows the folly of churches and exposes hypocrites, till he imagines that all are religious and himself the single one on earth that ever broke a net.

" Now hear a plain fact: Swedenborg has not written one new truth.

" Now hear another: He has written all the old falsehoods.

" And now hear the reason : He conversed with Angels who are all religious and conversed not with Devils who all hate religion; for he was incapable, through his conceited notions.

" Thus Swedenborg's writings are a recapitulation of all superficial opinions, and an analysis of the more sublime, but no further.

" Hear now another plain fact: Any man of mechanical talents may, from the writings of Paracelsus or Jacob Behmen, produce ten thousand volumes of equal value with Swedenborg's; and from those of Dante or Shakespeare, an infinite number. But when he has done this, let him not say that he knows better than his master, for he only holds a candle in sunshine."

This also we will leave for those to decide who please, and attend to the next and final vision. That the fire of inspiration should absorb and convert to its own nature all denser and meaner elements of mind, was the prophet's sole idea of redemption : the dead cloud of belief consumed becomes the vital flame of faith.

" A Memorable Fancy.

" Once I saw a Devil in a flame of fire, who arose before an Angel that sat on a cloud, and the Devil uttered these words.

" The worship of God is : Honouring his gifts in other men, each according to his genius, and loving the greatest men best; those who envy or calumniate great men hate God, for there is no other God.

" The Angel hearing this became almost blue, but mastering himself, he grew yellow, and at last white, pink, and smiling ; and then replied, Thou Idolator, is not God one ? and is not he visible in Jesus Christ ? and has not Jesus Christ given his sanction to the law of ten commandments ? and are not all other men fools, sinners, and nothings ?

" The Devil answered ; Bray a fool in a mortar with wheat, yet shall not his folly be beaten out of him : if Jesus Christ is the greatest man, you ought to love him in the greatest degree ; now hear how he has given his sanction to the law of the ten commandments : did he not mock at the sabbath, and so mock the sabbath's God ? murder those who were murdered, because of him ? turn away the law from the woman taken in adultery ? steal the labour of others to support him ? bear false witness when he omitted making a defence before Pilate ? covet when he prayed for his disciples, and when he bid them shake off the dust of their feet against such as refused to lodge them ? I tell you, no virtue can exist without breaking these ten commandments. Jesus was all virtue, and acted from impulse, not from rules.

" When he had so spoken, I beheld the Angel who stretched out his arms embracing the flame of fire, and he was consumed, and arose as Elijah.

" Note. This Angel, who is now become a Devil, is my particular friend : we often read the Bible together in its infernal or diabolical sense, which the world shall have if they behave well.

" I have also the Bible of Hell, which the world shall have, whether they will or no."

Under this title at least the world was never favoured with it ; but we may presumably taste some savour of that Bible in these pages. After this the book is wound up in a lyric rapture, not without some flutter and tumour of style, but full of clear high music and flame-like aspiration. Epilogue and prologue are both nearer in manner to the dubious hybrid language of the succeeding books of prophecy than to the choice and noble prose in which the rest of this book is written. The overture must be read by the light of its meaning; of the mysterious universal mother and her son, the latest birth of the world, we have already taken account. The date of 1790 must here be kept in mind, that all may remember what appearances of change were abroad, what manner of light and tempest was visible upon earth, when the hopes of such men as Blake made their stormy way into speech or song.

"A SONG OF LIBERTY.

1. The Eternal Female groan'd! it was heard over all the Earth.

2. Albion's coast is sick silent; the American meadows faint!

3. Shadows of Prophecy shiver along by the lakes and the rivers, and mutter across the ocean. France, rend down thy dungeon;

4. Golden Spain, burst the barriers of old Rome;

5. Cast thy keys, O Rome, into the deep down falling, even to eternity down falling;

6. And weep.

7. In her trembling hands she took the new-born terror howling:

8. On those infinite mountains of light now barred out by the Atlantic sea, the new-born fire stood before the starry King!

9. Flag'd with grey-browed snows and thunderous visages the jealous wings waved over the deep.

10. The speary hand burned aloft, unbuckled was the shield, forth went the hand of jealousy among the flaming hair, and hurled the new-born wonder thro' the starry night.

11. The fire, the fire is falling!

12. Look up! look up! O citizen of London, enlarge thy countenance: O Jew, leave counting gold! return to thy oil and wine; O African! black African! (go, winged thought, widen his forehead.)

13. The fiery limbs, the flaming hair, shot like the sinking sun into the western sea.

14. Waked from his eternal sleep, the hoary element roaring fled away.

15. Down rushed, beating his wings in vain, the jealous King; his grey-browed councillors, thunderous warriors, curled veterans, among helms and shields, and chariots, horses, elephants; banners, castles, slings and rocks;

16. Falling, rushing, ruining! buried in the ruins, on Urthona's dens;

17. All night beneath the ruins, then their sullen flames faded emerge round the gloomy King.

18. With thunder and fire, leading his starry hosts thro' the waste wilderness, he promulgates his ten commands, glancing his beamy eyelids over the deep in dark dismay;

19. Where the son of fire in his eastern cloud, while the morning plumes her golden breast,

20. Spurning the clouds written with curses, stamps the stony law to dust, loosing the eternal horses from the dens of night, crying, Empire is no more! and now the lion and the wolf shall cease.

CHORUS.

Let the Priests of the Raven of dawn no longer in deadly black with hoarse note curse the sons of joy; Nor his accepted brethren, whom, tyrant, he calls free, lay the bound or build the roof; Nor pale religious letchery call that virginity that wishes but acts not;

For everything that lives is Holy."

And so, as with fire and thunder—" thunder of thought, and flames of fierce desire"—is this *Marriage of Heaven and Hell* at length happily consummated; the prophet, as a fervent paranymph, standing by to invoke upon the wedded pair his most unclerical benediction. Those who are not bidden to the bridegroom's supper may as well keep away, lest worse befall them, not having a wedding garment. For us there remains little to say, now that the torches are out, the nuts scattered, the songs silent, and the saffron faded from the veil. We will wish them a quiet life, and an heir who may combine the merits and capacities of either parent. It were pleasant enough, but too superfluous, to

dwell upon the beauty of this nuptial hymn ; to bid men
remark what eloquence, what subtlety, what ardour of
wisdom, what splendour of thought, is here ; how far it
outruns, not in daring alone but in sufficiency, all sayings
of minor mystics who were not also poets ; how much
of lofty love and of noble faith underlies and animates
these rapid and fervent words ; what greatness of spirit
and of speech there was in the man who, living as Blake
lived, could write as Blake has written.   Those who
cannot see what is implied may remain unable to tolerate what is expressed ; and those who can read aright
need no index of ours.*

---

* Before we dismiss the matter from view, it may be permissible to cast up
in a rough and rapid way the sum of Blake's teaching in these books, if only
because this was also the doctrine or moral of his entire life and life's work.   I
will therefore, as leave has been given, append a note extracted from a manuscript now before me, which attempts to embody and enforce, if only by dint of
pure and simple exposition, the pantheistic evangel here set forth in so strange a
fashion.   Thus at least I read the passage ; if misinterpreted, my correspondent
has to thank his own laxity of expression.   "These poems or essays at prophecy "
(he says) "seem to me to represent in an obscure and forcible manner the real
naked question to which all theologies and all philosophies must in the end be
pared down.   Strained and filtered clear of extraneous matter, pruned of foreign
fruit and artificial foliage, this radical question lies between Theism and Pantheism.   When the battles of the creeds have been all fought out, this battle will
remain to fight.   I do not see much likelihood on either hand of success or
defeat.   Faith and reason, evidence and report, are alike inadequate to decide the
day.   This prophet or that prophet, this God or that God, is not here under
debate.   Histories, religions, all things born of rumour or circumstance, accident
or change, are out of court ; are, for the moment, of necessity set aside.   Gentile
or Jew, Christian or Pagan, Eastern or Western, can but be equal to us—for the
moment.   No single figure, no single book, stands out for special judgment or
special belief.   On the right hand, let us say (employing the old figure of speech),
is the Theist—the 'man of God,' if you may take his own word for it ; the believer
in a separate or divisible deity, capable or conceivably capable of existence apart
from ours who conceive of it ; a conscious and absolute Creator.   On the left
hand is the Pantheist ; to whom such a creed is mainly incredible and wholly insufficient.   His creed is or should be much like that of your prophet here ;" (I
must observe in passing that my correspondent seems so unable to conceive of a
comment apart from the text, an exponent who is not an evangelist,—so inclined
to confuse the various functions of critic and of disciple, and assume that you
must mean to preach or teach whatever doctrine you may have to explain—in a

The decorations of this great work, though less large
and complete than those of the subsequent prophecies,
are full of noble and subtle beauty. Over every page
faint fibres and flickering threads of colour weave a net of
intricate design. Skies cloven with flame and thunder,

word, so obtuse or perverse on this point that he might be taken for a professional
man-of-letters or sworn juryman of the press ; but I will hope better things of
him, though anonymous ;) "and that creed, as I take it, is simply enough expressible in Blake's own words, or deducible from them ; that 'all deities reside
in the human breast' ; that except humanity there is no divine thing or person.
Clearly therefore, in the eyes of a Theist, he lies open to the charge of atheism
or antitheism.   The real difference is perhaps this ; God appears to a Theist as
the root, to a Pantheist as the flower of things.   It does not follow logically or
actually that to this latter all things are alike.   For us (he might say), for us,
within the boundaries of time and space, evil and good do really exist, and live no
empirical life—for a certain time, and within a certain range.   'There is no God
unless man can become God.'   That is no saying for an Atheist.   'There is no
man unless the child can become a man' ; is that equivalent to a denial of manhood ?   But if a man is to be born into the world, the mother must abstain from
the drugs that produce abortion, the child from strong meats and drinks, the
man from poisons.   So it is in the spiritual world ; tyranny and treachery, indolence and dulness, cannot but impede and impair the immutable law of nature
and necessary growth.   These and their like must be and must pass away ; the
eternal body of things must change.   As the fanatic abstains through fear of God
or of hell, the free-thinker abstains from what he sees or thinks to be evil (*i. e.*,
adverse or alien to his nature at its best) through respect for what he is and
reverence for what he may be.   Pantheism therefore is no immoral creed, and
cannot be, if only because it is based upon faith in nature and rooted in respect
for it.   By faith in sight it attains to sight through faith.   It follows that pure
Theism is more immediately the contrary of this belief, more unacceptable and
more delusive in the eyes of its followers, than any scheme of doctrine or code of
revelation.   These, as we see by your Blake" (again), "the Pantheist may seize
and recast in the mould of his own faith.   But Theism, but the naked distinct
figure of God, whether or not he assume the nature of man, so long as this is mere
assumption and not the essence of his being—the clothes and not the body, the
body and not the soul—this is to him incredible, the source of all evil and error.
Grant such a God his chance of existence, what reason has the Theist to suppose
or what right to assume his wisdom or his goodness ? why this and not that?
whence his acceptance and whence his rejection of anything that is? 'Shall the
clay demand of the potter, why hast thou made me thus ?'   Shall it not ? and
why ?   Of whom else should a man ask ? and if sure of his God, what better
should he do ? Theism is not expansive, but exclusive : and the creeds begotten
or misbegotten on this lean body of belief are 'Satanic' in the eyes of a
Pantheist, as his faith is in the eyes of their followers."   There is much more,
but it were superfluous to mix a narcotic over strong : and in pursuit of his
flying "faith" my friend's ideal "Pantheist" is apt to become heretical.

half-blasted trees round which huddled forms of women or men cower and cling, strange beasts and splendid flowers, alternate with the engraved text; and throughout all the sunbeams of heaven and fires of hell shed fiercer or softer light. In minute splendour and general effect the pages of Blake's next work fall short of these; though in the *Visions of the Daughters of Albion* the separate designs are fuller and more composed. This poem, written in a sort of regular though quasi-lyrical blank verse, is more direct and lucid in purpose than most of these books ; but the style is already laxer, veers more swiftly from point to point, stands weaker on its feet, and speaks with more of a hurried and hysterical tone. With " formidable moral questions," as the biographer has observed, it does assuredly deal ; and in a way somewhat formidable. This, we are told, " the exemplary man had good right to do." Exemplary or not, he in common with all men had undoubtedly such a right ; and was not slow to use it. Nowhere else has the prophet so fully and vehemently set forth his doctrine of indulgence ; too Albigensian or antinomian this time to be given out again in more decorous form. Of pure mythology there is happily little ; of pure allegory even less. " The eye sees more than the heart knows ;" these words are given on the title-page by way of motto or key-note. Above this inscription a single design fills the page ; in it the title is written with characters of pale fire upon cloud and rainbow ; the figure of the typical woman, held fast to earth but by one foot, seems to soar and yearn upwards with straining limbs that flutter like shaken flame : appealing in vain to the mournful and merciless

Creator, whose sad fierce face looks out beyond and over her, swathed and cradled in bloodlike fire and drifted rain. In the prologue we get a design expressive of plain and pure pleasure; a woman gathers a child from the heart of a blossom as it breaks, and the sky is full of the golden stains and widening roses of a sundawn. But elsewhere, from the frontispiece to the end, nothing meets us but emblems of restraint and error; figures rent by the beaks of eagles though lying but on mere cloud, chained to no solid rock by the fetters only of their own faiths or fancies; leafless trunks that rot where they fell; cold ripples of barren sea that break among caves of bondage. The perfect woman, Oothoon, is one with the spirit of the great western world; born for rebellion and freedom, but half a slave yet, and half a harlot. "Bromion," the violent Titan, subject himself to ignorance and sorrow, has defiled her;* "Theotormon," her lover, emblem of man held in bondage to creed or law, will not become one with her because of her shame; and she, who gathered in time of innocence the natural flower of delight, calls now for his eagles to rend her polluted flesh with cruel talons of remorse and ravenous beaks of shame: enjoys his infliction, accepts her agony, and reflects his severe smile in the mirrors of her purged spirit.†

---

* That is, woman has become subject to oppression of customs; suffers violence at the hands of marriage laws and other such condemnable things. "Emancipation" and the cognate creeds of which later days have heard so much never had a more violent and vehement preacher. Not love, not the plucking of the flower, but error, fear, submission to custom and law, is that which "defiles" a woman in the sight of our prophet.

† Even thus told, the myth is plain enough; a word or two of briefer translation may serve also to light up future allusions. "I plucked Leutha's flower," says Oothoon in the prelude of this poem, "and I was not ashamed;" the flower that brings forth a child, which nature permits and desires her to gather :

But he

> " sits wearing the threshold hard
> With secret tears ; beneath him sound like waves on a desert shore
> The voice of slaves beneath the sun, and children bought with money."

From her long melodious lamentation we give one continuous excerpt here. Sweet and lucid as *Thel,* it is more subtle and more strong ; the allusions to American servitude and English aspiration, which elsewhere distract and distort the sense and scheme of the poem, are here well cleared away.

> " I cry Arise, O Theotormon ; for the village dog
> Barks at the breaking day ; the nightingale has done lamenting ;
> The lark does rustle in the green corn, and the eagle returns
> From nightly prey and lifts his golden beak to the pure east ;
> Shaking the dust from his immortal pinions, to awake
> The sun that sleeps too long. Arise my Theotormon, I am pure
> Because the night is gone that closed me in its deadly black.
> They told me that the night and day were all that I could see ;
> They told me that I had five senses to enclose me up,
> And they enclosed my infinite beam into a narrow circle,
> And sank my heart into the abyss, a red round globe hotburning
> Till all from life I was obliterated and erased:
>
> Instead of morn arises a bright shadow like an eye
> In the eastern cloud ; instead of night a sickly charnel-house.

Leutha is the spirit emblematic of physical pleasure, of sensual impulse and indulgence, from whom comes the "loose Bible" of Mahomet (*Song of Los*). But crossing the seas eastward to find her lover, the strong enslaved spirit of Europe, she, type of womanhood and freedom, is caught and chained as he by the force of conventional error and tyrannous habit, which makes her seem impure in his eyes ; so they sit bound back to back, afraid to love ; the eagles that tear her flesh are emblems of her lover's scorn ; vainly, a virgin at heart, she appeals to all the fair and fearless face of nature against her rival, the prurient modesty of custom, a virgin in face, a harlot at heart ; against unnatural laws of restraint upon youths and maidens, whose inevitable outcome is in the licentious alternative not less unnatural ; he will not answer but with vain and vague lamentation, will not turn himself and love her for all her crying : the mystery of things and thoughts, the tyranny of times and laws, is heavy upon them to the end. All forms of life but these are free to be fair and happy : only from east to west the prison-houses are full of the wailing of women.

But Theotormon hears me not : to him the night and morn
Are both alike ; a night of sighs, a morning of fresh tears.
And none but Bromion can hear my lamentations.

With what sense is it that the chicken shuns the ravenous hawk ?
With what sense does the tame pigeon measure out the expanse ?
With what sense does the bee form cells ? have not the mouse and frog
Eyes and ears and sense of touch ? yet are their habitations
And their pursuits as different as their forms and as their joy.
Ask the wild ass why he refuses burdens, and the meek camel
Why he loves man : is it because of eye, ear, mouth or skin,
Or breathing nostrils ? no : for these the wolf and tiger have.
Ask the blind worm the secrets of the grave and why her spires
Love to curl around the bones of death : and ask the ravenous snake
Where she gets poison ; and the winged eagle why he loves the sun ;
And then tell me the thoughts of man, that have been hid of old.

Silent I hover all the night, and all day could be silent,
If Theotormon once would turn his loved eyes upon me ;
How can I be defiled when I reflect thy image pure ?
Sweetest the fruit that the worm feeds on, and the soul prey'd on by
    woe ;
The new-washed lamb tinged with the village smoke, and the bright
    swan
By the red earth of our immortal river ; I bathe my wings
And I am white and pure to hover round Theotormon's breast.

Then Theotormon broke his silence, and he answered ;
Tell me what is the night or day to one overflowed with woe ?
Tell me what is a thought ? and of what substance is it made ?
Tell me what is joy ? and in what gardens do joys grow ?
And in what rivers swim the sorrows ? and upon what mountains
Wave shadows of discontent ? and in what houses dwell the wretched
Drunken with woe forgotten, and shut up from cold despair ?

Tell me where dwell the thoughts forgotten till thou call them forth ?
Tell me where dwell the joys of old ? and where the ancient loves ?
And when will they renew again and the night of oblivion be past ?
That I might traverse times and spaces far remote and bring
Comfort into a present sorrow and a night of pain !
Where goest thou, O thought ? to what remote land is thy flight ?
If thou returnest to the present moment of affliction
Wilt thou bring comforts on thy wings and dews and honey and balm
Or poison from the desert wilds, from the eyes of the envier ? "

After this Bromion, with less musical lamentation, asks

whether for all things there be not one law established ?
" Thou knowest that the ancient trees seen by thine eyes
have fruit; but knowest thou that trees and fruits flou-
rish upon the earth to gratify senses unknown, in worlds
over another kind of seas ? " Are there other wars,
other sorrows, and other joys than those of external life ?
But the one law surely does, exist " for the lion and the ox,"
for weak and strong, wise and foolish, gentle and fierce ;
and for all who rebel against it there are prepared from
everlasting the fires and the chains of hell. So speaks
the violent slave of heaven ; and after a day and a night
Oothoon lifts up her voice in sad rebellious answer and
appeal.

" O Urizen, Creator of men ! mistaken Demon of heaven !
Thy joys are tears : thy labour vain, to form man to thine image ;
How can one joy absorb another ? are not different joys
Holy, eternal, infinite ? and each joy is a Love.

Does not the great mouth laugh at a gift ? and the narrow eyelids mock
At the labour that is above payment ? and wilt thou take the ape
For thy counsellor, or the dog for a schoolmaster to thy children ?
    *   *   *   *
Does the whale worship at thy footsteps as the hungry dog ?
Or does he scent the mountain prey, because his nostrils wide
Draw in the ocean ? does his eye discern the flying cloud
As the raven's eye ? or does he measure the expanse like the vulture ?
Does the still spider view the cliffs where eagles hide their young ?
Or does the fly rejoice because the harvest is brought in ?
Does not the eagle scorn the earth and despise the treasures beneath ?
But the mole knoweth what is there, and the worm shall tell it thee."

Perhaps there is no loftier note of music and of thought
struck anywhere throughout these prophecies. For the
rest, we must tread carefully over the treacherous hot
ashes strewn about the latter end of this book : which
indeed speaks plainly enough for once, and with high

equal eloquence; but to no generally acceptable effect. The one matter of marriage laws is still beaten upon, still hammered at with all the might of an insurgent prophet : to whom it is intolerable that for the sake of mere words and mere confusions of thought "she who burns with youth and knows no fixed lot" should be "bound by spells of law to one she loathes," should "drag the chain of life in weary lust," and "bear the wintry rage of a harsh terror driven to madness, bound to hold a rod over her shrinking shoulders all the day, and all the night to turn the wheel of false desire;" intolerable that she should be driven by "longings that wake her womb" to bring forth not men but some monstrous "abhorred birth of cherubs," imperfect, artificial, abortive ; counterfeits of holiness and mockeries of purity ; things of barren or per-verse nature, creatures inhuman or diseased, that live as a pestilence lives and pass away as a meteor passes ; "till the child dwell with one he hates, and do the deed he loathes, and the impure scourge force his seed into its unripe birth ere yet his eyelids can behold the arrows of the day :" the day whose blinding beams had surely somewhat affected the prophet's own eyesight, and left his eyelids lined with strange colours of fugitive red and green that fades into black. However, all these things shall be made plain by death ; for "over the porch is written Take thy bliss, O man ! and sweet shall be thy taste, and sweet thy infant joys renew." On the one hand is innocence, on the other modesty ; infancy is "fearless, lustful, happy;" who taught it modesty, "subtle modesty, child of night and sleep?" Once taught to dissemble, to call pure things impure, to "catch virgin joy, and brand it with the name of whore and sell it in the night;" once corrupted and misled, "religious dreams and holy vespers light thy smoky fires: once were thy fires lighted by the eyes of honest morn." Not pleasure but hypocrisy is the unclean thing; Oothoon is no harlot, but "a virgin filled with virgin fancies, open to joy and to delight wherever it appears; if in the morning sun I find it, there my eyes are fixed in happy copulation:" and so forth—further than we need follow.

"Is it because acts are not lovely that thou seekest solitude
Where the horrible darkness is impressed with reflections of desire?—

Father of Jealousy, be thou accursed from the earth!
Why hast thou taught my Theotormon this accursed thing?
Till beauty fades from off my shoulders, darkened and cast out,
A solitary shadow wailing on the margin of non-entity;"

as in a later prophecy Ahania, cast out by the jealous God, being the type or embodiment of this sacred natural love "free as the mountain wind."

"Can that be love which drinks another as a sponge drinks water?
That clouds with jealousy his nights, with weepings all the days?
  *   *   *   *   *   *
Such is self-love, that envies all; a creeping skeleton
With lamp-like eyes watching around the frozen marriage-bed."

But instead of the dark-grey "web of age" spun around man by self-love, love spreads nets to catch for him all wandering and foreign pleasures, pale as mild silver or ruddy as flaming gold; beholds them without grudging drink deep of various delight, "red as the rosy morning, lustful as the first-born beam." No single law for all things alike; the sun will not shine in the miser's secret chamber, nor the brightest cloud drop fruitful rain on his stone threshold; for one thing night

is good and for another thing day: nothing is good
and nothing evil to all at once.

" 'The sea-fowl takes the wintry blast for a covering to her limbs,
And the wild snake the pestilence, to adorn him with gems and gold;
And trees and birds and beasts and men behold their eternal joy.
Arise, you little glancing wings, and sing your infant joy!
Arise and drink your bliss! For everything that lives is holy.'

Thus every morning wails Oothoon, but Theotormon sits
Upon the margined ocean, conversing with shadows dire.

The daughters of Albion hear her woes, and echo back her sighs."

It may be feared that Oothoon has yet to wait long
before Thetoormon will leave off "conversing with
shadows dire;" nor is it surprising that this poem won
such small favour; for had it not seemed inexplicable it
must have seemed unbearable. Blake, as evidently as
Shelley, did in all innocence believe that ameliorated
humanity would be soon qualified to start afresh on
these new terms after the saving advent of French and
American revolutions. "All good things are in the
West;" thence in the teeth of "Urizen" shall human
deliverance come at length. In the same year Blake's
prophecy of *America* came forth to proclaim this message over again. Upon this book we need not dwell so
long; it has more of thunder and less of lightning than
the former prophecies; more of sonorous cloud and less
of explicit fire. The prelude, though windy enough,
is among Blake's nobler myths: the divine spirit of
rebellious redemption, imprisoned as yet by the gods of
night and chaos, is fed and sustained in secret by the
"nameless" spirit of the great western continent; nameless and shadowy, a daughter of chaos, till the day of
their fierce and fruitful union.

" Silent as despairing love and strong as jealousy,
The hairy shoulders rend the links, free are the wrists of fire."

At his embrace "she cast aside her clouds and smiled her first-born smile, as when a black cloud shows its lightnings to the silent deep."

" Soon as she saw the terrible boy then burst the virgin's cry ;
I love thee ; I have found thee, and I will not let thee go.
Thou art the image of God who dwells in darkness of Africa,
And thou art fallen to give me life in regions of dark death."

Then begins the agony of revolution, her frost and his fire mingling in pain ; and the poem opens as with a sound and a light of storm. It is throughout in the main a mere expansion and dilution of the "Song of Liberty" which we have already heard ; and in the interludes of the great fight between Urizen and Orc the human names of American or English leaders fall upon the ear with a sudden incongruous clash : not perhaps unfelt by the author's ear also, but unheeded in his desire to make vital and vivid the message he came to deliver. The action is wholly swamped by the allegory ; hardly is it related how the serpent-formed "hater of dignities, lover of wild rebellion and transgressor of God's Law," arose in red clouds, " a wonder, a human fire;" "heat but not light went from him ;" "his terrible limbs were fire ;" his voice shook the ancient Druid temple of tyranny and faith, proclaiming freedom and "the fiery joy that Urizen perverted to ten commands ;" the "punishing demons" of the God of jealousy

" Crouch howling before their caverns deep like skins dried in the wind ;
They cannot smite the wheat nor quench the fatness of the earth ;
They cannot smite with sorrows nor subdue the plough and spade ;

For terrible men stand on the shores, and in their robes I see
Children take refuge from the lightnings.　＊　　　＊　　　＊　　　＊
Ah vision from afar! ah rebel form that rent the ancient heavens!
　　＊　　　＊　　　＊　　　＊　　　Red flames the crest rebellious
And eyes of death; the harlot womb oft opened in vain
Heaves in eternal circles, now the times are returned upon thee."

"Thus wept the angel voice" of the guardian-angel of
Albion; but the thirteen angels of the American provinces rent off their robes and threw down their sceptres
and cast in their lot with the rebel; gathered together
where on the hills

　　　　　　　" called Atlantean hills,
Because from their bright summits you may pass to the golden world,
An ancient palace, archetype of mighty emperies,
Rears its immortal pinnacles, built in the forest of God
By Ariston the king of beauty for his stolen bride."

A myth of which we are to hear no more, significant
probably of the rebellion of natural beauty against the
intolerable tyranny of God, from which she has to seek
shelter in the darkest part of his creation with the angelic
or dæmonic bridegroom (one of the descended "sons of
God") who has wedded her by stealth and built her a
secret shelter from the strife of divine things; where at
least nature may breathe freely and take pleasure;
whither also in their time congregate all other rebellious
forces and spirits at war with the Creator and his laws.
But the speech of "Boston's angel" we will at least transcribe: not without a wish that he had never since then
spoken more incoherently and less musically.

"Must the generous tremble and leave his joy to the idle, to the pestilence,
That mock him? who commanded this? what God? what Angel?
To keep the generous from experience, till the ungenerous
Are unrestrained performers of the energies of nature,
Till pity is become a trade and generosity a science

That men get rich by; and the sandy desert is given to the strong?
What God is he writes laws of peace and clothes him in a tempest?
What pitying Angel lusts for tears and fans himself with sighs?
What crawling villain preaches abstinence and wraps himself
In fat of lambs? no more I follow, no more obedience pay."

This is perhaps the finest and clearest passage in the book; and beyond this point there is not much extractable from the clamorous lyrical chaos. Here again besides the mere outward violence of battle, the visible plague and fire of war, we have sight of a subtler and wider revolution.

" For the female spirits of the dead pining in bonds of religion
Run from their fetters reddening and in long-drawn arches sitting.
They feel the nerves of youth renew, and desires of ancient times."

Light and warmth and colour and life are shed from the flames of revolution not alone on city and valley and hill, but likewise

" Over their pale limbs, as a vine when the tender grape appears;
    *   *   *   *   *   *
The heavens melted from north to south; and Urizen who sat
Above all heavens in thunders wrapt, emerged his leprous head
From out his holy shrine; his tears in deluge piteous
Falling into the deep sublime."

Notwithstanding for twelve years it was fated that "angels and weak men should govern o'er the strong, and then their end should come when France received the demon's light:" and the ancient European guardians " slow advance to shut the five gates of their law-built heaven, filled with blasting fancies and with mildews of despair, with fierce disease and lust;" but these gates were consumed in the final fire of revolution that went forth upon the world. So ends the poem; and of the decoration we have barely space to say enough. On one page are the visions of the renewed world, on another the emblems of oppression and war : children sleeping nestled in the fleece of a sleeping ram with heavy horns and quiet mouth pressing the soft ground, while overhead shapely branches droop and gracious birds are perched; or what seems the new-born body of Orc cast under the sea, enmeshed in a web of water whose waves are waves of corn when you come to look ; maidens and infants that bridle a strong dragon, and behind them a flight of birds through the clouds of a starry moonlit night, where a wild swan with vast wings and stretching neck is bestridden by a spirit looking eagerly back as he clutches the rein ; eagles that devour the dead on a stormy sea-beach, while underneath fierce pikes and sharks make towards a wrecked corpse that has sunk without drifting, and seasnakes wind about it in soft loathsome coils ; women and children embrace in bitter violence of loving passion among ripples of fruitful flame, out of which rise roots and grasses of the field and laden branches of the vine. Of all these we cannot hope to speak duly ; nor can we hope to give more than a glimpse of the work they illustrate.

Throughout the Prophecy of *Europe* the fervent and intricate splendours of text and decoration are whirled as it were and woven into spreading webs or twining wheels of luminous confusion. The Museum copy, not equal in nobility of colour to some others, is crowded with MS. notes and mottos of some interest and significance. To the frontispiece a passage of Milton is appended ; to the first page is prefixed a transcript of some verses by Mrs. Radcliffe concerning a murdered pilgrim, sufficiently execrable and explanatory; and so throughout. These notes will help us at least to measure the amount of connexion between the text and the designs; an amount easily measurable, being in effect about the smallest possible. Fierce fluctuating wind and the shaken light of meteors flutter or glitter upon the stormy ways of vision; serving rather for raiment than for symbol. The outcast gods of star and comet are driven through tempestuous air: "forms without body" leap or lurk under cloud or water; War, a man coated with scales of defiled and blackening bronze, handling a heavy sword-hilt, averts his face from appealing angels; Famine slays and eats her children; fire curls about the caldron in which their limbs are to be sodden for food; starved plague-stricken shapes of women and men fall shrieking or silent as the bell-ringer, a white-haired man with slouched hat drawn down and long straight cassock, passes them bell in hand; a daughter clings to her father in the dumb pain of fear, while he with arms thrust out in repulsion seems to plead against the gathering deluges that "sweep o'er the yellow year;" mildews are seen incarnate as foul flushed women with strenuous limbs contorted, blighting ears of corn with the violent breath of their inflated mouths; "Papal Superstition," with the triple crown on a head broader across cheek and jowl than across the forehead, with bat's wings and blood-like garments dripping and rent, leers across the open book on his knees; behind his reptile face a decoration as of a cleft mitre, wrought in the shape of Gothic windows that straiten as it ascends, shows grey upon the dead black air; this is "Urizen seen on the Atlantic; and his brazen book that kings and priests had copied on earth, expanded from north to south;" all the creeping things of the prison-house, bloated leaf and dropping spider, crawl or curl above a writhing figure overgrown with horrible scurf of corruption as with network; the gaoler leaves his prisoner fast bound by the ankles, with limbs stained and discoloured; (the motto to this is from "The Two Noble Kinsmen," Act ii., Sc. 1., "The vine shall grow, but we shall never see it," &c.); snakes and caterpillars, birds and gnats, each after their own kind take their pleasure and their prey among the leaves and grasses they defile and devour; flames chase the naked or swooning fugitives from a blazing ruin. The prelude is set in the frame of two large designs; one of the assassin waiting for the pilgrim as he turns round a sharp corner of rock; one of hurricane and storm in which "Horror, Amazement and Despair" appear abroad upon the winds. A sketch of these violent and hideously impossible figures is pasted into the note-book on a stray slip of paper. The MS. mottos are mostly from Milton and Dryden; Shakespeare and Fletcher, Rowe and Mason, are also dragged into service. The prophecy itself is full of melody and mist; of music not wholly unrecognisable and vapour not wholly impermeable. In a lull of intermittent war, the gods of time and space awake with all their children; Time bids them "seize all the spirits of life and bind their warbling joys to our loud strings, bind all the nourishing sweets of earth to give us bliss." Orc, the fiery spirit of revolution, first-born of Space, his father summons to arise; "and we will crown thy head with garlands of the ruddy vine ; for now thou art bound ; and I may see thee in the hour of bliss, my eldest born." Allegory, here as always, is interfused with myth in a manner at once violent and intricate ; but in this book the mere mythologic fancy of Blake labours for the most part without curb or guide.   Enitharmon, the universal or typical woman, desires that " woman may have dominion " for a space over all the souls upon earth ; she descends and becomes visible in the red light of Orc ; and she charges other spirits born of her and Los to " tell the human race that woman's love is sin," for thus the woman will have power to refuse or accede, to starve or satiate the perverted loves and lives of man; "that an eternal life awaits the worms of sixty winters, in an allegorical abode where existence hath never come; forbid all joy, and from her childhood shall the little female spread nets in every secret path."   To this end the goddess of Space calls forth her chosen children, the " horned priest" of animal nature, the " silver-bowed queen " of desolate places, the " prince of the sun " with his innumerable race " thick as the summer stars ; each one, ramping, his golden mane shakes, and thine eyes rejoice because of strength, O Rintrah, furious King." Moon and sun, spirit and flesh, all lovely jealous forces and mysteries of the natural world are gathered together under her law, that throughout the eighteen Christian centuries she may have her will of the world.   For so long nature has sat silent, her harps out of tune ; the goddess herself has slept out all those years, a dream among dreams, the ghostly regent of a ghostly generation. The angels of Albion, satellites once of the ancient Titan, are smitten now with their own plagues, crushed in their own council-house, and rise again but to follow after Rintrah, the fiery minister of his mother's triumph. Him the chief "Angel" follows to "his ancient temple serpent-formed," ringed round with Druid oaks, massive with pillar and porch built of precious stones; "such eternal in the heavens, of colours twelve, few known on earth, give light in the opaque."

> "Placed in the order of the stars, when the five senses whelmed
> In deluge o'er the earth-born man : then bound the flexile eyes
> Into two stationary orbs concentrating all things:
> The ever-varying spiral ascents to the heaven of heavens
> Were bended downward, and the nostril's golden gates shut,
> Turned outward, barred and petrified against the infinite.
> Thought changed the infinite to a serpent ; that which pitieth
> To a devouring flame ; and man fled from its face and hid
> In forests* of night ; then all the eternal forests were divided
> Into earths rolling in circles of space, that like an ocean rushed
> And overwhelmed all except this finite wall of flesh.
> Then was the serpent temple formed, image of (the) infinite
> Shut up in finite revolutions,† and man became an Angel ;
> Heaven a mighty circle turning ; God a tyrant crowned."

Thus again recurs the doctrine that the one inlet left us for spiritual perception—that namely of the senses—is but one and the least of many inlets and channels of communication now destroyed or perverted by the creative demon ; a tenet which once well grasped and digested by the disciple will further his understanding of Blake more than anything else can : will indeed, pushed to the full extreme of its logical results, elucidate and justify much

---

* Night, or the darkness of worlds yet undivided and chaotic, is always typified by Blake as a "forest" dark with involved and implicated leaf or branch. Compare "The Tiger."

† Along this page a serpent of imperious build rears the strong and sinuous length of his dusky glittering body, and spits forth keen undulating fire.

that seems merely condemnable and chaotic. To resume our somewhat halting and bewildered fable : the southern porch of this temple, " planted thick with trees of blackest leaf, and in a vale obscure, enclosed the stone of night ; oblique it stood, o'erhung with purple flowers and berries red ; " image of the human intellect " once open to the heavens " as the south to the sun ; now, as the head of fallen man, " overgrown with hair and covered with a stony roof ;" sunk deep " beneath the attractive north," where evil spirits are strongest, where the whirlpool of speculation sucks in the soul and entombs it. Standing on this, as on a watch-tower, the " Angel" beholds Religion enthroned over Europe, and the pale revolution of cloud and fire through the night of space and time ; beholds " Albion," the home once of ancient freedom and faith, trodden underfoot by laws and churches, that the God of religion may have wherewithal to " feed his soul with pity." At last begins the era of rebellion and change; the fires of Orc lay hold upon law* and gospel ; yet for a little while the ministers of his mother have power to fight against him, and she, allied now and making common cause with the God alien to her children, " laughs in her sleep," seeing through the veil and vapour of dreams the subjection of male to female, the false attribute of unnatural power given to women by faith and fear. Not as yet can the Promethean fire utterly dissolve the clouds of Urizen, though the flesh of the ministering angel of religion is already consumed or consuming ;

---

* It is possible that Blake intended here some grotesque emblematic reference to the riots witnessed by himself, in which Lord Mansfield's house and MSS. were destroyed by fire. At all events, here alone is there any visible allusion to a matter of recent history.

nor as yet can the trumpet of revolution summon the
dead to judgment. That first blast of summons must
be blown by material science, which destroys the letter
of the law and the text of the covenant. When the
" mighty spirit " of Newton had seized the trumpet
and blown it,

> " Yellow as leaves of Autumn the myriads of Angelic hosts
> Fell thro' the wintry skies seeking their graves,
> Rattling their hollow bones in howling and lamentation ; "

as to this day they do, and did in Blake's time, throughout whole barrowfuls of controversial "apologies" and
" evidences." Then the mother-goddess awoke from her
eighteen centuries of sleep, the " Christian era" being now
wellnigh consummated, and all those years "fled as if
they had not been ;" she called her children around her,
by many monstrous names and phrases of chaotic invocation ; comfort and happiness here, there sweet pestilence
and soft delusion ; the "seven churches of Leutha" seek
the love of " Antamon," symbolic of Christian faith recon-
ciled to " pagan" indulgence and divorced from Jewish
prohibition; even as we find in the prophet himself equal
faith in sensual innocence and spiritual truth. Of " the
soft Oothoon " the great goddess asks now " Why wilt
thou give up woman's secrecy, my melancholy child ?
Between two moments bliss is ripe." Last she calls
upon Orc ; "Smile, son of my afflictions ; arise and give
our mountains joy of thy red light."

> " She ceased ; for all were forth at sport beneath the solemn moon,
> Waking the stars of Urizen with their immortal songs,
> That nature felt thro' all her pores the enormous revelry.
> Till morning oped her eastern gate ;
> Then every one fled to his station ; and Enitharmon wept."

But with the dawn of that morning Orc descended in fire, " and in the vineyards of red France appeared the light of his fury." The revolution begins ; all space groans ; and lion and tiger are gathered together after their prey : the god of time arises as one out of a trance,

> " And with a cry that shook all nature to the utmost pole
> Called all his sons to the strife of blood."

Our study of the *Europe* might bring more profit if we could have genuine notes appended to the text as well as to the designs. Such worth or beauty as the poem has burns dim and looms distant by comparison ; but there is in it more of either than we have here time or means to indicate. At least the prelude so strangely selected for citation and thrown loose upon the pages of the biography in so crude and inexplicable a manner, may now be seen to have some tangible or presumable sense. The spirit of Europe rises revealed in the advent of revolution, sick of time and travail ; pleading with the mother-goddess, Cybele of this mythology ; wrapping about her veils of water and garments of cloud, in vain ; " the red sun and moon and all the overflowing stars rain down prolific pains." Out of her overlaboured womb arise forms and forces of change, fugitive fires of wrath, sonorous shapes of fear ; and they take substance in space, but bring to their mother no help or profit, no comfort or light ; to the virgin daughter of America freedom has come and fruitful violence of love, but not to the European mother. She has no hope in all the infinity of space and time ; " who shall bind the infinite with an eternal band, to compass it with swaddling bands ? " By comparison of the two preludes the relations of the two kindred poems may be better understood: the one is plaintive as the voice of a world in pain, and decaying kingdom by kingdom; the other fierce and hopeful as the cry of a nation in travail, whose agony is not that of death, but rather that of birth.

The First Book of Urizen is perhaps more shapeless and chaotic at a first glimpse than any other of these prose poems. Clouds of blood, shadows of horror, worlds without form and void, rise and mingle and wane in indefinite ways, with no special purpose or appreciable result. The myth here is of an active but unprolific God, warring with shapes of the wilderness, and at variance with the eternals: beaten upon by Time, who figures always in all his various shapes and actions as the saviour and friend of man. "Earth was not, nor globes of attraction; the will of the Immortal expanded or contracted at will his all-flexible senses. Death was not; but eternal life sprang." (1. Urizen, ii. 1.) Urizen, the God of restraint, creator of prohibition, whose laws are forbearance and abstinence, is for ages divided from Eternity and at war with Time; "long periods in burning fires labouring, till hoary, and age-broken, and aged, in despair and the shadows of death." (1. Urizen, iii. 6.) In time the formless God takes form, creating and assuming feature by feature; bones, heart, eyes, ears, nostrils, throat with tongue, hands with feet; an age of agony being allotted to each of the seven created features; still toiling in fire and beset by snares, which the Time-Spirit kindles and weaves to avert and destroy in its birth the desolate influence of the Deity who forbids and restrains.

These transformations of Urizen make up some of Blake's grandest and strangest prophetic studies. First the spinal skeleton, with branchwork of rib and savage nudity of joint and clavicle, shaped mammoth-wise, in grovelling involution of limb. In one copy at least these bones are touched with dim green and gold colour ; such a faint fierce tint as one might look for on the cast scales or flakes of dragons left astrand in the ebb of a deluge. Next a huge fettered figure with blind shut eyes over-flowing into tears, with convulsed mouth and sodden stream of beard : then bones painfully gathering flesh, twisted forms round which flames break out fourfold, tortured elemental shapes that plunge and writhe and moan. Until Time, divided against himself, brings forth Space, the universal eternal female element, called Pity among the gods, who recoil in fear from the dawn of human creation and division. Of these two divinities, called in the mythology Los and Enitharmon, is born the man-child Orc. "The dead heard the voice of the child and began to awake from sleep ; all things heard the voice of the child and began to awake to life." (vii. 5.) Here again we may spare a word or two for that splendid figure (p. 20) of the new-born child falling aslant through cloven fire that curls and trembles into spiral blossoms of colour and petals of feverish light. And the children of Urizen were Thiriel, born from cloud ; Utha, from water ; Grodna, from earth ; Fuzon, "first-begotten, last-born," from fire—"and his daughters from green herbs and cattle, from monsters and worms of the pit. He cursed both sons and daughters ; for he saw that no flesh nor spirit could keep his iron laws one moment." (viii. 3, 4.)

Then from his sorrows for these his children begotten on the material body of nature, the web of religion begins to unwind and expand, "throwing out from his sorrowing soul, the dungeon-like heaven dividing" (viii. 6)—and the knotted meshes of the web to involve all races and cities. "The Senses inward rushed shrinking beneath the dark net of infection : till the shrunken eyes, clouded over, discerned not the woven hypocrisy ; but the streaky slime in their heavens, brought together by narrowing perceptions, appeared transparent air ; for their eyes grew small like the eyes of a man. Six days they shrank up from existence, and the seventh day they rested, and they blessed the seventh day, in sick hope ; and forgot their eternal life." (1. Urizen, ix. 1, 2, 3.) Hence grows the animal tyranny of gravitation, and hence also the spiritual tyranny of law ; "they lived a period of years, then left a noisome body to the jaws of devouring darkness ; and their children wept, and built tombs in the desolate places ; and formed laws of prudence and called them the eternal laws of God." (ix. 4, 5.) Seeing these his brethren degraded into life and debased into flesh, the son of the fire, Fuzon, called together "the remaining children of Urizen ; and they left the pendulous earth : they called it Egypt, and left it. And the salt ocean rolled englobed." (ix. 8, 9.) The freer and stronger spirits left the world of men to the dominion of earth and water ; air and fire were withdrawn from them, and there were left only the heaviness of imprisoning clay and the bitterness of violent sea.

This is a hurried and blotted sketch of the main myth, which is worth following up by those who would enter on any serious study of Blake's work; all that is here indicated in dim hints being afterwards assumed as the admitted groundwork of later and larger myths. In this present book (and in it only) the illustrative work may be said almost to overweigh and stifle the idea illustrated. Strange semi-human figures, clad in sombre or in fiery flesh, racing through fire or sinking through water, allure and confuse the fancy of the student. Every page vibrates with light and colour; on none of his books has the artist lavished more noble profusion of decorative work. It is worth observing that while some copies are carefully numbered throughout "First Book," in others the word "First" is erased from every leaf: as in effect the Second Book never was put forth under that title. Next year however the *Book of Ahania* came out—if one may say as much of a quarto of six leaves which has hardly yet emerged into sight of two or three readers. This we may take—or those may who please—to be the *Second Book of Urizen*. It is among the choicer spoils of Blake, not as yet cast into the public treasury; for the Museum has no copy, though possessing (in its blind confused way) duplicates of *America, Albion,* and *Los.* Some day, one must hope, there will at least be a complete accessible collection of Blake's written works arranged in rational order for reference. Till the dawn of that day people must make what shift they can in chaos.

In *Ahania*, though a fine and sonorous piece of wind-music, we have not found many separate notes worth striking. Formless as these poems may seem, it is often the floating final impression of power which makes them

memorable and valuable, rather than any stray gleam of
purple or glitter of pearl on the skirt. Thus the myth
runs—to the best of its power; but the tether of it is but
short.

Fuzon, born of the fiery part of the God of nature, in
revolt against his father, divides him in twain as with a
beam of fire; the desire of Urizen is separated from him;
this divided soul, "his invisible lust," he sees now as she
is apart from himself, and calls Sin; seizes her on
his mountains of jealousy; kisses and weeps over her,
then casts her forth and hides her in cloud, in dumb
distance of mysterious space; "jealous though she was
invisible." Divided from him, she turns to mere shadow
"unseen, unbodied, unknown, the mother of Pestilence."
But the beam cast by Fuzon was light upon earth—
light to "Egypt," the house of bondage and place of
captivity for the outcast human children of Urizen.
Thus far the book floats between mere allegory and
creative myth; not difficult however to trace to the root
of its purport. From this point it grows, if not wilder
in words, still mistier in build of limb and shape of
feature. Fuzon, smitten by the bow of Urizen, seems to
typify dimly the Christian or Promethean sacrifice; the
revolted God or son of God, who giving to men some help
or hope to enlighten them, is slain for an atonement to
the wrath of his father : though except for the mythical
sonship Prometheus would be much the nearer parallel.
The bow, formed in secresy of the nerves of a slain
dragon "scaled and poisonous-horned," begotten of the
contemplations of Urizen and destroyed by him in combat, must be another type, half conceived and hardly at

all wrought out, of the secret and jealous law of intro-
spective faith divided against itself and the god of its
worship, but strong enough to smite the over-confident
champion of men even in his time of triumph, when he
"thought Urizen slain by his wrath : I am God, said he,
eldest of things." (II. 8.) Suddenly the judgment of
the jealous wrath of God falls upon him ; the rock hurled
as an arrow "enters his bosom ; his beautiful visage, his
tresses that gave light to the mornings of heaven, were
smitten with darkness.—But the rock fell upon the earth,
Mount Sinai, in Arabia : " being indeed a type of the
moral law of Moses, sent to destroy and suppress the
native rebellious energies and active sins of men. Here
one may catch fast hold of one thing—the identity of
Blake's " Urizen," at least for this time, with the Deity of
the earlier Hebrews ; the God of the Law and Decalogue
rather than of Job or the Prophets. " On the accursed
tree of mystery" that shoots up under his heel from
"tears and sparks of vegetation " fallen on the barren
rock of separation, where " shrunk away from Eternals,"
alienated from the ancient freedom of the first Gods or
Titans, averse to their large and liberal laws of life, the
jealous God sat secret—on the topmost stem of this tree
Urizen "nailed the corpse of his first-begotten." Thence-
forward there fell upon the half-formed races of men
sorrow only and pestilence, barren pain of unprofitable
fruit and timeless burden of desire and disease. One
need not sift the myth too closely ; it would be like
winnowing water and weighing cloud with scale or sieve.
The two illustrations, it may here be said, are very slight
—mere hints of a design, and merely touched with colour.

In the frontispiece Ahania, divided from Urizen, floats
upon a stream of wind between hill and cloud, with hag-
gard limbs and straightened spectral hair; on the last
leaf a dim Titan, wounded and bruised, lies among rocks
flaked with leprous lichen and shaggy with bloodlike
growths of weed and moss.   One final glimpse we may
take of Ahania after her division—the love of God, as it
were, parted from God, impotent therefore and a shadow,
if not rather a plague and blight; mercy severed from
justice, and thus made a worse thing than useless.   Such
may be the hinted meaning, or at least some part of it;
but the work, it must be said, holds by implication dim
and great suggestions of something more than our analytic ingenuities can well unravel by this slow process of
suggestion.   Properly too Ahania seems rather to represent the divine generative desire or love, translated on
earth into sexual expression; the female side of the
creative power—mother of all things made.

"The lamenting voice of Ahania weeping upon the void and round the
Tree of Fuzon. Distant in solitary night her voice was heard, but no form
had she; but her tears from clouds eternal fell round the Tree.   And the
voice cried 'Ah Urizen! Love! Flower of morning! I weep on the verge
of non-entity: how wide the abyss between Ahania and thee! I lie on
the verge of the deep, I see thy dark clouds ascend; I see thy black forests
and floods, a horrible waste to my eyes.   Weeping I walk over the rocks,
over dens, and through valleys of death.   Why dost thou despise Ahania,
to cast me from thy bright presence into the world of loneness? I cannot
touch his hand; nor weep on his knees; nor hear his voice and bow; nor
see his eyes and joy; nor hear his footsteps, and my heart leap at the
lovely sound; I cannot kiss the place where his bright feet have trod:
but I wander on the rocks with hard necessity.   Where is my golden
palace? where my ivory bed? where the joy of my morning hour? where
the sons of eternity singing to awake bright Urizen my king to arise to
the mountain sport, to the bliss of eternal valleys, to awake my king in
the morn, to embrace Ahania's joy on the breath of his open bosom; from
my soft cloud of dew to fall in showers of life on his harvest?   When he

gave my happy soul to the sons of eternal joy; when he took the daughters of life into my chambers of love; when I found babes of bliss on my beds and bosoms of milk in my chambers, filled with eternal seed. O! eternal births sung round Ahania in interchange sweet of their joys; swelled with ripeness and fat with fatness, bursting in clouds my odours, my ripe figs and rich pomegranates, in infant joy at thy feet, O Urizen, sported and sang: then thou with thy lap full of seed, with thy hand full of generous fire, walkedst forth from the clouds of morning, on the virgins of springing joy, on the human soul, to cast the seed of eternal science. The sweat poured down thy temples, to Ahania returned in evening; the moisture awoke to birth my mother's joys sleeping in bliss. But now alone over rocks, mountains—cast out from thy lovely bosom— cruel jealousy! selfish fear! self-destroying! how can delight renew in these chains of darkness, where bones of beasts are strewn on the bleak and snowy mountains, where bones from the birth are buried before they see the light?' "—*Ahania*, ch. v., v. 1—14.

With the prolonged melody of this lament the *Book of Ahania* winds itself up; one of the most musical among this crowd of singing shadows. In the same year the last and briefest of this first prophetic series was engraved. The *Song of Los*, broken into two divisions headed *Africa* and *Asia*, has more affinity to *Urizen* and *Ahania* than to *Europe* and *America*. The old themes of delusion and perversion are once again rehandled; not without vigorous harmonies of choral expression. The illustrations are of special splendour, as though designed to atone for the lean and denuded form in which *Ahania* had been sent forth. In the frontispiece a grey old giant, clothed from the waist only with heavy raiment of livid and lurid white, bows down upon a Druid altar before the likeness of a darkened sun low-hung in heaven, filled with sombre and fiery forms of things, and shooting out upon each quarter a broad reflected ray like the reflection struck by sunlight from a broad bare sword-blade, but touched also, as with strange infection, with flakes of deadly colour that vibrate upon the starless solid ground of an intolerable night. Less of menace with more of sadness is in the landscape and sky on the title-page: a Titan, with one weighty hand lying on a gigantic skull, rests at the edge of a green sloping moor, himself seeming a grey fragment of moorland rock; brown fire of waste grass or rusted flower stains crag and bent all round him; the sky is all night and fire, bitter red and black. On the first page a serpent, splendid with blood-red specks and scales of greenish blue, darts the cloven flame of its tongue against a brilliant swarm of flies; and again throughout the divided lines a network of fair tortuous things, of flickering leaf and sinuous tendril and strenuous root, flashes and curls from margin to margin.

This song is the song of Time, sung to the four harps of the world, each continent a harp struck by Time as by a harper. In brief dim words it celebrates the end of the world of the patriarchs where faith and freedom were one, the advent of the iron laws and ages, when God the Accuser gave his laws to the nations by the hands of the children of time: when to the extreme east was given mere abstract philosophy for faith instead of clear pure belief, and man became slave to the elements, the slave and not the lord of the nature of things; but not yet was philosophy a mere matter of the five senses. Thus they fared in the east; meantime the spirits of the patriarchal world shrank beneath waters or fled in fires, Adam from Eden, Noah from Ararat; and "Moses beheld upon Mount Sinai forms of dark delusion." Over each religion, Indian and

Jewish and Grecian, some special demon or god of the mythology is bidden preside ; Christianity, the expression of human sorrow, human indulgence and forgiveness, was given as gospel to " a man of sorrows " by the two afflicted spirits who typify man and woman, in whom the bitter errors and the sore needs of either several sex upon earth are reproduced in vast vague reflection ; to them therefore the gentler gospel belongs as of right. Next comes Mahometanism, to give some freedom and fair play to the controlled and abused senses ; but northwards other spirits set on foot a code of war to satiate their violent delight. So on all sides is the world overgrown with kingdoms and churches, codes and creeds ; inspiration is crushed and erased ; the sons of Time and Space reign alone ; Har and Heva, the spirits of loftier and purer kind who were not as the rest of the Titan brood that " lived in war and lust," are fled and fallen, become as mere creeping things ; and the world is ripe to bring forth for its cruel and mournful God the final fruit of reason debased and faith distorted.

> " Thus the terrible race of Los and Enitharmon gave
> Laws and Religions to the sons of Har, binding them more
> And more to Earth, closing and restraining ;
> Till a Philosophy of Five Senses was complete ;
> Urizen wept, and gave it into the hands of Newton and Locke."

These " terrible sons " of time and space are the presiding demons of each creed or code ; the sons of men are in their hands now, for the father and mother of men are fallen gods, oblivious and transformed : and these minor demons are all subservient to the Creator, whose soul, sorrowful but not merciful, animates the whole pained world. So, with cloud of menace and fire of wrath shed out about the deceased gods and the new philosophies, the first part ends. In the second part the clouds have broken and the fire has come forth; revolution has begun in Europe; the ancient lords of Asia are startled from their dens and cry in bitterness of soul for help of the old oppressions; for councillors and for taxes, for plagues and for priests, " to turn man from his path; to restrain the child from the womb; to cut off the bread from the city, that the remnant may learn to obey : that the pride of the heart may fail; that the lust of the eye may be quenched; that the delicate ear in its infancy may be dulled, and the nostrils closed up; to teach mortal worms the path that leads from the gates of the grave." At their cry Urizen arose, the lord of Asia from of old, ever since he cast down the patriarchal law and set up the Mosaic code; " his shuddering waving wings went enormous above the red flames," to contend with the rekindled revolution, " the thick-flaming thought-creating fires of Orc ;"

> " His books of brass, iron, and gold
> Melted over the land as he flew,
> Heavy-waving, howling, weeping.
> And he stood over Judea,
> And stayed in his ancient places,
> And stretched his clouds over Jerusalem.
> For Adam, a mouldering skeleton,
> Lay bleached on the garden of Eden ;
> And Noah, as white as snow,
> On the mountains of Ararat."

Thus, with thunder from eastward and fire from westward, the God of jealousy and the Spirit of freedom met together; earth shrank at the meeting of them.

> " Forth from the dead dust rattling bones to bones
> Came; shaking, convulsed, the shivering clay breathes;
> And all flesh naked stands; Fathers and Friends;
> Mothers and Infants; Kings and Warriors;
> The Grave shrieks with delight, and shakes
> Her hollow womb, and clasps the solid stem;
> Her bosom swells with wild desire;
> And milk and blood and glandous wine
> In rivers rush and shout and dance
> On mountain, dale and plain.
>   The Song of Los is ended.
>   Urizen wept."

So much for the text; which has throughout a contagious power of excitement in the musical passion of its speech. For these books, above all, it is impossible to read continuously and not imbibe a certain half-nervous enjoyment from their long cadences and tempestuous undulations of melody. Such passion went to the writing of them that some savour of that strong emotion infects us also in reading pages which seem still hot from the violent touch of the poet. The design of Har and Heva flying from their lustful and warlike brethren across green waste land before a late and thunder-coloured sky, he grasping her with convulsive fear, she looking back as she runs with lifted arm and flame-like hair and fiery flow of raiment; and that succeeding where they reappear fallen to mere king and queen of the vegetable world, themselves half things of vegetable life; are both noble if somewhat vehement and reckless. In this latter, the deep green-blue heaven full of stars like flowers is set with sweet and deep effect against the darkening green of the vast lily-leaves supporting the fiery pallor of those shapely chalices which enclose as the heart of either blossom the queen lying at her length, and the king sitting with bright plucked-out pistil in hand by way of sceptre or sword; and below them the dim walls of the world alone are wholly black : his robes of soft shot purple and red, her long chrysalid shell or husk of tarnished gold, are but signs of their bondage and fall from deity ; they are fallen to be mere flowers.   More might be said of the remaining designs ; the fierce glory of sweeping branches and driven leaves in a strong wind, the fervent sky and glimmering hill, the crouching figures above and under, the divine insane luxuriance of cloudy and flowery colour which makes twice luminous the last page of the poem ; the strange final design where a spirit with huge childlike limbs and lifted hair seems to smite with glittering mallet the outer rim of a huger blood-red sun ; but for this book we have no more space; and much laborious travel lies ahead of us yet.

With the *Song of Los* the first or London series of prophecies came to a close not unfit or unmelodious.   As their first word had been Revelation, their last was Revolution.   We have now to deal with the two later and larger books written at Felpham, but not put forth till 1804.   To one of these at least we must allow some tolerably full notice.   The *Milton* shall here take precedence.   This poem, though sufficiently vexatious to the human sense at first sight, is worth some care and some admiration.   Its preface must here be read in full.

" The stolen and perverted writings of Homer and Ovid, of Plato and Cicero, which all men ought to contemn, are set up by artifice against the sublime of the Bible ; but when the New Age is at leisure to pronounce, all will be set right, and those grand works of the more ancient and consciously and professedly inspired men, will hold their proper rank ; and the daughters of memory shall become the daughters of inspiration. Shakespeare and Milton were both curbed by the general malady and infection from the silly Greek and Latin slaves of the sword. Rouse up, O young men of the New Age ! set your foreheads against the ignorant hirelings ! For we have hirelings in the camp, the court, and the university; who would, if they could, for ever depress mental and prolong corporeal war. Painters ! on you I call ! Sculptors ! Architects ! suffer not the fashionable fools to depress your powers by the prices they pretend to give for contemptible works or the expensive advertising boasts that they make of such works : believe Christ and his Apostles, that there is a class of men whose whole delight is in destroying. We do not want either Greek or Roman models if we are but just and true to our own imaginations, those worlds of eternity in which we shall live for ever, in Jesus our Lord.

> And did those feet in ancient time
> Walk over England's mountains green ?
> And was the holy Lamb of God
> On England's pleasant pastures seen ?
>
> And did the Countenance Divine
> Shine forth upon our clouded hills ?
> And was Jerusalem builded here,
> Among these dark Satanic mills ?
>
> Bring me my bow of burning gold ;
> Bring me my arrows of desire ;
> Bring me my spear : O clouds, unfold ;
> Bring me my chariot of fire.
>
> I will not cease from mental fight,
> Nor shall my sword sleep in my hand,
> Till we have built Jerusalem
> In England's green and pleasant land.

' Would to God that all the Lord's people were prophets.'—Numbers xi. 29."

After this strange and grand prelude, which, though taken in the letter it may read like foolishness, is in the spirit of it certainty and truth for all time, we pass again under the shadow and into the land that shifts and slips under our feet. Something however out of the chaos of fire and wind and stormy colour may be caught at by fits and stored up for such as can like it. Thus the poem opens, with not less fervour and splendour of sound than usual.

> "Daughters of Beulah! Muses who inspire the Poet's Song!
> Record the journey of immortal Milton thro' your realms
> Of terror and mild moony lustre, in soft sexual delusions
> Of varied beauty, to delight the wanderer and repose
> His burning thirst and freezing hunger! Come into my hand,
> By your mild power descending down the Nerves of my right arm
> From out the Portals of my Brain, where by your ministry
> The Eternal Great Humanity Divine planted his Paradise
> And in it caused the Spectres of the Dead to take sweet forms
> In likeness of himself."

(Observe here the answer by anticipation to the old foolish charge of madness and belief in mere material visions ; a charge indeed refuted and confuted at every turn we take. Thus, and no otherwise, did Blake believe in his dead visitors and models : as spectres formed into new and significant shape by God, after his own likeness ; *not* called up as by some witch of Endor and reclothed with the rags and rottenness of their dead old bodies ; creatures existing within the brain and imagination of the workman, not as they were once externally and by accident, but as they will be for ever by the essence and substance of their nature. For the "vegetated shadow" or "human vegetable" no mystic ever had deeper or subtler contempt than Blake ; nor was ever a man less likely to care about raising or laying it after death.)

> "Tell also of the False Tongue! vegetated
> Beneath your land of shadows; of its sacrifices, and
> Its offerings: even till Jesus, the image of the Invisible God,
> Became its prey; a curse, an offering, and an atonement
> For Death Eternal, in the heavens of Albion, and before the gates
> Of Jerusalem his Emanation, in the heavens beneath Beulah."

Let the Súfis of the West make what construction they can of that doctrine. We will help them, before passing on, with another view of the Atonement, taken from *The Everlasting Gospel.*

> " But when Jesus was crucified,
>   Then was perfected his galling pride.
>   In three days he devoured his prey,
>   *And still he devours the body of clay ;*
>   For dust and clay is the serpent's meat,
>   Which never was meant for man to eat."

That is, the spirit must be eternally at work consuming and destroying the likeness of things material and the religions made out of them. This over-fervent prophet of freedom for the senses as well as the soul would have them free, one may say, only for the soul's sake : talking as we see he did of redemption from the body and salvation by the spirit at war with it, in words which literally taken would hardly have misbecome a monk of Nitria.

Returning to the *Milton,* we are caught again in the mythologic whirlpools and cross-currents of symbol and doctrine ; our ears rung deaf and dazed by the hammers of Los (Time) and our eyes bewildered by the wheels and woofs of Enitharmon (Space) : " her looms vibrate with soft affections, weaving the Web of Life out from the ashes of the Dead." This is a fragment of the main myth, whose details Los and Enitharmon themselves for the present forbid our following out.

> " The Three Classes of men regulated by Los's hammer, and woven
> By Enitharmon's Looms, and spun beneath the Spindle of Tirzah :
> The first : The Elect from before the foundation of the World ;
> The second : The Redeemed. The Third : the Reprobate and formed
> To destruction from the mother's womb."

Into the myth of the harrow and horses of Pala-mabron, more Asiatic in tone than any other of Blake's, and full of the vast proportion and formless fervour of Hindoo legends, we will not haul any reluctant reader. Let him only take enough by way of extract to understand how thoroughly one vein of fiery faith runs through all the prophetic books, and one passionate form of doctrine is enforced and beaten in upon the disciple again and again; not hitherto with much material effect.

" And in the midst of the Great Assembly Palamabron prayed;
O God, protect me from my friends that they have not power over me;
Thou hast given me power to protect myself from my bitterest enemies."

Then the wrath of Rintrah, the most fiery of the spirits who are children of Time, having entered by lot into Satan, who was of the Elect from the first, "seeming a brother, being a tyrant, even thinking himself a brother while he is murdering the just," "with incomparable mildness," believing "that he had not oppressed"—a symbolic point much insisted on—

" He created Seven deadly Sins, drawing out his infernal scroll
Of moral laws and cruel punishments upon the clouds of Jehovah,
To pervert the divine voice in its entrance to the earth
With thunders of war and trumpet's sound, with armies of disease;
Punishments and deaths mustered and numbered; saying, I am God alone,
There is no other; let all obey my principles of moral individuality
I have brought them from the uppermost innermost recesses
Of my Eternal Mind; transgressors I will rend off for ever;
As now I rend this accursed Family from my covering."

This is the Satan of Blake, sufficiently unlike the Miltonic. Of himself he cannot conceive evil and bring forth destruction; the absolute Spirit of Evil is alien

from this mythology ; he must enter into the body of
a law or system and put on the qualities of spirits
strange to himself (Rintrah); he is divided, inconsistent, a mystery and error to himself; he represents Monotheism with its stringent law and sacerdotal
creed, Jewish or Christian, as opposed to Pantheism
whereby man and God are one, and by culture and
perfection of humanity man makes himself God. The
point of difference here between Blake and many other
western Pantheists is that in his creed self-abnegation
(in the mystic sense, not the ascetic—the Oriental, not
the Catholic) is the highest and only perfect form of
self-culture : and as Satan (under "names divine"—
see the Epilogue to the *Gates of Paradise*) is the
incarnate type of Monotheism, so is Jesus the incarnate
type of Pantheism. To return to our myth ; the stronger
spirit rears walls of rocks and forms rivers of fire round
them ;

" And Satan, *not having the Science of Wrath but only of Pity,* *
Rent them asunder ; and Wrath was left to Wrath, and Pity to Pity."

This is Blake's ultimate conception of active evil ; not
wilful wrong-doing by force of arm or of spirit; but mild
error, tender falsehood innocent of a purpose, embodied in
an external law of moral action and restrictive faith, and
clothed with a covering of cruelty which adheres to and
grows into it (Decalogue and Law). A subtle and rather

* That is, being unable to reconcile qualities, to pass beyond the legal and
logical grounds of good and evil into the secret places where they are not. The
whole argument hinges on this difference between Pantheism, which can, and
Theism, which cannot, and is therefore no surer or saner than a mere religion
based on Church or Bible, nor less incompetent to include, to expound, to redeem
the world.

noble conception, developing easily and rapidly into what was once called the Manichean doctrine as to the Old Testament.

> " If the guilty should be condemned, he must be an Eternal Death,
> And one must die for another throughout all Eternity;
> Satan is fallen from his station and can never be redeemed,
> But must be new-created continually moment by moment,
> And therefore the class of Satan shall be called the Elect, and those
> Of Rintrah the Reprobate, and those of Palamabron the Redeemed;
> For he is redeemed from Satan's law, the wrath falling on Rintrah.
> And therefore Palamabron cared not to call a solemn Assembly
> Till Satan had assumed Rintrah's wrath in the day of mourning,
> In a feminine delusion * of false pride self-deceived."

The words of the text recur not unfrequently in the prophetic books. A single final act of redemption by sacrifice and oblation of one for another is not admitted as sufficient, or even possible. The favourite dogma is this, of the eternity of sacrifice; endless redemption to be bought at no less a price than endless self-devotion. To this plea of " an Eternal" before the assembly succeeds the myth of Leutha " offering herself a ransom for

---

* Compare, for the doctrine as to delusion and jealousy being *feminine* principles (destructive by their weakness, not by their strength), this strange expostulation with God, recalling the tone of earlier prophets :—

> " Why art thou silent and invisible,
>   Father of Jealousy ?
> Why dost thou hide thyself in clouds
>   From every searching eye ?
>
> Why darkness and obscurity
>   In all thy words and laws,
> That none dare eat the fruit but from
>   The wily serpent's jaws ?
> Or is it because Jealousy †
>   Gives feminine applause ? "

---

† (This word, half rubbed off in the MS., may be "secrecy"; and the point would remain the same.)

Satan :"* a myth, not an allegory ; for of allegory pure and simple there is scarcely a trace in Blake.

> " I formed the Serpent
> Of precious stones and gold turned poison on the sultry waste.
> To do unkind things with kindness ; with power armed, to say
> The most irritating things in the midst of tears and love ;
> These are the stings of the Serpent."

This whole myth of Leutha is splendid for colour, and not too subtle to be thought out : the imaginative action of the poem plays like fire and palpitates like blood upon every line, as the lips of caressing flame and the tongues of cleaving light in which the text is set fold and flash about the margins.

> " The Elect shall meet the Redeemed, on Albion's rocks they shall meet,
> Astonished at the Transgressor, in him beholding the Saviour.
> And the Elect shall say to the Redeemed ; We behold it is of Divine
> Mercy alone, of free gift and Election, that we live ;
> Our Virtues and cruel Goodnesses have deserved Eternal Death."

Forgiveness of sin and indulgence, the disciple perceives, is not enough for this mythology ; it must include forgiveness of virtue and abstinence, the hypocritic holiness made perfect in the body of death for six thousand years under the repressive and restrictive law called after the name of the God of the Jews, who " was leprous."

---

* Leutha, the spirit or guardian goddess of natural pleasure and physical beauty, is sacrificed as a ransom to redeem the spirit or guardian god of prohibitive law or judicial faith ; to him she is sacrificed that through her he may be saved. Thus, in the *Visions of the Daughters of Albion*, the maiden who "plucks Leutha's flower," who trusts and indulges Nature, has her " virgin mantle torn in twain by the terrible thunders" of religious and moral law : woman was sacrificed and man "fast bound in misery" during the eighteen centuries—through which the mother goddess lay asleep, to weep over her children at her waking ; as in the Prophecy of *Europe* Time the father and Space the mother of men are afflicted and spellbound until the sleep of faith be slept out. There again the emblematic name of Leutha recurs in passing.

Thus prophesies Blake, in a fury of supra-Christian dogmatism.

Here ends the "Song of the Bard" in the First Book. "Many condemned the high-toned song, saying, Pity and Love are too venerable for the imputation of guilt. Others said, If it is true!" Let us say the same, and pass on : listening only to the Bard's answer :—

> "I am inspired! I know it is Truth! for I sing
> According to the Inspiration of the Poetic Genius
> Who is the Eternal all-protecting divine Humanity
> To whom be Glory and Power and Dominion evermore. Amen."

Then follows the incarnation and descent into earth and hell of Milton, who represents here the redemption by inspiration, working in pain and difficulty before the expiration of the six thousand Satanic years. His words are worth quoting :—

> "When will the Resurrection come, to deliver the sleeping body
> From corruptibility? O when, Lord Jesus, wilt thou come?
> Tarry no longer ; for my soul lies at the gates of death :
> I will arise and look forth for the morning of the grave :
> I will go down to the sepulchre and see if morning breaks.
> I will go down to self-annihilation and eternal death
> Lest the Last Judgment come and find me unannihilate
> And I be seized and given into the hands of my own selfhood."

This grand dogma, that personal love and selfishness make up the sin which defies redemption, is in a manner involved in that former one of the necessary "eternity of sacrifice," for

> "I in my selfhood am that Satan ; I am that Evil One ;
> He is my Spectre."

Now by the light of these extracts let any student examine the great figure at p. 13, where "he beheld his own

Shadow—and entered into it." Clothed in the colours of pain, crowned with the rays of suffering, it stands between world and world in a great anguish of transformation and change : Passion included by Incarnation. Erect on a globe of opaque shadow, backed by a sphere of aching light that opens flower-wise into beams of shifting colour and bitter radiance as of fire, it appeals with a doubtful tortured face and straining limbs to the flat black wall and roof of heaven. All over the head is a darkness not of transitory cloud or night that will some time melt into day ; recalling that great verse : " Neither could the bright flames of the stars endure to lighten that horrible night."

" As when a man dreams he reflects not that his body sleeps,
Else he would wake ; so seemed he entering his Shadow ; but
With him the Spirits of the Seven Angels of the Presence
Entering, they gave him still perceptions of his Sleeping Body
Which now arose and walked with them in Eden, as an Eighth
Image, Divine tho' darkened, and tho' walking as one walks
In Sleep ; and the Seven comforted and supported him."

The whole passage is full of a deep and dim beauty which grows clearer and takes form of feature to those only who bring with them eyes to see and patience to desire it. Take next this piece of cosmography, worth comparing with Dante's vision of the worlds :—

" The nature of infinity is this ; That everything has its
Own vortex : and when once a traveller thro' Eternity
Has passed that vortex, he perceives it roll backward behind
His path into a globe itself enfolding, like a sun
Or like a moon or like a universe of starry majesty,
While he keeps onward in his wondrous journey thro' the earth,
Or like a human form, a friend with whom he lived benevolent :
As the eye of man views both the east and west encompassing
Its vortex, and the north and south, with all their starry host ;

> Also the rising and setting moon he views surrounding
> His cornfields and his valleys of five hundred acres square ;
> Thus is the earth one infinite plane, and not as apparent
> To the weak traveller confined beneath the moony shade ;
> Thus is the heaven a vortex passed already, and the earth
> A vortex not yet passed by the traveller thro' Eternity."

One curious piece of symbolism may be extracted from the myth, as the one reference to anything actual :—

> " Then Milton knew that the Three Heavens of Beulah were beheld
> By him on earth in his bright pilgrimage of sixty years
> In those three Females whom his Wives, and those three whom his
>   Daughters
> Had represented and contained, that they might be resumed
> By giving up of Selfhood."

But of Milton's flight, of the cruelties of Ulro, of his journey above the Mundane Shell, which "is a vast concave earth, an immense hardened shadow of all things upon our vegetated earth, enlarged into dimension and deformed into indefinite space," we will take no more account here ; nor of the strife with Urizen, " one giving life, the other giving death, to his adversary ;" hardly even of the temptation by the sons and daughters of Rahab and Tirzah, when

> " The twofold Form Hermaphroditic, and the Double-sexed,
> The Female-male and the Male-female, self-dividing stood
> Before him in their beauty and in cruelties of holiness."

(Compare the beautiful song " To Tirzah," in the Songs of Experience.) This Tirzah, daughter of Rahab the holy, is " Natural Religion " (Theism as opposed to Pantheism), which would fain have the spiritual Jerusalem offered in sacrifice to it.

" Let her be offered up to holiness : Tirzah numbers her :
She numbers with her fingers every fibre ere it grow :
Where is the Lamb of God ? where is the promise of his coming ?
Her shadowy sisters form the bones, even the bones of Horeb
Around the marrow ; and the orbed scull around the brain ;
She ties the knot of nervous fibres into a white brain ;
She ties the knot of bloody veins into a red-hot heart ;
She ties the knot of milky seed into two lovely heavens,
Two yet but one ; each in the other sweet reflected ; these
Are our Three Heavens beneath the shades of Beulah, land of rest."

Here and henceforward the clamour and glitter of the
poem become more and more confused; nevertheless every
page is set about with jewels ; as here, in a more comprehensible form than usual :—

" God sent his two servants Whitfield and Wesley; were they prophets ?
Or were they idiots and madmen ? ' Show us Miracles ' ?
Can you have greater Miracles than these ? Men who devote
Their life's whole comfort to entire scorn, injury, and death ? "

Take also these scraps of explanation mercifully vouchsafed us :—

" Bowlahoola is named Law by Mortals : Tharmas founded it
Because of Satan : 　　*　　*　　*　　*
But Golgonooza is named Art and Manufacture by mortal men.
In Bowlahoola Los's Anvils stand and his Furnaces rage.
Bowlahoola thro' all its porches feels, tho' too fast founded
Its pillars and porticoes to tremble at the force
Of mortal or immortal arm ; 　　*　　*　　*
The Bellows are the Animal Lungs; the Hammers the Animal Heart ;
The Furnaces the Stomach for digestion ; "

(Here we must condense instead of transcribing. While
thousands labour at this work of the Senses in the halls
of Time, thousands "play on instruments stringed or
fluted " to lull the labourers and drown the painful sound
of the toiling members, and bring forgetfulness of this

slavery to the flesh : a myth of animal life not without beauty, and to Blake one of great attraction.)

> "Los is by mortals named Time, Enitharmon is named Space;
> But they depict him bald and aged who is in eternal youth
> All-powerful, and his locks flourish like the brows of morning;
> He is the Spirit of Prophecy, the ever-apparent Elias.
> Time is the mercy of Eternity; without Time's swiftness
> Which is the swiftest of all things, all were eternal torment."

At least this last magnificent passage should in common charity and sense have been cited in the biography, if only to explain the often-quoted words Los and Enitharmon. Neither blindness to such splendour of symbol, nor deafness to such music of thought, can excuse the omission of what is so wholly necessary for the comprehension of extracts already given, and given (as far as one can see) with no available purpose whatever.

The remainder of the first book of the *Milton* is a vision of Nature and prophecy of the gathering of the harvest of Time and treading of the winepress of War ; in which harvest and vintage work all living things have their share for good or evil.

> "How red the sons and daughters of Luvah ! here they tread the grapes,
> Laughing and shouting, drunk with odours ; many fall o'erwearied,
> Drowned in the wine is many a youth and maiden ; those around
> Lay them on skins of Tigers and of the spotted Leopard and the wild Ass
> Till they revive, or bury them in cool grots, making lamentation.
> This Winepress is called War on Earth ; it is the printing-press
> Of Los, there he lays his words in order above the mortal brain
> As cogs are formed in a wheel to turn the cogs of the adverse wheel."

All kind of insects, of roots and seeds and creeping things—"all the armies of disease visible or invisible"— are there ;

"The slow slug; the grasshopper that sings and laughs and drinks
(Winter comes, he folds his slender bones without a murmur);"

wasp and hornet, toad and newt, spider and snake,

"They throw off their gorgeous raiment; they rejoice with loud jubilee
Around the winepresses of Luvah, naked and drunk with wine.
There is the nettle that stings with soft down; and there
The indignant thistle whose bitterness is bred in his milk;
Who feeds on contempt of his neighbour; there all the idle weeds
That creep around the obscure places show their various limbs
Naked in all their beauty, dancing round the winepresses.
But in the winepresses the human grapes sing not nor dance,
They howl and writhe in shoals of torment, in fierce flames consuming;"

tortured for the cruel joy and deadly sport of Luvah's
sons and daughters;

"They dance around the dying and they drink the howl and groan;
They catch the shrieks in cups of gold, they hand them one to another;
These are the sports of love, and these the sweet delights of amorous play;
Tears of the grape, the death-sweat of the cluster; the last sigh
Of the mild youth who listens to the luring songs of Luvah."

Take also this from the speech of Time to his reapers.

"You must bind the sheaves not by nations or families,
You shall bind them in three classes; according to their classes
So shall you bind them, separating what has been mixed
Since men began to be woven into nations.   *   *
     *   *   *   The Elect is one class; you
Shall bind them separate; they cannot believe in eternal life
Except by miracle and a new birth. The other two classes,
The Reprobate* who never cease to believe, and the Redeemed
Who live in doubts and fears, perpetually tormented by the Elect,
These you shall bind in a twin bundle for the consummation."

The constellations that rise in immortal order, that keep
their course upon mountain and valley, with sound of harp

---

* That is of course the reprobate according to theology, such as the heretical
prophet himself: the class of men upon which is laid the burden of the sins of
the elect, as Satan's upon Rintrah in the myth.

and song, "with cups and measures filled with foaming
wine;" that fill the streams with light of many visions
and leave in luminous traces upon the extreme sea the
peace of their passage; these too are sons of Los, and
labour in the vintage.   The gorgeous flies on meadow or
brook, that weave in mazes of music and motion the
delight of artful dances, and sound instruments of song as
they touch and cross and recede; the trees shaken by the
wind into sound of heavy thunder till they become
preachers and prophets to men; these are the sons of
Los, these the visions of eternity; and we see but as it
were the hem of their garments.

A noble passage follows, in which are resumed the
labours of the sons of time in fashioning men and the
stations of men.   They make for doubts and fears
cabinets of ivory and gold; when two spectres "like
lamps quivering" between life and death stand ready for
the blind malignity of combat, they are taken and
moulded instead into shapes fit for love, clothed with soft
raiment by softer hands, drawn after lines of sweet
and perfect form. Some "in the optic nerve" give to the
poor infinite wealth of insight, power to know and enjoy
the invisible heaven, and to the rich scorn and ignorance
and thick darkness.   Others build minutes and hours
and days;

> "And every moment has a couch of gold for soft repose
> (A moment equals a pulsation of the artery)
> And every minute has an azure tent with silken veils,
> And every hour has a bright golden gate carved with skill,
> And every day and night has walls of brass and gates of adamant
> Shining like precious stones and ornamented with appropriate signs,
> And every month a silver-paved terrace builded high,

And every year invulnerable barriers with high towers,
And every age is moated deep, with bridges of silver and gold,
And every Seven Ages are encircled with a flaming fire."

There is much more of the same mythic sort concerning the duration of time, the offices of the nerves (*e.g.*, in the optic nerve sleep was transformed to death by Satan the father of sin and death, even as we have seen sensual death re-transformed by Mercy into sleep), and such-like huge matters; full, one need not now repeat, of subtle splendour and fanciful intensity. But enough now of this over-careful dredging in such weedy waters; where nevertheless, at risk of breaking our net, we may at every dip fish up some pearl.

At the opening of the second book the pearls lie close and pure. From this (without explanation or reference) has been taken the lovely and mutilated extract at p. 197 of the *Life*. Thus it stands in Blake's text :—

" Thou hearest the nightingale begin the song of spring ;
    The lark, sitting upon his earthy bed, just as the morn
    Appears, listens silent ; then, springing from the waving corn-field, loud
    He leads the choir of day : trill—trill—trill—trill—
    Mounting upon the wings of light into the great expanse,
    Re-echoing against the lovely blue and shining heavenly shell
    His little throat labours with inspiration ; every feather
    On throat, and breast, and wing, vibrate with the effluence divine.
    All nature listens to him silent ; and the awful Sun
    Stands still upon the mountains, looking on this little bird
    With eyes of soft humility, and wonder, love, and awe.
    Then loud, from their green covert, all the birds began their song,—
    The thrush, the linnet and the goldfinch, robin and the wren,
    Awake the Sun from his sweet reverie upon the mountains ;
    The nightingale again essays his song, and through the day
    And through the night warbles luxuriant ; every bird of song
    Attending his loud harmony with admiration and love.

(This is a vision of the lamentation of Beulah over Ololon.)

Thou perceivest the flowers put forth their precious odours,

And none can tell how from so small a centre come such sweets,
Forgetting that within that centre eternity expands
Its ever-during doors that Og and Anak fiercely guard.*
First ere the morning breaks joy opens in the flowery bosoms,
Joy even to tears, which the sun rising dries; first the wild thyme
And meadow-sweet downy and soft waving among the reeds,
Light springing on the air, lead the sweet dance; they wake
The honeysuckle sleeping on the oak, the flaunting beauty
Revels along upon the wind; the white-thorn, lovely May,
Opens her many lovely eyes; listening, the rose still sleeps,
None dare to wake her : soon she bursts her crimson-curtained bed
And comes forth in the majesty of beauty; every flower,
The pink, the jessamine, the wallflower, the carnation,
The jonquil, the mild lily, opes her heavens; every tree
And flower and herb soon fill the air with an innumerable dance,
Yet all in order sweet and lovely; men are sick with love.
Such is a vision of the lamentation of Beulah over Ololon."

This Beulah is "a place where contrarieties are equally
true;" "it is a pleasant lovely shadow where no dispute

---

* This line appears to have been too much for the writer in the *Life*, who here
breaks his quotation short off by the head, annihilating with a quite ingenious
violence at once grammar, sense, and sound.   It is but a small nut to have
broken his critical tooth upon ; the evident meaning being simply this : that
within the centre of everything living by animal or vegetative life there is by
way of kernel something imperishable ; the fleshly or material life of form contains the infinite spiritual life, lurking under leaf or latent under limb : man
and flower and beast have each the separate secret of a soul or divisible indestructible spirit (compare even the *Songs of Innocence*) ; but while the earthly and
fleshly form remains there stand as wardens of the ways the two material
giants, Strength and Force, binding the soul in the body with chains of flesh and
sex, the spirit in the petals with bonds of vegetable form, fashioned fastenings
of chalice and anther, sprinklings of dusty gold on leaf or pistil ; always, without
hammer or rivet of Vulcanic forging, able to hold fast Prometheus in blind
bondage to the flesh and form of things ; so that except by inspiration there can
be no chance of seeing what does exist and work in man or beast or flower ; only
by vision or by death shall one be brought safe past the watch guarded by the sen-
tinels of material form and bodily life, the crude tributary "Afrites" (as in the
Æschylean myth) of the governing power which fashions and fetters life in men
and things. And thus this, the singing of birds and dancing of flowers, the springing
of colour and kindling of music at each day's dawn, is a symbol—"a vision of
the lamentation of Beulah over Ololon"—of the dwellers in that milder and moon-
light-coloured world of reflex mortal spirits over the imperishable influences of
a higher spiritual world, which descending upon earth must be clothed with

can come because of those who sleep : " made to shelter, before they " pass away in winter," the temporary emanations " which trembled exceedingly neither could they live, because the life of man was too exceeding unbounded." Of the incarnation and descent of Ololon, of the wars and prophecies of Milton, and of all the other Felpham visions here put on record, we shall say no more in this place ; but all these things are written in the Second Book. The illustrative work is also noble and worth study in all ways. One page for example is covered by a design among the grandest of Blake's. Two figures lie half embraced, as in a deadly sleep without dawn of dream or shadow of rest, along a bare slant ledge of rock washed against by wintry water. Over these two stoops an eagle balanced on the heavy-laden air, with stretching throat and sharpened wings, opening beak, and eyes full of a fierce perplexity of pity. All round the greenish and black slope of moist sea-cliff the weary tidal ripple plashes and laps, thrusting up as it were faint tongues and listless fingers tipped with foam. On an earlier page, part of the text of which we have given, crowd and glitter all shapes and images of insect or reptile life, sprinkling between line and margin keen points of jewel-

material mystery and become subject to sensuous form and likeness in the body of the shadow of death. This glorious passage, almost to be matched for wealth of sound, for growth and gradation of floral and musical splendour, for mastery of imperial colour, even against the great interlude or symphony of flowers in *Maud*, was not cast at random into the poem, but has also a " soul " or meaning in it—though the ways of seeing and understanding are somewhat too closely guarded by " Og and Anak." Reading it as an excerpt indeed one need hardly wish to see beyond the form or material figure. That " innumerable dance " of tree and flower and herb is not unfit for comparison with the old ἀνήριθμου γέλασμα of the waves of the sea.

coloured light and soft flashes as of starry or scaly brilliance.

The same year 1804 saw the huge advent of *Jerusalem.* Of that terrible "emanation," hitherto the main corner-stone of offence to all students of Blake, what can be said within any decent limit? or where shall any traveller find a rest for feet or eyes in that noisy and misty land? It were a mere frenzy of discipleship that would under-take by force of words to make straight these crooked ways or compel things incoherent to cohere. *Supra hanc petram*—and such a rock it is to begin any church-building upon! Many of the unwary have stumbled over it and broken their wits. Seriously, one cannot imagine that people will ever read through this vast poem with pleasure enough to warrant them in having patience with it.

Several things, true in the main of all the prophetic books, are especially true and memorable with regard to those written or designed during the "three years' slumber" at Felpham. They are the results of intense and active solitude working upon the capricious nerves and tremulous brain of a man naturally the most excit-able and receptive of men. They are to be read by the light of his earlier work in the same line; still more per-haps by the light of those invaluable ten letters printed in Vol. II. of the *Life,* for which one can hardly give thanks enough. The incredible fever of spirit under the sting and stress of which he thought and laboured all his life through, has left marks of its hot and restless presence as clearly on this short correspondence as on the volumi-nous rolls of prophecy. The merit or demerit of the work done is never in any degree the conscious or deliberate result of a purpose. Possessed to the inmost nerve and core by a certain faith, consumed by the desire to obey his instinct of right by preaching that faith, utterly regardless of all matters lying outside of his own inspiration, he wrote and engraved as it was given him to do, and no otherwise. As to matter and argument, the enormous *Jerusalem* is simply a fervent apocalyptic discourse on the old subjects—love without law and against law, virtue that stagnates into poisonous dead matter by moral isolation, sin that must exist for the sake of being forgiven, forgiveness that must always keep up with sin—must even maintain sin that it may have something to keep up with and to live for. Without forgiveness of sins, the one thing necessary, we lapse each man into separate self-righteousness and a cruel worship of natural morality and religious law. For nature, oddly enough as it seems at first sight, is assumed by this mystical code to be the cruellest and narrowest of absolute moralists. Only by worship of imaginative impulse, the grace of the Lamb of God, which admits infinite indulgence in sin and infinite forgiveness of sin—only by some such faith as this shall the world be renewed and redeemed. This may be taken as the rough result, broadly set down, of the portentous book of revelation. Never, one may suppose, did any Oriental heretic drive his deductions further or set forth his conclusions in obscurer form. Never certainly did a man fall to his work with keener faith and devotion. Sin itself is not so evil—but the remembrance and punishment of sin! "Injury the Lord heals; but vengeance cannot be

healed." Next or equal in hatefulness to the division of
qualities into evil and good (see above, *Marriage of
Heaven and Hell*) is the separation of sexes into male
and female : hence jealous love and personal desire, that
set itself against the mystical frankness of fraternity :
hence too (contradictory as it may seem till one thinks it
out) the hermaphroditic emblem is always used as a
symbol seemingly of duplicity and division, perplexity
and restraint. The two sexes should not combine and
contend ; they must finally amalgamate and be annihilated.* All this is of course more or less symbolic, and

* One may fear that some such symbolic stuff as this is really at the root of the
admirable poem christened by its editor with the name of *Broken Love:* which I
gravely suspect was meant for insertion in some fresh instalment of prophetic
rhapsody by way of complement or sequel to *Jerusalem.* The whole tone of it,
and especially that of some rejected stanzas, is exactly in the elemental manner
of the scenes (where scene is none) between Albion, Jerusalem, and Vala the
Spectre of Jerusalem (books 1st and 2nd) :—

> "Thou hast parted from my side—
> Once thou wast a virgin bride :
> Never shalt thou a true love find—
> My Spectre follows thee behind.
>
> " When my love did first begin,
> Thou didst call that love a sin ;
> Secret trembling, night and day,
> Driving all my loves away."

These two stanzas (recalling so many other passages where Blake has enforced his
doctrines as to the fatal tendency of the fears and jealousies, the abstinence and
doubt, produced by theoretic virtue and hatched by artificial chastity) stood originally as third and fourth in the poem. They are cancelled in Blake's own MS. ;
but in that MS. the poem ends as follows, in a way (I fear) conclusive as to the
justice of my suggestion; I mark them conjecturally, as I suppose the dialogue
to stand, by way of helping the reader to some glimpse of the point here and
there.

> " When wilt thou return and view
> My loves and them to life renew ?
> When wilt thou return and live ?
> When wilt thou pity as I forgive ?"

not to be taken in literal coarseness or folly of meaning.
The whole stage is elemental, the scheme one of patriarchal

> "Never, never, I return ;
> Still for victory I burn.
> Living, thee alone I'll have ;
> And when dead I'll be thy grave.

> "Through the heaven and earth and hell
> Thou shalt never, never quell :
> I will fly and thou pursue ;
> Night and morn the flight renew."

(This I take to be the jealous lust of power and exclusive love speaking through the incarnate "female will." See *Jerusalem* again.)

> "And I, to end thy cruel mocks,
> Annihilate thee on the rocks,
> And another form create
> To be subservient to my fate.

> "Till I turn from female love
> And root up the infernal grove,
> I shall never worthy be
> To step into eternity."

(This stanza ought probably to be omitted ; but I retain it as being carefully numbered for insertion by Blake : though he by some evident slip of mind or pen has put it before the preceding one.)

> "Let us agree to give up love
> And root up the infernal grove,
> Then shall we return and see
> The worlds of happy eternity.

> "And throughout all eternity
> I forgive you, you forgive me ;
> As our dear Redeemer said,
> This the wine and this the bread."

That is perfect *Jerusalem* both for style and matter. The struggle of either side for supremacy—the flight and pursuit—the vehemence and perversion—the menace and the persuasion—the separate Spectre or incarnation of sex "annihilated on the rocks" of rough law or stony circumstance and necessity—the final vision of an eternity where the jealous divided loves and personal affections "born of shame and pride" shall be destroyed or absorbed in resignation of individual office and quality—all this belongs but too clearly to the huge prophetic roll. Few however will be desirous, and none will be wise, to resign for these gigantic shadows of formless and baseless fancy the splendid exposition given by the editor (p. 76 of vol. ii). Seen by that new external illumination, though it be none of the author's kindling, his poem stands on firmer feet and is clothed with a nearer light.

vapour, and the mythologic actors mere Titans outlined in cloud. Reserving this always, we shall not be far out in interpreting Blake's dim creed somewhat as above. One distinction it is here possible to make, and desirable to keep in mind : Blake at one time speaks of Nature as the source of moral law, "the harlot virgin-mother," "Rahab," "the daughter of Babylon," origin of religious restrictions and the worship of abstinence ; mother of "the harlot modesty," and spring of all hypocrisies and prohibitions ; to whom the religious and moral of this world would fain offer up in sacrifice the spiritual Jerusalem, the virgin espoused, named among men Liberty, forbidding nothing and enjoying all, but therefore clean and not unclean : by whom comes indulgence, after whom follows redemption. At another time this same prophet will plead for freedom on behalf of "natural" energies, and set up the claims of nature to energetic enjoyment and gratification of all desires, against the moral law and government of the creative and restrictive Deity— "Urizen, mistaken Demon of Heaven." With a like looseness of phrase he uses and transposes the words "God" and "Satan," even to an excess of laxity and consequent perplexity ; not, it may be suspected, without a grain of innocent if malign pleasure at the chance of inflicting on men of conventional tempers bewilderment and offence. But as to this question of the term "Nature" the case seems to lie thus : when, as throughout the *Marriage of Heaven and Hell*, he uses it in the simple sense of human or physical condition as opposed to some artificial state of soul or belief, he takes it as the contrary of conventional ideas and habits (of religion and morality as vulgarly conceived or practised) ; but when, as throughout the *Milton* and *Jerusalem*, he speaks of nature as opposed to inspiration, it must be taken as the contrary of that higher and subtler religious faith which he is bent on inculcating, and which itself is the only perfect opposite and efficient antagonist to the conventional faith and (to use another of his quasi-technical terms) the " deistical virtue " which he is bent on denying. Blake, one should always remember, was not infidel but heretic ; his belief was peculiar enough, but it was not unbelief ; it was farther from that than most men's. To him, though for quite personal reasons and in a quite especial sense, much of what is called inspired writing was as sacred and infallible as to any priest of any church. Only before reading he inverted the book.

> " Both read the Bible day and night,
> But thou read'st black where I read white."
> (*Everlasting Gospel*, MS.)

Thus, by his own showing, in the recorded words of Christ he found authority for his vision and sympathy with his faith ; in the published creed of reason or rationalism, he found negation of his belief and antipathy to his aims. Hence in his later denunciation he brackets together the Churches of Rome and England with the Churches of Ferney and Lausanne ; it was all uninspired—all "nature's cruel holiness—the deceits of natural religion"'; all irremediably involved, all inextricably interwoven with the old fallacies and the old prohibitions.

Such points as these do, above most others, deserve, demand, and reward the trouble of clearing up ; and these once understood, much that seemed the aimless unreflecting jargon of crude or accidental rhetoric assumes a distinct if unacceptable meaning. It is much otherwise with the external scheme or literal shell of the *Jerusalem.* Let no man attempt to define the post or expound the office of the "terrible sons and daughters." These, with all their flock of emanations and spectrous or vegetating shadows, let us leave to the discretion of Los; who has enough on his hands among them all. Neither let any attempt to plant a human foot upon the soil of the newly-divided shires and counties, partitioned though they be into the mystic likeness of the twelve tribes of Israel. Nor let any questioner of arithmetical mind apply his skill in num-bers to the finding of flaws or products in the twelves, twenty-fours, and twenty-sevens which make up the sum of their male and female emanations. In earnest, the externals of this poem are too incredibly grotesque —the mythologic plan too incomparably tortuous—to be fit for any detailed coherence of remark. Nor indeed were they meant to endure it. Such things, and the expression of such things, as are here treated of, are not to be reasoned out; the matter one may say is above reasoning; the manner (taken apart from the matter) is below it : the spirit of the work is too strong and its form too faulty for any rule or line. It will upon the whole suffice if this be kept in mind; that to Blake, in a literal perhaps as well as a mystical sense, Albion was as it were the cradle and centre of all created exist-ence; he even calls on the Jews to recognize it as the parent land of their history and their faith. Its incar-

nate spirit is chief among the ancient giant-gods, Titans
of his mythology, who were lords of the old simple
world and its good things, its wise delights and strong
sweet instincts, full of the vigorous impulse of innocence;
lords of an extinct kingdom, superseded now and transformed by the advent of moral fear and religious jealousy,
of pallid faith and artificial abstinence. In this manner Albion is changed and overthrown; hence at length
he dies, stifled and slain by his children under the new
law. His one friend, not misled or converted to the
dispensations of bodily virtue and spiritual restraint,
but faithful from of old and even after his change and
conversion to moral law, is Time; whose Spectre, or
mere outside husk and likeness, is indeed (as it must
needs be) fain to range itself on the transitory side of
things, fain to follow after the fugitive Emanation embodied in these new forms of life and allied to the
faith and habit of the day against the old liberty;* but
for all the desire of his despair and fierce entreaties to
be let go, he is yet kept to work, however afflicted and
rebellious, and compelled to labour with Time's self at
the building up within every man of that spiritual city
which is redemption and freedom for all men (ch. i.).
All the myth of this building of "Golgonooza," (that is,

---

* In the mythologic scheme, also, Los god of time and Albion father of the
races of men are rival powers; and the "Spectre" or satellite deity reproaches
his lord with resignation of the world and all its ways and generations (which
should have been subject only to the Time-Spirit) to the guidance of the nations
sprung from the patriarch Albion (called in Biblical records after Jewish names,
here spoken of by their English or other titles, more or less burlesque and
barbaric) who have taken upon themselves to subdue even Time himself to this
work and divide his spoils. So closely is the bare mythical construction enwound
with the symbolic or doctrinal passages which are meant to give it such vitality
and such coherence as they may.

we know, inspired art by which salvation must come) is noticeable for sweet intricacy of beauty; only after a little some maddening memory (surely not pure inspiration this time, but rather memory?) of the latter chapters of Ezekiel, with their interminable inexplicable structures and plans, seizes on Blake's passionate fancy and sets him at work measuring and dividing walls and gates in a style calculated to wear out a hecatomb of scholiasts, for whole pages in which no subtilized mediæval intellect, though trained under seraphic or cherubic doctors, could possibly find one satisfactory hair to split. For it merely trebles the roaring and rolling confusion when some weak grain of symbolism is turned up for a glimpse of time in the thick of a mass of choral prose consisting of absolute fancy and mere naked sound.

Not that there is here less than elsewhere of the passion and beauty which redeem so much of these confused and clamorous poems. The merits and attractions of this book are not such as can be minced small and served up in fragments. To do justice to its melodious eloquence and tender subtlety, we should have to analyze or transcribe whole sections : to give any fair notion of the grandeur and variety of its decorations would take up twice the space we can allow to it. Let this brief prologue stand as a sample of the former qualities.

> " Reader ! lover of books ! lover of heaven
> And of that God from whom all things are given ;
> Who in mysterious Sinai's awful cave
> To Man the wondrous art of writing gave ;
> Again he speaks in thunder and in fire,
> Thunder of thought and flames of fierce desire ;

Even from the depths of Hell his voice I hear
Within the unfathomed caverns of my ear;
Therefore I print; nor vain my types shall be;
Heaven, Earth, and Hell henceforth shall live in harmony."

" We who dwell on earth," adds the prophet, speaking of the measure and outward fashion of his poem, " can do nothing of ourselves; everything is conducted by Spirits no less than digestion or sleep." It is to be wished then that the spirits had on this occasion spoken less like somnambulists and uttered less indigested verse. For metrical oratory the plea that follows against ordinary metre may be allowed to have some effective significance; however futile if applied to purer and more essential forms of poetry.

It will be enough to understand well and bear well in mind once for all that the gist of this poem, regarded either as a scheme of ethics or as a mythological evangel, is simply this: to preach, as in the Saviour's opening invocation, the union of man with God :—(" I am not a God afar off;—Lo ! we are One; forgiving all evil ; not seeking recompense ") : to confute the dull mournful insanity of disbelief which compels " the perturbed man" to avert his ear and reject the divine counsellor as a " Phantom of the over-heated brain." This perverted humanity is incarnate in Albion, the fallen Titan, imprisoned by his children ; the " sons of Albion" are dæmonic qualities of force and faith, the " daughters" are reflex qualities or conditions which emanate from these. As thus ; reason supplants faith, and law, moral or religious, grows out of reason ; Jerusalem, symbol of imaginative liberty, emanation of his unfallen days, is the faith cast out by the " sons" or spirits who substitute reason for faith, the freedom trodden under by the " daughters" who substitute moral law for moral impulse : " Vala," her Spectre, called " Tirzah" among men, is the personified form in which " Jerusalem" becomes revealed, the perverted incarnation, the wrested medium or condition in which she exists among men. Thus much for the scheme of allegory with which the prophet sets out ; but when once he has got his theogony well under way and thrown it well into types, the antitypes all but vanish : every condition or quality has a god or goddess of its own ; every obscure state and allegorical gradation becomes a personal agent : and all these fierce dim figures threaten and complain, mingle and divide, struggle and embrace as human friends or foes. The main symbols are even of a monotonous consistency ; but no accurate sequence of symbolic detail is to be looked for in the doings and sayings of these contending giants and gods. To those who will remember this distinction and will make allowance for the peculiar dialect and manner of which some account has already been taken, this poem will not seem so wholly devoid of reason or of charm.

For its great qualities are much the same in text as in design : plenteous, delicate, vigorous. There is a certain real if rough and lax power of dramatic insight and invention shown even in the singular divisions of adverse symbol against symbol ; in such allegories as that which opposes the " human imagination in which all things exist"—do actually exist to all eternity—and the reflex fancy or belief which men confound with this ; nay, which they prefer to dwell in and ask comfort from. These two the poet calls the " states" of Beulah and Jerusalem.

As the souls of men are attracted towards that "mild heaven" of dreams and shadows where only the reflected image of their own hopes and errors can abide, the imagination, most divine and human, most actual and absolute, of all things, recedes ever further and further among the clouds of smoke, vapours of "abstract philosophy," and is caught among the " starry wheels" of religion and law, whose restless and magnetic revolution attracts and absorbs her.

> " O what avail the loves and tears of Beulah's lovely daughters ?
> They hold the immortal form in gentle bands and tender tears,
> But all within is opened into the deeps "—

the deeps of " a dark and unknown night " in which " philosophy wars against imagination." Here also the main myth of the *Europe* is once more rehandled ; to " create a female will," jealous, curious, cunning, full of tender tyranny and confusion, this is " to hide the most evident God in a hidden covert, even in the shadows of a woman and a secluded holy place, that we may pry after him as after a stolen treasure, hidden among the dead and mured up from the paths of life." Thus is it with the Titan Albion and all his race of mythologic men, when for them " Vala supplants Jerusalem," the husk replaces the fruit, the mutable form eclipses the immutable substance.

But into these darker parts of the book we will not go too deep. Time, patience, and insight on the part of writer and reader might perhaps clear up all details and lay bare much worth sight and study ; but only at the expense of much labour and space. It is feasible, and would be worth doing ; but not here. If the singular amalgam called Blake's works should ever get published, and edited to any purpose, this will have to be done by an energetic editor with time enough on his hands and wits enough for the work. We meantime will gather up a few strays that even under these circumstances appear worth hiving. In the address (p. 27) to the Jews, &c., Blake affirms that " Britain was the primitive seat of the patriarchal religion": therefore, in a literal as well as in a mystical sense, Jerusalem was the emanation of the giant Albion. (This it should seem was, according to the mythology, before the visible world was created ; in the time when all things were in the divine undivided world of the gods.) "Ye are united, O ye inhabitants of Earth, in one Religion : the most Ancient, the Eternal, and the Everlasting Gospel. The Wicked will turn it to Wickedness ; the Righteous, to Righteousness." If there be truth· in the Jewish tradition, he adds further on, that man anciently contained in his mighty limbs all things in heaven and earth, "and they were separated from him by cruel sacrifices ; and when compulsory cruel sacrifices had brought Humanity into a feminine tabernacle in the loins of Abraham and David, the Lamb of God, the Saviour, became apparent on earth as the prophets had foretold : the return of Israel is a return to mental sacrifice and war," to noble spiritual freedom and labour, which alone can supplant "corporeal war" and violence of error.

The second address (p. 52) "to the Deists" is more singular and more eloquent. Take a few extracts given not quite at random. "He," says Blake, " who preaches natural religion or morality is a flatterer who means to

betray, and to perpetuate tyrant pride and the laws of
that Babylon which he foresees shall shortly be destroyed
with the spiritual and not the natural sword ; he is in the
state named Rahab." The prophet then enforces his law
that "man is born a spectre or Satan and is altogether
an Evil," and "must continually be changed into his
direct contrary." Those who persuade him otherwise are
his enemies. For "man must and will have some religion ; if he has not the religion of Jesus he will have
the religion of Satan." Again, "Will any one say, Where
are those who worship Satan under the name of God ?—
where are they ? Listen. Every religion that preaches
vengeance for sin is the religion of the enemy and
avenger, and not of the forgiver of sin : and their God
is Satan named by the Divine Name." This, he says,
must be at root the religion of all who deny revelation
and adore nature ;* for mere nature is Satanic. Adam
the first man was created at the same time with Satan,
when the earth-giant Albion was cast into a trance of
sleep : the first man was a part of the universal fluent
nature made opaque ; the first fiend, a part contracted ;
and only by these qualities of opacity and contraction
can man or devil have separate natural existence. Those,
the prophet adds in his perverse manner, who profess
belief in natural virtue are hypocrites ; which those
cannot be who "pretend to be holier than others, but
confess their sins before all the world." *Therefore* there
was never a religious hypocrite ! "Rousseau thought

---

* Who adore nature as she appears to the Deist, who select this and reject that,
assume and presume according to moral law and custom, instead of accepting the
Pantheistic revelation which consecrates all things and absorbs all contraries.

men good by nature ; he found them evil, and found no
friend.   Friendship cannot exist without forgiveness of
sins continually."   And so forth.

At p. 66 is a passage recalling the myth of the "Mental
Traveller," and which seems to bear out the interpretation we gave to that misty and tempestuous poem.
This part of the prophecy, describing the blind pitiful
cruelty of divided qualities set against each other, is full
of brilliant and noble passages.   Even the faint symbolic
shapes of Tirzah and all her kind assume now and then
a splendour of pathos, utter words of stately sound, complain and appeal even to some recognizable purpose.   So
much might here be cited that we will prefer to cite
nothing but this slight touch of myth.   In the world of
time " they refuse liberty to the male : not like Beulah,

Where every female delights to give her maiden to her husband."

The female searches sea and land for gratification to the
male genius, who in return clothes her in gems and gold
and feeds her with the food of Eden : hence all her
beauty beams.   But this is only in the " land of dreams,"
where dwell things "stolen from the human imagination
by secret amorous theft : " and when the spectres of the
dead awake in that land, " all the jealousies become mur-
derous :—forming a commerce to sell loves with moral
law ; an equal balance, not going down with decision :
therefore—mutual hate returns and mutual deceit and
mutual fear."   In fact, the divorce batteries are here open
again.

The third address " to the Christians " is too long to
transcribe here ; and should in fairness have been given

in the biography. Its devout passion and beauty of words
might have won notice, and earned tolerance for the more
erratic matter in which it lies embedded. "What is the
joy of heaven but improvement in the things of the
spirit ? What are the pains of hell but ignorance, bodily
lust, idleness, and devastation of the things of the spirit?"
Mental gifts, given of Christ, "always appear to the
ignorance-loving hypocrite as sins ; but that which is a
sin in the sight of cruel man is not so in the sight of our
kind God." Every Christian after his ability should
openly engage in some mental pursuit ; for " to labour in
knowledge is to build up Jerusalem ; and to despise
knowledge is to despise Jerusalem and her builders." A
little before he has said : " I know of no other Christianity and no other Gospel than the liberty both of body
and mind to exercise the divine arts of imagination."
God being a spirit, and to be worshipped in spirit and in
truth, are not all his gifts spiritual gifts ? " The Christians then must give up the religion of Caiaphas, the dark
preacher of death, of sin, of sorrow, and of punishment,
typified as a revolving wheel, a devouring sword ; and
recognize that the labours of Art and Science alone are
the labours of the Gospel." As to religion, "Jesus died
because he strove against the current of this wheel—
opposing nature ; it is natural religion. But Jesus is the
bright preacher of life, creating nature from this fiery
law, by self-denial and forgiveness of sin." So speaks to
the prophet " a Watcher and a Holy One ;" bidding him

> " Go therefore, cast out devils in Christ's name,
>   Heal thou the sick of spiritual disease ;
>   Pity the evil ; for thou art not sent

> To smite with terror and with punishments
> Those that are sick.   *   *   *   *
> But to the publicans and harlots go:
> Teach them true happiness; but let no curse
> Go forth out of thy mouth to blight their peace.
> For hell is opened to heaven; thine eyes behold
> The dungeons burst, the prisoners set free.
>   England, awake! awake! awake!
>   Jerusalem thy sister calls;
>   Why wilt thou sleep the sleep of death
>   And chase her from thy ancient walls?
>   Thy hills and valleys felt her feet
>   Gently upon their bosoms move;
>   Thy gates beheld sweet Zion's ways;
>   Then was a time of joy and love.
>   And now the time returns again;
>   Our souls exult; and London's towers
>   Receive the Lamb of God to dwell
>   In England's green and pleasant bowers."

Much might also be said, had one leave of time, of the last chapter; of the death of the earth-giant through jealousy, and his resurrection when the Saviour appeared to him revealed in the likeness and similitude of Time: of the ultimate deliverance of all things, chanted in a psalm of high and tidal melody; a resurrection wherein all things, even " Tree, Metal, Earth and Stone," become all

> " Human forms identified; living, going forth, and returning wearied
> Into the planetary lives of years, months, days, and hours: reposing
> And then awaking into his bosom in the life of immortality.
> And I heard the name of their emanations: they are named Jerusalem."

We will add one reference, to pp. 61-62, where God shows to Jerusalem in a vision " Joseph the carpenter in Nazareth, and Mary his espoused wife." Through the vision of their story the forgiveness of Jerusalem also, when she has gone astray from her Lord, is made manifest to her.

"And I heard a voice among the reapers saying,
'Am I Jerusalem the lost adulteress? or am I Babylon
come up to Jerusalem?' And another voice answered
saying, 'Does the voice of my Lord call me again? am I
pure through his mercy and pity? am I become lovely
as a virgin in his sight, who am indeed a harlot drunken
with the sacrifice of idols?—O mercy, O divine humanity,
O forgiveness and pity and compassion, if I were pure I
should never have known thee: if I were unpolluted I
should never have glorified thy holiness, or rejoiced in
thy great salvation.'" The whole passage—and such are
not so unfrequent as at first glimpse they seem—is, if
seen with equal eyes, whether its purport be right or
wrong, "full of wisdom and perfect in beauty." But we
will dive after no more pearls at present in this huge
oyster-bed; and of the illustrations we can but speak in
a rough swift way. These are all generally noble: that
at p. 70 is great among the greatest of Blake's. Spires
of serpentine cloud are seen before a strong wind below a
crescent moon; Druid pillars enclose as with a frame
this stormy division of sky; outside them again the vapour twists and thickens; and men standing on desolate
broken ground look heavenward or earthward between
the pillars. Of others a brief and admirable account is
given in the *Life*, more final and sufficient than we can
again give; but all in fact should be well seen into by
those who would judge fitly of Blake's singular and
supreme gift for purely imaginative work. Flowers
sprung of earth and lit from heaven, with chalices of
floral fire and with flower-like women or men growing
up out of their centre; fair large forms full of labour or

of rest ; sudden starry strands and reaches of breathless heaven washed by drifts of rapid wind and cloud ; serrated array of iron rocks and glorious growth of weedy lands or flowering fields ; reflected light of bows bent and arrows drawn in heaven, dividing cloud from starlit cloud ; stately shapes of infinite sorrow or exuberant joy ; all beautiful things and all things terrible, all changes of shadow and of light, all mysteries of the darkness and the day, find place and likeness here : deep waters made glad and sad with heavy light that comes and goes; vast expansion of star-shaped blossom and swift aspiration of laborious flame ; strong and sweet figures made subject to strange torture in dim lands of bondage ; mystic emblems of plumeless bird and semi-human beast ; women like the daughters of giants, with immense shapeliness and vigour of lithe large limbs, clothed about with anguish and crowned upon with triumph ; their deep bosoms pressed against the scales of strong dragons, their bodies and faces strained together in the delight of monstrous caresses ; similitudes of all between angel and reptile that divide illimitable spaces of air or defile the overlaboured furrows upon earth.

It is easier to do complete justice to the minor prophecies than to give any not inadequate conception of this great book, so vast in reach, so repellent in style, so rich, vehement, and subtle beyond all other works of Blake ; the chosen crown and treasured fruit of his strange labours. Extracts of admirable beauty might be gathered up on all hands, more eligible it may be than any here given ; none I think more serviceable by way of sample and exposition, as far as such can at all be attained.

That the book contains much of a personal kind referring in a wild dim manner to his own spiritual actions and passions, is evident : but even by the new light of the Felpham correspondence one can hardly see where to lay finger on these passages and separate them decisively from the loose floating context. Not without regret, yet not with any sense of wilful or scornful oversight, we must be content now to pass on, and put up with this insufficient notice.

The only other engraved work of a prophetic kind did not appear for eighteen years more. This last and least in size, but not in worth, of the whole set is so brief that it may here be read in full.

THE GHOST OF ABEL.
A REVELATION IN THE VISIONS OF JEHOVAH.
SEEN BY WILLIAM BLAKE.

To Lord Byron in the Wilderness.—What dost thou here, Elijah ?
Can a Poet doubt the Visions of Jehovah ? Nature has no Outline :
But Imagination has.   Nature has no Time ; but Imagination has.
Nature has no Supernatural, and dissolves ; Imagination is Eternity.

SCENE.—*A rocky Country.* EVE *fainted over the dead body of* ABEL *which lays near a grave.* ADAM *kneels by her.* JEHOVAH *stands above.*

JEHOVAH. Adam !
  ADAM. It is in vain : I will not hear thee more, thou Spiritual
            Voice.
Is this Death ?
  JEHOVAH.   Adam !
  ADAM.   It is in vain ; I will not hear thee
Henceforth. Is this thy Promise that the Woman's Seed
Should bruise the Serpent's Head ? Is this the Serpent ? Ah !
Seven times, O Eve, thou hast fainted over the Dead. Ah ! Ah !

(EVE *revives.*)

  EVE. Is this the Promise of Jehovah ? O it is all a vain delusion,
This Death and this Life and this Jehovah.

JEHOVAH.   Woman, lift thine eyes.

(A VOICE *is heard coming on.*)

VOICE.   O Earth, cover not thou my blood! cover not thou my blood!

(*Enter the* GHOST *of* ABEL.)

EVE.   Thou visionary Phantasm, thou art not the real Abel.

ABEL.   Among the Elohim a Human Victim I wander: I am their House,
Prince of the Air, and our dimensions compass Zenith and Nadir.
Vain is thy Covenant, O Jehovah: I am the Accuser and Avenger
Of Blood; O Earth, cover not thou the blood of Abel.

JEHOVAH.   What vengeance dost thou require?

ABEL.   Life for Life! Life for Life!

JEHOVAH.   He who shall take Cain's life must also die, O Abel;
And who is he? Adam, wilt thou, or Eve, thou, do this?

ADAM.   It is all a vain delusion of the all-creative Imagination.
Eve, come away, and let us not believe these vain delusions.
Abel is dead, and Cain slew him; We shall also die a death
And then—what then? be as poor Abel, a Thought; or as
This? O what shall I call thee, Form Divine, Father of Mercies,
That appearest to my Spiritual Vision? Eve, seest thou also?

EVE.   I see him plainly with my mind's eye: I see also Abel living;
Tho' terribly afflicted, as we also are: yet Jehovah sees him
Alive and not dead; were it not better to believe Vision
With all our might and strength, tho' we are fallen and lost?

ADAM.   Eve, thou hast spoken truly; let us kneel before his feet.

(*They kneel before* JEHOVAH.)

ABEL.   Are these the sacrifices of Eternity, O Jehovah? a broken spirit
And a contrite heart? O, I cannot forgive; the Accuser hath
Entered into me as into his house, and I loathe thy Tabernacles.
As thou hast said so is it come to pass: My desire is unto Cain
And he doth rule over me: therefore my soul in fumes of blood
Cries for vengeance: Sacrifice on Sacrifice, Blood on Blood.

JEHOVAH.   Lo, I have given you a Lamb for an Atonement instead
Of the Transgressor, or no Flesh or Spirit could ever live.

ABEL.   Compelled I cry, O Earth, cover not the blood of Abel.

(ABEL *sinks down into the grave, from which arises* SATAN *armed in glittering scales with a crown and a spear.*)

SATAN.   I will have human blood and not the blood of bulls or goats,
And no Atonement, O Jehovah; the Elohim live on Sacrifice
Of men: hence I am God of men; thou human, O Jehovah.

By the rock and oak of the Druid, creeping mistletoe and thorn,
Cain's city built with human blood, not blood of bulls and goats,
Thou shalt thyself be sacrificed to me thy God on Calvary.

    JEHOVAH. Such is my will—(*Thunders*)—that thou thyself go to
        Eternal Death
In self-annihilation, even till Satan self-subdued put off Satan
Into the bottomless abyss whose torment arises for ever and ever.

        (*On each side a Chorus of Angels entering sing the following.*)

The Elohim of the Heathen swore Vengeance for Sin ! Then thou stood'st
Forth, O Elohim Jehovah, in the midst of the darkness of the oath all
    clothed
In thy covenant of the forgiveness of Sins. Death, O Holy! is this
    Brotherhood ?
The Elohim saw their oath eternal fire ; they rolled apart trembling over
    the
Mercy-Seat, each in his station fixed in the firmament, by Peace, Brother-
    hood, and Love.

        The Curtain falls.

    (1822. W. Blake's original stereotype was 1788.)

On the skirt of a figure, rapid and "vehemently sweeping," engraved underneath (recalling that vision of Dion made memorable by one of Wordsworth's nobler poems) are inscribed these words—"The Voice of Abel's Blood." The fierce and strenuous flight of this figure is as the motion of one "whose feet are swift to shed blood," and the dim face is full of hunger and sorrowful lust after revenge. The decorations are slight but not ineffective ; wrought merely in black and white. This small prose lyric has a value beyond the value of its occasional beauty and force of form ; it is a brief comprehensible expression of Blake's faith seen from its two leading sides ; belief in vision and belief in mercy. Into the singular mood of mind which made him inscribe it to the least imaginative of all serious poets we need by no means strive to enter ; but in the trustful admiration and the loyal goodwill which this quaint inscription seems to imply, there must be something not merely laughable : as, however rough and homespun the veil of eccentric speech may seem to us at first, we soon find it interwoven with threads of such fair and fervent colour as make the stuff of splendid verse ; so, beyond all apparent aberrations of relaxed thought which offend us at each turn, a purpose not ignoble and a sense not valueless become manifest to those who will see them.

Here then the scroll of prophecy is finally wound up ; and those who have cared to unroll and decipher it by such light as we can attain or afford may now look back across the tempest and tumult, and pass sentence, according to their pleasure or capacity, on the message delivered from this cloudy and noisy tabernacle. The complete and exalted figure of Blake cannot be seen in full by those who avert their eyes, smarting and blinking, from the frequent smoke and sudden flame. Others will see more clearly, as they look more sharply, the radical sanity and coherence of the mind which put forth its shoots of thought and faith in ways so strange, at such strange times. Faith incredible and love invisible to most men were alone the springs of this turbid and sonorous stream. In Blake, above all other men, the moral and the imaginative senses were so fused together as to compose the final artistic form. No man's fancy, in that age, flew so far and so high on so sure a wing. No man's mind, in that generation, dived so deep or gazed so long after the chance of human redemption. To serve art and to love liberty seemed to him the two things (if indeed they were not one thing) worth a man's life and work ; and no servant was ever trustier, no lover more constant than he. Knowing that without liberty there can be no loyalty, he did not fear, whether in his work or his life, to challenge and to deride the misconstruction of the foolish and the fraudulent. It does not appear that he was ever at the pains to refute any senseless and rootless lie that may have floated up during his life on the muddy waters of rumour, or drifted from hand to hand and mouth to mouth along the putrescent weed-beds of tradition. Many such lies, I am told, were then set afloat, and have not all as yet gone down. One at least of these may here be swept once for all out of our way. Mr. Linnell, the truest friend of Blake's age and genius, has assured me—and has expressed a wish that I should make public his assurance—that the legend of Blake and his wife, sitting as Adam and Eve in their garden, is simply a legend—to those who knew them, repulsive and absurd ; based probably, if on any foundation at all, on some rough and rapid expression of Blake's in the heat and flush of friendly talk, to the effect (it may be) that such a thing, if one chose to do it, would be in itself innocent and righteous,—wrong or strange only in the eyes of a world whose views and whose deeds were strange and wrong. So far Blake would probably have gone ; and so far his commentators need not fear to go. But one thing does certainly seem to me loathsome and condemnable ; the imputation of such a charge as has been brought against Blake on this matter, without ground and without excuse. The oral flux of fools, being as it is a tertian or quotidian malady or ague of the tongue among their kind, may deserve pity or may not, but does assuredly demand rigid medical treatment. The words or thoughts of a free thinker and a free speaker, falling upon rather than into the ear of a servile and supine fool, will probably in all times bring forth such fruit as this. By way of solace or compensation for the folly which he half perceives and half admits, the fool must be allowed his little jest and his little lie. Only when it passes into tradition and threatens to endure, is it worth while to set foot on it. It seems that Blake never cared to do this good office for himself ; and in effect it can only seem worth doing on rare occasions to any workman who respects his work. This contempt, in itself noble and rational, became injurious when applied to the direct service of things in hand. Confidence in future friends, and contempt of present foes, may have induced him to leave his highest achievements impalpable and obscure. Their scope is as wide and as high as heaven, but not as clear ; clouds involve and rains inundate the fitful and stormy space of air through which he spreads and plies an indefatigable wing. There can be few books in the world like these ; I can remember one poet only whose work seems to me the same or similar in kind ; a poet as vast in aim, as daring in detail, as unlike others, as coherent to himself, as strange without and as sane within. The points of contact and sides of likeness between William Blake and Walt Whitman are so many and so grave, as to afford some ground of reason to those who preach the transition of souls or transfusion of spirits. The great American is not a more passionate preacher of sexual or political freedom than the English artist. To

each the imperishable form of a possible and universal
Republic is equally requisite and adorable as the temporal and spiritual queen of ages as of men. To each all
sides and shapes of life are alike acceptable or endurable.
From the fresh free ground of either workman nothing
is excluded that is not exclusive. The words of either
strike deep and run wide and soar high. They are both
full of faith and passion, competent to love and to loathe,
capable of contempt and of worship. Both are spiritual,
and both democratic ; both by their works recall, even to
so untaught and tentative a student as I am, the fragments vouchsafed to us of the Pantheistic poetry of the
East. Their casual audacities of expression or speculation are in effect wellnigh identical. Their outlooks and
theories are evidently the same on all points of intellectual and social life. The divine devotion and selfless
love which make men martyrs and prophets are alike
visible and palpable in each. It is no secret now, but a
matter of public knowledge, that both these men, being
poor in the sight and the sense of the world, have given
what they had of time or of money, of labour or of love,
to comfort and support all the suffering and sick, all the
afflicted and misused, whom they had the chance or the
right to succour and to serve. The noble and gentle
labours of the one are known to those who live in his
time ; the similar deeds of the other deserve and demand
a late recognition. No man so poor and so obscure as
Blake appeared in the eyes of his generation ever did
more good works in a more noble and simple spirit. It
seems that in each of these men at their birth pity and
passion, and relief and redress of wrong, became incarnate

and innate. That may well be said of the one which
was said of the other : that " he looks like a man." And
in externals and details the work of these two constantly
and inevitably coheres and coincides. A sound as of a
sweeping wind ; a prospect as over dawning continents at
the fiery instant of a sudden sunrise ; a splendour now
of stars and now of storms ; an expanse and exultation
of wing across strange spaces of air and above shoreless
stretches of sea ; a resolute and reflective love of liberty
in all times and in all things where it should be ; a
depth of sympathy and a height of scorn which complete and explain each other, as tender and as bitter as
Dante's ; a power, intense and infallible, of pictorial con-
centration and absorption, most rare when combined with
the sense and the enjoyment of the widest and the
highest things ; an exquisite and lyrical excellence of
form when the subject is well in keeping with the poet's
tone of spirit ; a strength and security of touch in small
sweet sketches of colour and outline, which bring before
the eyes of their student a clear glimpse of the thing
designed—some little inlet of sky lighted by moon or
star, some dim reach of windy water or gentle growth
of meadow-land or wood ; these are qualities common to
the work of either. Had we place or time or wish to
touch on their shortcomings and errors, it might be
shown that these too are nearly akin ; that their poetry
has at once the melody and the laxity of a fitful storm-
wind ; that, being oceanic, it is troubled with violent
groundswells and sudden perils of ebb and reflux, of
shoal and reef, perplexing to the swimmer or the sailor ;
in a word, that it partakes the powers and the faults of

elemental and eternal things ; that it is at times noisy
and barren and loose, rootless and fruitless and informal ;
and is in the main fruitful and delightful and noble,
a necessary part of the divine mechanism of things.
Any work or art of which this cannot be said is superfluous and perishable, whatever of grace or charm it
may possess or assume. Whitman has seldom struck a
note of thought and speech so just and so profound as
Blake has now and then touched upon ; but his work is
generally more frank and fresh, smelling of sweeter air,
and readier to expound or expose its message, than this
of the prophetic books. Nor is there among these any
poem or passage of equal length so faultless and so
noble as his " Voice out of the Sea," or as his dirge over
President Lincoln—the most sweet and sonorous nocturn
ever chanted in the church of the world. But in breadth
of outline and charm of colour, these poems recall the
work of Blake ; and to neither poet can a higher tribute
of honest praise be paid than this.

We have now done what in us lay to help the works
of a great man on their way towards that due appreciation
and that high honour of which in the end they will not
fail. Much, it need not be repeated, has been done for
them of late, and admirably done ; much also we have
found to do, and have been compelled to leave undone
still more. If it should now appear to any reader that
too much has been made of slight things, or too little
said of grave errors, this must be taken well into
account : that praise enough has not as yet been given,
and blame enough can always be had for the asking ;
that when full honour has been done and full thanks

rendered to those who have done great things, then and then only will it be no longer an untimely and unseemly labour to map out and mark down their shortcomings for the profit or the pleasure of their inferiors and our own; that however pleasant for common palates and feeble fingers it may be to nibble and pick holes, it is not only more profitable but should be more delightful for all who desire or who strive after any excellence of mind or of achievement to do homage wherever it may be due; to let nothing great pass unsaluted or unenjoyed; but as often as we look backwards among past days and dead generations, with glad and ready reverence to answer the noble summons—" Let us now praise famous men, and our fathers who were before us." Those who refuse them that are none of their sons; and among all these " famous men, and our fathers," no names seem to demand our praise so loudly as theirs who while alive had to dispense with the thanksgiving of men. To them doubtless, it may be said, this is now more than ever indifferent; but to us it had better not be so. And especially in the works and in the life of Blake there is so strong and special a charm for those to whom the higher ways of work are not sealed ways that none will fear to be too grudging of blame or too liberal of praise. A more noble memory is hardly left us; and it is not for his sake that we should contend to do him honour.

THE END.

LIST OF AUTHORITIES

1. LIFE OF WILLIAM BLAKE. By Alexander Gilchrist. 1863.
2. POETICAL SKETCHES. By W. B. 1783.
3. SONGS OF INNOCENCE. 1789.
4. THE BOOK OF THEL. 1789.
5. THE MARRIAGE OF HEAVEN AND HELL. 1790.
6. VISIONS OF THE DAUGHTERS OF ALBION. 1793.
7. AMERICA: A PROPHECY. 1793.
8. SONGS OF EXPERIENCE. 1794.
9. EUROPE: A PROPHECY. 1794.
10. THE FIRST BOOK OF URIZEN. 1794.
11. THE BOOK OF AHANIA. 1795.
12. THE SONG OF LOS. 1795.
13. MILTON: A POEM IN TWO BOOKS. 1804.
14. JERUSALEM, AN EMANATION OF THE GIANT ALBION. 1804.
15. IDEAS OF GOOD AND EVIL. (MS.)
16. TIRIEL. (MS.)

NOTE

There are men whose fame is as universal as the appeal of their work to the sympathy and gratitude of all men but such as seek their single chance of notoriety by denying or decrying the claim and the station of the greatest among all the sons of men. There are others whose fame is as limited as the appeal of their work to the sympathies of those alone who can appreciate and assimilate the exceptional influence and the peculiar charm of it. These may not impossibly be liable to overvalue the actual excellence which the average critic will assuredly depreciate or deny. The greatest English poet except Collins who had the fortune or misfortune to be born into a century far greater in progress than in poetry—in the advance of humanity than in the ascent of imagination—is perhaps the most notable example on record of this hardly less happy and only less illustrious class of poets, or of artists, or of men.

The genius of William Blake—and his genius is one with his character: at one with it on all points and in every way—has so peculiar a charm that no one not incapable of feeling its fascination can ever outlive his delight in it. While we were able to regard this Londoner born and bred as not only a fellow-townsman of Milton's but a fellow-countryman of Shakespeare's, it did seem an almost insoluble problem to explain or to conjecture how so admirable and adorable a genius could be so deeply flawed and so continually vitiated by such unutterable and unimaginable defects. But if we regard him as a Celt rather than an Englishman, we shall find it no longer so difficult to understand from whence he derived his amazing capacity for such illimitable emptiness of mock-mystical babble as we find in his bad imitations of so bad a model as the Apocalypse: his English capacity for occasionally superb and serious workmanship we may rationally attribute to his English birth and breeding. Some Hibernian commentator on Blake, if I rightly remember a fact so insignificant, has somewhere said something to some such effect as that I, when writing about some fitfully audacious and fancifully delirious deliverance of the poet he claimed as a countryman, and trying to read into it some coherent and imaginative significance, was innocent of any knowledge of Blake's meaning. It is possible, if the spiritual fact of his Hibernian heredity has been or can be established, that I was: for the excellent reason that, being a Celt, he now and then too probably had none worth the labour of deciphering—or at least worth the serious attention of any student belonging to a race in which reason and imagination are the possibly preferable substitutes for fever and fancy. But in that case it must be gladly and gratefully admitted that the Celtic tenuity of his sensitive and prehensile intelligence throws into curious relief the occasional flashes of inspiration, the casual fits of insight, which raise him to the momentary level of a deep and a free thinker as well as a true and an immortal poet.

The vein of sound reason in Blake's eccentric and fitful intelligence has never been adequately acknowledged or perceived. He assailed Voltaire as a mocker: but he said the best and truest and deepest thing ever said of that great deliverer when he affirmed, after his fashion, that Voltaire had said to him in a vision, 'I blasphemed the Son of Man, and it shall be forgiven me; but my enemies blasphemed the Holy Ghost in me, and it shall not be forgiven them.' He brought the same charge against Rousseau, with whom he had more in common than with any other contemporary man of genius; but to match the antitheistic audacity of his passionate theanthropy we must turn from these milder heretics of Diderot himself. Antitheism, opposition to the God of man's making and man's worshipping, could hardly find bolder or better expression than in this memorable deliverance of 'a memorable fancy':

'The worship of God is, Honouring his gifts in other men each according to his genius, and loving the greatest men best: those who envy or calumniate great men hate God, for there is no other God.'

So hard-headed a materialist as Diderot is no fiercer or more fervent an antagonist of all religions built on creeds and propped by sacraments than so imaginative an irrationalist as Blake. Underneath all his incessant denunciations of 'the holy reasoning power' which comes to its consummation in grammars of assent and creeds of things incredible, there was actually a spiritual bedrock of natural righteousness and reason which preserved his intelligence and delivered his conscience from the farthest aberration and the worst perversion of all.

EDITOR'S NOTES

Swinburne's citations of Blake's verse are here located in the two editions of Blake now considered standard: The Complete Writings of William Blake, *Oxford University Press, 1966, edited by Sir Geoffrey Keynes; and* The Poetry and Prose of William Blake, *Doubleday, 1965, edited by David V. Erdman. "K38" indicates page 38 of the Keynes edition; "E38" page 38 of the Erdman edition. The Keynes edition preserves the pagination of the 1957 Nonesuch Centennial edition.*

p 1, epigraph. "All great poets, naturally and inevitably, become critics. I feel sorry for those poets who are guided by instinct alone; I believe them to be incomplete. In the imaginative life of the former, a point unfailingly comes when they wish to analyse their art, to discover the hidden laws by virtue of which they have written, and to draw from that study a series of precepts whose divine goal is infallibility in poetic creation. It would be miraculous for a critic to become a poet; but every poet contains a critic." From Baudelaire's *Richard Wagner et Tannhauser à Paris* (Paris, 1861). Swinburne possessed a copy of this pamphlet inscribed to him by Baudelaire.

p 7, line 9 of note. K817/E692.

p 9, line 10. *The Maid's Tragedy,* II, i, 68.

p 10, lines 15–22. K7/E405.

p 11, lines 5–12. K5/E403–4. From "Fair Elenor," lines 41–42, 45–47, 49–51. Since this poem is not included in Gilchrist, the omissions, as well as the alteration of Blake's "summer's noon" to "summer moon," must be taken as Swinburne's own.

p 11, final lines. K3/E402.

p 12, lines 17–18. K14/E412.

p 13, line 2. *Joseph and his Brethren,* by Charles Jeremiah Wells, was published in 1824, under the pseudonym of "H. L. Howard." It was re-issued in 1876 with an essay by Swinburne serving as introduction.

p 21, line 26. K770/E265.

p 25, lines 28–29. These lines from Job xvii, 14 appear on p. 45 of Blake's Notebook (the Rossetti Manuscript), transcribed in *A Concordance to the Writings of William Blake,* ed. David V. Erdman, Cornell University Press, 1966, II, 2315, Appendix B. Cf. K770/E265.

p 26, lines 1–2. K771/E266.

pp 26–27, final and beginning lines. K771/E266.

p 27, lines 11–12. Psalms cii, 6.

pp 28–29, final and beginning lines. K808.

pp 31–32, final and beginning lines. K187/E491. The omitted lines (Erdman's text) read: "That from his body it neer could be parted/ Till to the last trumpet it was farted" and "And so feeling he begd him to turn again/ And ease poor Klopstocks nine fold pain/ Thrice Blushing he redend round/ And the Spell turned & unwound/ It spun Back on the Stile/ Whereat Klopstock did smile/ If Blake could do this when he rose up from shite/ What might he not do if he sat down to write."

p 32 lines 23–24. K808.

p 33, lines 8–12. K803/E682.

p 33, lines 19–20. K803/E682.

pp 33–34, final and beginning lines. K804/E682.

p 34, note. The lines are from "Ce que dit la bouche d' ombre" ("What the mouth of the phantom said"), from Book Six of Victor Hugo's *Les Contemplations* (see Victor Hugo, *Oeuvres Poetiques,* ed. Pierre Albouy, Bibliothèque de la Pleiade, 1967, II, 801). They may be translated: "near the dolmen which dominates Rozel/ A the point where the promontory extends as a peninsula." A "dolmen" is a "structure usually regarded as a tomb, consisting of two or more large, upright stones set with a space between and capped by a horizontal stone." The bay of Rozel is situated in the northwest of the channel island of Jersey.

p 35, lines 2–3. K825.

p 35, lines 10–13. K825.

p 35, final line. The Latin phrase may be translated as "wine of the spirits."

p 36, lines 6–7. K800/E681.

p 36, lines 7–16. K812/E688.

p 38, lines 20-21. K539/E497.

p 39, line 26. K809/E685.

p 39–40, final and beginning lines. K809/E685.

p 40, lines 2–11. K809/E685.

p 40, lines 18–21. K815/E691.

p 40, final lines. K816–17/E692.

p 41, line 30. K818/E693.

p 42, lines 22–27. K818/E693.

p 43, lines 1–6. K818/E693.

p 43, lines 26–27. K818/E693.

p 44, line 28. K823/E697.

p 44, lines 29–31. K812/E688.

p 45, lines 10–18. K823/E697.

p 46, lines 23–24. Exodus, xix, 18.

p 47, lines 6–9 and note. Not identified.

p 49, note, line 5. The Greek phrase may be translated "Do not disturb Camarina"—proverbial for "let sleeping dogs lie."

p 53, note. For the epigrams, see K543/E472.

p 55–56, final and beginning lines. K558/E472.

p 61, line 10. "You would say Arcadian herds were bellowing" (Persius 3, 9).

p 61, lines 22–3. K432/E482.

p 65, lines 17–20. K446/E626.

p 70, line 19. *Macbeth,* III, ii, 2506.

p 78, lines 19–20. Cf. Shelley's sonnet "England 1819."

p 86, lines 22–23. Not identified.

p 91, note, final line. "So forever, brother, hail and farewell" (a slight modification of Catullus 101, 10). Swinburne saw the erroneous report of Baudelaire's death in April, 1866 (see *Letters,* I, 164), and immediately set about to write "a little notice of his death." In May, 1867, he is "writing a sort of lyric dirge for my poor Baudelaire" (*Letters,* I, 246). The finished elegy, entitled "Ave atque Vale" and undoubtedly one of the very best of Swinburne's poems, was published in 1868, some four months after Baudelaire's actual death on August 31, 1867.

p 93, line 15. "Beware of the dog" (Petronius, *Satyricon*, 29, 1).

p 94, line 6. Cf. K502/E113 ("the spiritual fourfold London"), K632/E154 ("the great city of Golgonooza fourfold"), etc.

p 94, lines, 8–11. K152/E38.

p 100, lines 25–29. Not identified.

p 106, lines 21–23. K716/E229.

p 106, line 26. *Hamlet*, III, ii, 393.

p 111, line 16. "nitwit god of the bourgeois."

p 111, lines 21–22. "He is quick-tempered and sharp wrath sits continuously at his nostrils" (Theocritus 1, 17).

p 115, lines 3–14. K119/E14.

p 115, lines 27–30. K115/E9.

p 117, lines 13–22. K210/E18.

p 118, lines 4–13. K210/E18.

p 118, lines 24–30. K210-11/E18.

p 119, lines 9–10. K211/E19.

p 120, beginning lines. K214/E24.

p 120, note. For the manuscript variations of "The Tyger," see K172–73/E717.

p 121, lines 4–11. K217/E27.

p 121, lines 18–19. K160/E44.

p 121, line 25. K217/E27.

p 122, lines 13–14. K506/E116.

p 122, line 28. K220/E30.

p 123, lines 9–10. K164/E459.

p 123, note. For the manuscript variations of "A Cradle Song," see K164–65/E769.

p 124, lines 4–11. K183/E490.

p 125, lines 8–11. K220/E31.

p 125, note, lines 17–18. K176/E721.

p 126, note, lines 6–7. Ecclesiastes, iv, 1.

p 126, note, lines 14–17. K180/E716.

p 217, lines 12–16. K673/E183.

p 128–29, final and beginning lines. K558–59/E472–73

p 130, note. K440/E408.

p 133, lines 5–7. K10/E408.

p 133, lines 22–30. K168/E462.

p 134–35, final and beginning lines. K427/E478.

p 135, final lines. K176/E464.

p 135, note. K176/E772.

p 137, beginning lines. K178/E465.

p 137, lines 15–18. K176/E460.

p 137–139, "Infant Sorrow." K166–67/E719–721.

p 138, note. For the manuscript variations, see *ibid.*

p 140, lines 15–16. K172/E463.

p 141, lines 3–10. K162/E459.

p 141, final lines. K163/E459.

p 142–43. Final and beginning lines. K178/E466.

p 143, note. K188/E473.

p 144, lines 10–13. K552/E470.

p 145, lines 17–24. K436/E489.

p 147, note. K147/E27.

p 149, lines 2–3. K614/E553.

p 149, line 22. K158/E42.

p 152–154. "The Everlasting Gospel." K748–59/E510–516.

p 156, lines 12–13. K150/E35.

p 158, note. Not identified.

p 159, lines 24–31. K752/E511.

p 160, lines 15–16. K536/E492.

p 160, lines 20–21. K748/E510.

p 161, lines 3–20. K752/E511.

p 161–2, final and beginning lines. K750–51/E511–12.

p 162, lines 22–29. K753/E512.

p 163, lines 11–18. K753/E512.

p 164, lines 5–14. K753/E512.

p 164, lines 24–29. K756/E791.

p 165, lines 3–6. K751/E510.

p 165, lines 8–13. K751/E510.

p 166, note, line 19. "Outside of man there is no salvation."

p 167, lines 2–7. K751–52/E510–511.

p 167, lines 19–26. K552/E470.

p 168, lines 3–14. K749/E515.

p 168, lines 23–28. K755/E514.

p 169, lines 4–5. K755/E514.

p 170, line 7. K755/E514.

p 170, lines 8–15. K749/E515.

p 170, final lines. K749–E515.

p 171, lines 20–27. K756/E794.

p 172, lines 20–27. K756/E794.

p 173, beginning lines. K757/E794.

p 173, line 15. K756/E794.

p 173, note. For the full text of Hugo's poem, see Victor Hugo, *Oeuvres Poétiques, Biblothèque de la Pléiade,* ed. Pierre Albouy, II, 203–04. The lines may be translated:

Comments of a Conservative upon an Agitator
That man was one of those who hold nothing sacred,
He refused to respect the respectable.
In order to infect them with his questionable views,
He would gather together in the vilest places
Churls, sinners, bilious buffoons,
Filthy wretches who didn't have a cent.
That's the kind of rabble he ran with.

. . . . . .

Respectable men would step back into their houses
When that charlatan went by with his gang.

. . . . . .

He always had with him a kind of streetwalker.
He was always making speeches to undermine the family,
And religion, and society.
He subverted morals and property.

. . . . . .

As for the priests,
He tore them to pieces. Bluntly, he blasphemed.
And he did it in the streets. He would spout his detestable
    theories
To the first beggar to come along, coatless and ragged.
It was finally necessary—the law was quite explicit—
That he be crucified.

p 174, lines 3–5. K757/E794.
p 174, line 6. Not identified.
p 174, lines 8–9. K757/E794.
p 174, lines 15–16. K757/E794.
p 174, lines 21–22. K756/E796.
p 175, note. K758–9/E792–3.
p 176, lines 19–20. K429/E479–80.
p 177, lines 20–21. K428/E478.
p 177, lines 25–26. K428/E478.
p 179, line 18. K425/E475.
p 179, lines 21–22. K425/E475.
p 180, line 11. K425/E475.
p 180, note, line 3. K613/E552.
p 182, lines 19–22. K180/E466.

p 182, note, lines 5–7. K40/E437.

p 182, note, lines 8–12. The reference probably is to "An Island in the Moon," K44–63/E440–456.

p 189, lines 25–6.

p 190, lines 27–30.

p 192, line 27. K171/E462.

p 193, lines 9–10. K249/E83.

p 193, lines 10–11. K211/E18.

p 199, note, lines 14–16. K108/E280.

p 199, note, lines 35–37. K106/E278.

p 200, lines 9–10. K128/E5.

p 200, lines 15–16. *The Tempest*, IV, I, 157–58.

p 200, note, lines 3–4. K109/E281.

p 200, note, lines 6–16. K110/E282–83.

p 201, line 28. K129/E5.

p 205, lines 23–24. K151/E35.

p 207, lines 14–19. K151–52/E36–37.

p 207, lines 26–29. K151–52/E36–37.

p 208, lines 3–4. K130/E6.

p 208, lines 7–8. K151/E35.

p 208, lines 16–19. K151/E36.

p 208, lines 21–22. K755/E514.

p 208, lines 23–24. K152/E37.

p 209, lines 15–28. K812–13/E688.

p 210–211, final and beginning lines. K149–50/E35–36.

p 212, lines 10–11. K149/E34.

p 213, lines 3–15. K150/E35.

p 213, lines 22–23. K152/E36.

p 213–14, final and beginning lines. K153/E37.

p 214–15, final and beginning lines. K153–54/E37–38.

p 215, final lines. K154/E38–39.

p 216, lines 14–35. K155/E39.

p 218–220, final and beginning lines. K155–57/E40–41.

p 221, lines 12–35. K157–58/E41–42.

p 222, lines 5–36. K158/E42.

p 223–24, final and beginning lines. K159–60/E43–44.

p 224, lines 25–26. K621/E144.

p 227, lines 23–24. K189/E44.

p 228, note 2, lines 2–3. K189/E44.

p 229, lines 2–4. K190/E45.

p 229–30, final and beginning lines. K190–92/E46–47.

p 231, lines 2–5. K192/E47.

p 231, line 7. K192/E47.

p 231, lines 14–29. K192–93/E47–48.

p 232–3. All the citations are to K193–95/E48–49.

p 234, lines 3–10. K195/E49–50.

p 234, lines 19–20. Not identified.

p 234, line 30. K195/E50.

p 235, lines 1–9. K196/E50–51.

p 235, lines 21–28. K197–98/E51–52.

p 235–6, final and beginning lines. K199/E53.

p 236, line 7. K200/E53.

p 236, lines 12–16. K200/E54.

p 236–37, final and beginning lines. K200/E54.

p 237, lines 12–14. K202/E56.

p 237, lines 18–23. K202–3/E56.

p 237, lines 24–30. K203/E56.

p 240, lines 1–3. K242/E62.

p 240, lines 18. Cf. K243/E63.

p 240, lines 27–29. K239/E60.

p 240–41, final and beginning lines. K239/E60–61.

p 241, lines 7–8. K240/E61.

p 241, line 11. K240/E61.

p 241, lines 13–17. K240/E61.

p 241, lines 19–23. K240/E61.

p 242, lines 4–22. K241/E62.

p 243, lines 3–7. K241–42/E62.

p 243, lines 17–18. K242/E63.

p 243, lines 22–23. K243/E63.

p 244, lines 5–9. K243/E63–64.

p 244, lines 14–15. K243/E64.

p 244, lines 18–32. K244/E64–65.

p 245, lines 2–3. K245/E65.

p 245, lines 6–7. K245/E65.

p 245, lines 20–22. K238/E59.

p 245, final lines. K239/E60.

p 246, lines 16–19. K223/E70.

p 246, lines 22–24. K225/E72.

p 247, lines 19–21. K233/E79.

p 247, final lines. K234–35/E80.

p 248. All the citations are to K235–6/E81–82.

p 250, line 8. K249/E83.

p 250, lines 12–14. K250/E84.

p 250, line 29. K250/E84.

p 251, lines 5–11. K251/E85.
p 251, lines 18–25. K252/E85–86.
p 252–3, final and beginning lines. K253–5/E87–89.
p 254, lines 30–31. K245/E66.
p 255, line 4. K246/E66.
p 255, line 17. K246/E66.
p 255, lines 22–26. K246/E66.
p 266, lines 9–16. K247/E67–68.
p 266, lines 18–19. K248/E68.
p 266, lines 20–21. K247/E67.
p 256, lines 22–31. K248/E68.
p 257, lines 3–14. K248/E68.
p 258–9, final and beginning lines. K480–81/E94–95.
p 260, lines 4–13. K481/E95.
p 260, line 25. K496/E108.
p 260, line 25. K688/E204.
p 260, final lines. K481/E95.
p 261, lines 5–10. K755/E514.
p 261, lines 22–31. K486/E99.
p 262, lines 11–13. K489/E102.
p 262, lines 16–19. K486–487/E99–100.
p 262, lines 21–29. K489–90/E102.
p 263, line 13. K771/E266.
p 263, lines 19–20. K490/E103.
p 264, lines 4–13. K491–492/E104.
p 264–265, final and beginning lines. K492/E104.
p 264, note. K171/E462.
p 265, lines 3–7. K493/E105.
p 265, lines 14–18. K494/E106.
p 265, line 24. K494/E106.
p 265, note, lines 4–6. K189/E44.
p 266, lines 4–11. K495/E107.
p 266, lines 17–24. K495/E107.
p 266, lines 27–30. K496/E107.
p 266–267, final and beginning lines. K496/E108.
p 267, lines 11–13. Not identified.
p 267, lines 14–20. K496/E108.
p 267–8, final and beginning lines. K497/E108–9.
p 268, lines 9–14. K497–498/E109.
p 268, lines 16–19. K498/E110.
p 268, lines 20–27. K501/E112.
p 269, lines 1–10. K501/E112.

p 269, lines 15–18. K506/E117.
p 269, lines 21–29. K509/E119.
p 269, lines 31–32. K509/E120.
p 270, lines 3–8. K509–510/E120.
p 270, lines 22–29. K513/E123.
p 270, line 31. K513/E123.
p 271, lines 1–19. K513–514/E123–124.
p 271, lines 21–30. K510–511/E121.
p 272, lines 1–2. K511/E122.
p 272, lines 16–17. K515/124.
p 272, line 20. K515/E125.
p 272–273, final and beginning lines. K516/E125.
p 273–274, final and beginning lines. K520–521/E129–130.
p 274–275, final and beginning lines. K518/E128.
p 274, note, lines 22–23. K521/E130.
p 274, final lines. "Countless laughter" (*Prometheus Bound*, 90).
p 275, lines 2–4. K519/E128.
p 276, lines 10–11. "Upon this rock" (Matthew xvi, 18).
p 276, lines 19–20. K823/E697.
p 277–8, final and beginning lines. K648/E169.
p 278, note. All citations save the last are to K415–417/E467–68, lines beginning "My Spectre round me day & night" (portions of which were included in Gilchrist, Vol II, under the title of "Broken Love"). For the final citation, cf. K220/E30.
p 280, line 6. Cf. "Mystery the Virgin Harlot, Mother of War," K506/E116.
p 280, line 7. K643/E164.
p 280, line 9. Not identified; cf. "Subtil modesty child of night and sleep" K194/E48.
p 280, line 20. K192/E47.
p 281, lines 16–17. K748/E516.
p 281, lines 25–26. K527/E136.
p 282, lines 6–7. K623/E146.
p 284–85, final and beginning lines. K621/E144.
p 285, lines 5–8. K621/E144.
p 285, lines 19–24. K622/E145.
p 286, lines 27–28. K707/E221.
p 287, lines 1–2. Not identified.
p 287, lines 6–14. K624/E147.

p 287, lines 16–21. K661/E175.

p 287, line 23. Not identified.

p 288, lines 7–8. K649/E169.

p 288, lines 14–17. K649/E169.

p 288, lines 20–26. K652/E172.

p 288, line 27. K480/E94.

p 288–89, final and beginning lines. K861–82/E198.

p 289, lines 5–15. K682/E198–99.

p 289, lines 26–27. Cf. K682/E199.

p 289–90, final and beginning lines. K682/E199.

p 290, lines 16–21. K707/E221. The quotation actually ends with the end of the sentence in line 21, not at "husband" in line 17.

p 290, lines 21–23. Cf. K707/E221.

p 290, lines 24–28. K708/E221.

p 291, lines 3–17. K716–17/E229–30.

p 291, lines 19–24. Cf. K718/E230.

p 291, lines 24–28. K718/E230.

p 291–92, final and beginning lines. K718/E230–31.

p 292, lines 26–30. K747/E256.

p 292, lines 32–33. K694/E209.

p 293, lines 1–11. K695/E210.

p 293, line 14. Ezekiel, xxviii, 12.

p 295–297, final and beginning lines. K779–781/E268–270.

p 297, line 27. Romans, iii, 15.

p 304, lines 15–16. Ecclesiasticus, xliv, 1.

p 307, lines 12–18. The reference is undoubtedly to *The Works of William Blake*, edited by Edwin John Ellis and William Butler Yeats (London, 1893). Ellis and Yeats, who invented an Irish ancestry for Blake, comment in the Introduction to their Memoir that Swinburne "reigns as the one-eyed man of the proverb among the blind" as a critic of Blake (I, viii).